AGAINST | MANAGEMENT

AGAINST MANAGEMENT

ORGANIZATION IN THE AGE OF MANAGERIALISM

MARTIN PARKER

polity

First published in 2002 by Polity Press in association with Blackwell Publishers Ltd

Editorial office:
Polity Press
65 Bridge Street
Cambridge CB2 1UR, UK

Marketing and production:
Blackwell Publishers Ltd
108 Cowley Road
Oxford OX4 1JF, UK

Published in the USA by
Blackwell Publishers Inc.
350 Main Street
Malden, MA 02148, USA

A catalogue record for this book is available from the British Library.

Library of Congress Cataloging-in-Publication Data

Parker, Martin, 1962–
    Against management : organization in the age of managerialism / Martin Parker.
        p. cm.
Includes bibliographical references and index.
    ISBN 0–7456–2925–3 (alk. paper) – ISBN 0–7456–2926–1 (pbk. : alk. paper)
    1. Management. 2. Organizational effectiveness. I. Title.
    HD31 .P296 2002
    302.3'5 – dc21   2002000700

Typeset in 10.5 on 12 pt Sabon
by SNP Best-set Typesetter Ltd., Hong Kong
Printed in Great Britain by TJ International, Padstow, Cornwall

This book is printed on acid-free paper.

CONTENTS

ACKNOWLEDGEMENTS

As I have been writing over the last few years, it seems that many of my concerns have rotated around the themes that organize this book. This means that some of the material in this book has appeared else-where, but it was all extensively expanded, cannibalized and rewritten during the spring, summer and autumn of 2001. For the sake of completeness you will find endnotes in the appropriate places. However, any self-plagiarism I have engaged in is really only possible because of the amazing support I have received from my colleagues past and present in the Management Department and Centre for Social Theory and Technology at Keele since 1995. Very many of those people have commented on my work and given me hard things to think about. Particular thanks then to Peter Armstrong, Steve Brown, Bob Cooper, Kevin Hetherington, Matthew Higgins, Gavin Jack, Campbell Jones, Valerie Fournier, Bob Grafton-Small, John Hassard, Mihaela Kelemen, David Knights, John Law, Nick Lee, Geoff Lightfoot, Simon Lilley, Rolland Munro, Gordon Pearson and Warren Smith, and general thanks to everyone who has made Keele such a worthwhile place to spend my time. Campbell Jones, Mihaela Kelemen, Matthias Klaes and two anonymous reviewers for Polity were also kind enough to comment on the whole manuscript, so particular thanks to them for their patience. Also, my thanks to Steve Ackroyd, Gibson Burrell, Peter Case, Chris Grey, Phil Hancock, René ten Bos, Hugh Willmott and Ed Wray-Bliss, none of them lucky enough to work at Keele, but all have provoked my thinking too.

Finally, this book is for Ben, Max, Zoe and Spike, with love, and for Jude, for her love.

1

MANAGERIALISM AND
ITS DISCONTENTS

'The campaign captures in a visual way Cap Gemini Ernst & Young's essential brand equity of "entrepreneurial creativity". It demonstrates that Cap Gemini Ernst & Young has successfully distilled the brand essence of the newly merged company. The campaign is a celebration of having defined the global offer which distinguishes Cap Gemini Ernst & Young from its competitors. This campaign marks a new phase for Cap Gemini Ernst & Young as it continues its aim of achieving global domination in consultancy services. Creative execution of the campaign was developed with a total campaign budget of $30 million.'

Patrick Boccard, CGE&Y Communications Director, 2001

'Management of what? Management for what? Management. Management. Management. The word sticks in one's interface. Please excuse me if I dare laugh, but I know that each age, even each decade, has its little cant word coiled up inside real discourse like a tiny grub in the middle of an apple. Each age, even each decade, is overly impressed for a little while by half-way bright youngish men on the make who adeptly manipulate the current terminology at precisely the right moment to make precisely the right impression on those who are a little older, a little less intelligent and considerably less alert.'

Dennis Potter (1994: 47)

What sense does it make to be 'against' management? It is easy enough to be against many things – discrimination against different groups of people, the degradation of the environment, the rise of corporate power – but to be 'against' management? Surely to take such

1

a position on something like this is like being 'against' buildings, or air, or society? That is to say, it makes no sense to be against something that constitutes the world that we live in so completely. 'Management' is a fact of life, and we might try to discover how to do it better, or aim it at different ends, but it makes no sense to deny it so unconditionally. But it is precisely because this idea sounds so implausible that I want to try and explore it. Simply because something is everywhere doesn't mean it is good or necessary, and simply because being 'against management' is perverse does not mean that it isn't worth thinking about.

Three assumptions

'Management' has become an inextricable part of the common sense of my world, and almost certainly of yours too. It is difficult, perhaps impossible now, for citizens of the first world to imagine a state of affairs in which we could buy bananas from our local supermarket, or visit a hospital, or vote in elections, without some process of management having taken place behind the scenes. It has become a defining feature of an organization that it has a group of individuals called managers. Most of these managers will have undergone extensive training in how to do management, perhaps in a Management Department of a university which contains specialists who teach and research on management and how to improve it. The managers of these organizations will also employ management consultants who often work for global organizations and advise on various aspects of management functioning. In an unholy (but well-compensated) trinity of self-interest and back-slapping, management academics train managers who seek advice from management consultants who seek their legitimacy from management academics, and so on.

Given this state of affairs, it is hardly surprising than many people believe that management is a precondition for an organized society, for social progress and economic growth. If we have a difficulty, with our jobs, our lives, our government or our world, then the answer is often supposed to be better management. It is increasingly articulated as a universal solution to whatever problem presents itself. Management protects us against chaos and inefficiency, management guarantees that organizations, people and machines do what they claim to do. Management is both a civilizing process and a new civic religion. Even if we don't share the faith in today's management, we often seem to believe that the answer is 'better' management, and not something else altogether. There are some rather interesting general assumptions lying behind this faith and I want to begin this book by briefly untangling them in three ways. The first is control over nature, the second is control over human beings, and the third is an increasing control of our organizational abilities. All these themes help to support our faith in management, though they are rarely articulated in the starkly simplistic way that I do here.

Firstly, it is assumed that social progress is equivalent to our ability as human beings to increasingly control the natural world around us. History tells us of a long struggle against adversity, of the attempt to overcome crop failures, floods and diseases, and of the replacement of incorrect assumptions by a scientific and rational world view. Where we were once the victims of a wild, unruly nature, we are now becoming the masters. It is, so the story goes, because we are now capable of understanding and organizing the world that we have sent a man to the moon, and can buy golden even-sized bananas in cold countries at any time of the year. Disorder and chance have been conquered by order and understanding. In the future, as our understanding grows, we will be able to understand and control the very molecules that make rockets, humans and bananas what they are; conquer unhappiness; and perhaps even travel outwards to the furthest reaches of the universe, boldly going where no one has gone before. Management is one of the ways in which we articulate this control over things by making them manageable, subject to the control of human beings. So, management is a key element of a particular version of the progressive scientific attitude that allows for, or encourages, an increase in the sum total of control that human beings have over the world that they live in.

Secondly, management is also a way for human beings to be controlled. That is to say that human beings are also a potential source of disorder in organizing the world. Here we have some sense in which an internal 'human nature' is being progressively better understood through the various tools of behavioural and social science. This internal nature is sometimes depicted as just as wild and unruly as 'external' nature, and requires similar forms of domestication in order that it can be made amenable to the modern world. Often this nature is understood as individually or collectively selfish, or as easily swayed by unconscious mysticism and irrationalism. Left to our own monkey instincts, we would be lazy and brutish – victims of the monsters from the Id and the endless armies that have raped and pillaged in the name of yet another God. Yet, if we can better understand our nature, we can better structure human societies to the benefit of all.

3

So psychologists determine the nature of our deepest motivations, personality types and social development; sociologists describe the interactions and invisible structures of the organized world; economists discover the hidden mechanisms of the market and so on. Once all these matters can be better understood, then a world can be engineered which harmonizes our individual natures with collective betterment. By using these sciences of the human, management can shape and shepherd human beings towards a more productive future.

Finally, it might be noted that management is also implicated in a story about the development of control strategies themselves. According to this account, the forms of social organization that characterize early societies were autocratic and cruel: sacrifices to the sun, golden-topped pyramids of hubris built with slave labour and kings who demanded that their serfs leave their entrails on muddy battlefields. Management, on the other hand, is democratic and transparent. It is a form of organization that is premised on the efficient ordering of people and things in order that agreed collective goals can be achieved.[1] In its best form, it prevents the abuse of power and greed and turns human energy into measurable objectives. For nineteenth-century utopians like Saint-Simon, this was a matter of replacing ancient regimes of privilege with a meritocracy governed by experts who knew what they were talking about (Berneri 1971: 213). This bourgeois revolution is now complete, and management is dominant. Management is clear, is accountable and precise. Management does not waste human energy, and only demands that democratic market liberalism be recognized as the best solution for all. Management, therefore, is the most advanced form of human organization – a professional expertise that Whyte suggested was based on the idea that it is an 'expertise relatively independent of the content of what is being managed' (1961: 11).[2] When the cruel autocrat becomes the responsible manager, the greatest good of the greatest number will be achieved.

Given these kind of assumptions,[3] these stories that many human beings tell about progress, it is hardly surprising that management occupies such a central place in advanced industrial societies. If we want to control nature and ourselves, and do so in a transparent fashion, then management is an obvious answer. It is the consolidation of order and efficiency, and who could be against order and efficiency? The common subtext behind these accounts of modernization is that progress is defined as the process of defeating disorder. Chaos and disorganization are obstacles that need to be overcome. Ordering, producing a pattern which will transcend space and persist into the future, is the activity which defends us against being open-mouthed and hollow-eyed victims. The process of management allows us to control our individual and collective destinies. To return to an earlier metaphor, if someone in Stoke-on-Trent wants to eat a banana in winter, then management allows them to do it. And why should we not eat bananas in winter? Further, if someone from Stoke-on-Trent also wants to write a book which calls into question 'management', then management (of higher education, of research output, of publishers, of printers, of bookshops) is necessary. I could not do what I want to do without the thing that I want to dethrone. I will return to this awkward contradiction later in the book, but note in passing that this might also be taken to be further proof of management's superiority to all other forms of social organization. The cruel king would not allow me to write a book which called into question his authority, but management is so democratic that (if there is a market for this book) it will be published. I, in biting the hand that feeds me, merely demonstrate the incoherence and ingratitude of my attitude. But, as I said, more of that later.

Now, as the astute reader will have noticed, I have used the word 'management' in a very general sense so far. Indeed, I seem to be conflating management with modernity itself. But my point here is that what we understand as management nowadays is predicated on a very large story about social progress. In many pre-industrial societies, it would make no sense to disentangle something called 'management' from the everyday skills through which life was lived. We have some hint of this when we talk about 'managing' in the sense of 'coping' with a particular state of affairs. So it might be that the very separation of management from other words which concern our abilities to organize our lives reflects a certain self-consciousness about our abilities to detach a general technology of control from other, more specific and grounded ideas. Growing crops, looking after cattle, determining the inheritance of property, throwing pots, trading things with other people and so on were all specific matters which required quite specific solutions and knowledge. But the very generality of management reflects a claim that this is a form of knowledge that can be made widely applicable across a huge variety of domains. Once it has been learnt, management can be applied anywhere, to anything and on anyone. More than any other form of knowing or practice, management is claimed to be absolutely nomadic and universally useful. It is the synthesis and culmination of the stories of control of things, the control of people and even the control of control itself.

Three definitions

The etymology of the word 'management' reflects this gradual expansion of its claims. It seems to be derived from the Italian *mano*, hand, and its expansion into *maneggiarre*, the activity of handling and training a horse carried out by *maneggio*. From this, very specific, form of manual control, the word gets expanded into a general activity of training and handling people too. The later development of the word is also influenced by the French *mener* (to lead) and its development into *ménage* – household, or housekeeping – and the verb *ménager* – to economize (Weekley 1967; see also Jacques 1996: 88). So an intimate technology of the hand or of the household grows to become a technology of the workplace, and eventually of the state too. But the later imperialism of this word for handling beasts also follows from its subsequent division into three parts – a noun, a verb and an academic discipline. I will look at each of those in turn, in order to refine what management means more precisely.

management (1) [*manïj*ment] *n* group of executives directing an industrial undertaking.

First then, management is a plural noun for 'manager'. The management. We can describe them as an occupational group who have engaged in a very successful strategy of collective social mobility over a century or so. From a disparate collection of occupational nouns – owner, supervisor, superintendent, administrator, overman, foreman, clerk – this collective term has emerged that represents anyone engaged in the co-ordination of people and things. Further, these managers are no longer concentrated in industrial organizations, making things. Nowadays, we find managers everywhere – in hospitals, universities and football clubs. Managers manage hotels, railway stations and museums – they are universally essential. There is an unusual reversal at work here. As Adam Smith, Emile Durkheim and many others have argued (Durkheim 1991 [1983]: 1), the historical effects of the division of labour have usually been to subdivide tasks, and their attached labels, whilst this word is a successful attempt to undivide, to create a general term which covers many labours. Whilst there might be qualifiers added to the noun (Marketing Manager, Human Resource Manager) and there are other occupational terms that can be subsumed within management (Accountant, Director), the general category is one that would be recognized across most of the world, and in every sector of the economy. Through this undivision, this merging, a new class of people is created. Perhaps not a class in the classical Marxist sense, though that might not be too wide of the mark, but certainly a class in the sense of concepts. Importantly, the term is almost always a positive ascription. Whilst 'engineer' or 'teacher' are occupational terms that are descriptive and sectorally located, 'manager' is a term that can be applied anywhere, and that implies a degree of power and status within the organization. It may also be attached to the possession of certain credentials, an MBA for example, usually implies high reward, and (if airport bookstalls are evidence) requires a lot of travelling and the use of mobile phones, lap-top computers and expensive hotels.

management (2) [*man*ĭjment] *v/i* process or act of managing; skill in contriving, handling *etc.*

The management practise management. Which is to say that, as with a word like organization, the noun can also be translated into a verb. This is a verb that can be applied to the processes of ordering and controlling people and things. It implies a separation between the actual doing of whatever is being managed (engineering or teaching) and the higher-level function of control of these processes. In other words, management is not *about* engineering or teaching, but the co-ordination of the doing of these things. In some sense, management is constituted as a higher order of brain work which requires an elevation from mundane functions in order to gain a better overall perspective. Though management may be etymologically linked with the hand, it is no longer a practice that is 'hands-on'. In substantive terms, management usually refers to what managers do – marketing, strategy, finance and so on – but the word is spreading beyond such restrictive definitions. Thus there is increasing talk of the management of everything. A look on the internet recently gave me books on Managing Anger, Managing Your Divorce, Managing Money in Relationships, Managing the Morning Rush, Managing Attention and Learning Disorders, Managing Childhood Medical Emergencies, Managing Disagreement, Managing the Demands of Work and Home, Managing Your Health Care, Managing Your Children's Conflicts, Managing Loss, Managing to Make It, and (of course) Managing Your Children, Career, Home, Finances and Everything Else. This was a small sample from a much longer list.[4] In principal, anything that is problematic or chaotic is potentially a target for management. 'Knowledge management' is currently a very fashionable

7

term, but it leads me to wonder what happens to knowledge if it isn't managed properly.[5] What happened to knowledge, relationships, children and anger before management came along? The division performed here is between managing something, which is good, and not-managing, which is bad. The not-managing usually gets less attention but seems to include both bad management (mismanagement) and no management, in other words both doing things badly and leaving things alone altogether. Both can be repaired by better management.

management (3) [*manɪ̆*jment] *n* the academic discipline concerned with managing and administration; the part of an educational institution concerned with the same.

The place that this book is written from. The name of university departments that signifies (paid) engagement in the discipline of reading, writing and talking about what the management does and what management is, and sometimes talking to managers about what they do. This is certainly not a practice that can be isolated from the other two, simply because much of the output of this 'discipline' is shaped by, and in turn shapes, contemporary practices in both of the other areas. Management Departments, Business Schools and so on have become an ubiquitous part of further and higher education over the last fifty years or so. From origins in the USA, elements of commerce, economics, psychology and sociology have congealed into the B-School, the cash-cow of cash-hungry university managers and what Thomas Frank calls 'processing plants for the faking of intellectual authority' (2000: 177–8). Nowadays, Management claims to be a coherent discipline in itself, and employs specialists to teach and research in organizational behaviour, human resource management, accounting and finance, marketing, strategy, operations and production management, international business, business ethics, information systems as well as a dizzying variety of specialisms within, and crossovers between, all these areas. The vast majority of the output from this network of hundreds of thousands of texts, professors, journals, Ph.D. students, conferences is unquestioningly supportive of the growth of all three senses of management.[6] Oceans of ink have been drained to promulgate highly performative and machinic notions of what 'organizing' is, and what 'organizations' are and should be. In the simplest of terms, problems of organization are reduced to matters of human systems engineering. Even when the intent is avowedly 'soft' or 'humanist', the subtext stresses the imperatives of managing and the necessity of control. This is one of the largest institutional legitimation and public relations campaigns in the history of thought, though it is rarely recognized as such.

It would seem then that management, as person, practice and discipline, is almost everywhere nowadays. It has become one of the defining words of our time and both a cause and a symptom of our brave new world. It directly employs millions, and indirectly employs almost everyone else. It is altering the language we use in our conceptions of home, work and self, and both relies on and reinforces deeply held assumptions about the necessary relationship between control and progress. I make a living from writing and teaching about it. How can it possibly be a bad thing?

Against what?

In this book, I will try to persuade you that almost all these senses of management are both limiting and dangerous, and that managerialism is ultimately a form of thought and activity which is being used to justify considerable cruelty and inequality. I will also be suggesting that, in a variety of places, an odd variety of people seem to be coming to the same conclusion. In other words, that it is possible to identify cracks in the new religion as some of its converts begin to lapse and others intensify their protest. In order to do this, I will be drawing from a wide variety of sources – academic writing on management and organization, general social theories of the present, various books and films which use management as their backdrop, and the increasing range of anti-corporate protests and politics. The overall argument will be that we can see the beginnings of a cultural shift in the image of management, from saviour to problem, and that this is a significant historical move. In essence, though, this is a polemical book. I want to fan the flames of discontent. I want to try to persuade my readers that they have good reason to be suspicious of management by showing that many people already are, and that they have some rather good reasons. I want to encourage *you* to question the common sense that tells us that we need management, managers and management schools. I want, in a sense, to put myself out of a job.

This means that the book is partisan. I would argue that all books already are, and that there is no neutral academic voice, but that is another story. I am not going to spend a lot of space carefully sifting evidence in order to reach balanced conclusions, or appealing to established academic authority to convince you by weight of reputation. It seems to me that there has already been quite enough partisan writing concealed as serious advice, or breathlessly hysterical writing that has puffed and sold market managerialism and global corporate libertarianism for money. Take another look at your local bookshop if you don't believe me. There will be a vast teetering pile of *Seven Secrets of Successful Managers*, *Marketing Yourself for Fun and Profit* and *Managing People and Organizations* (eighth edition, with instructor's manual, website, OHP slides, class exercises and testbank). Open some of these books. You will see bullet points, flipchart summaries, cartoons, learning boxes and two by two matrices supported by legitimating references and case studies. Others will overwhelm you with hyperbole – world-class excellence, strategic future vision, high-impact global odyssey to tomorrow; currently fashionable terminology – knowledge management, emotional intelligence, spirit and passion, e-business; or brutal straightforwardness – scaling the corporate wall, how to succeed in business, discovering the leader within. Most of them are actually the same. Their hysterical attempts to differentiate themselves, to go beyond this, reassess that, or provide you with the essentials (principles, fundamentals) of the other, are merely expressions of wish-fulfilment – perhaps for both writers and readers. Whether wide-eyed and fashionable, warm and helpful, or dutifully academic, all these books praise management. They might attend to, or construct, debates *within* management, but these will be debates about the newest organizational form, or why companies should adopt relationship marketing as opposed to transactional marketing, or whatever. The king is dead, long live the king. Old management versus new management in other words, but very little which questions management itself. But this book comes to bury management, not praise it. This book seeks to attack these vast libraries of propaganda that masquerade as necessary common sense.

However, this opening is too insufficient and imprecise to be left as it is. Of course the argument gets more sophisticated and nuanced as you burrow into the book, but I can imagine too many objections to what I have written so far for me to leave it here. For a start, I think my broader target is 'managerialism', the generalized ideology of management. This lies behind all the three senses of management I outlined above, but does not include a more modest version of 'managing' as a local and temporary art. As I said, when we ask someone 'how are you managing?', or 'how did you manage?', it usually means something like 'cope' or 'deal with'. It suggests that an individual has a problem with something rather difficult – learning to juggle, moving house or the death of a friend – and that they could describe whether they found a personal way of dealing with it as best they could. This partial and modest sense of managing, perhaps like the practical art of *maneggiarre*, is not one of my targets. Rather, it is the application of a narrow conception of management as a generalized technology of control to everything – horses, humans and hospitals. This is management as the universal solution, not a personal assessment of a local problem.

This imperialism of management has found a particular home in large organizations, the 'corporations' which will be the particular focus of my chapter on anti-corporate protest. But taking the big organization as the breeding ground of managerialism is not intended to imply that only big organizations are managerial, or conversely that all organization is inherently managerial.[7] In terms of the former, I have already suggested above that the instrumentalism of management expertise has found its way into most organizations, big and small, as well as into the crevices of private life. I am not at all sure that this colonization is always helpful. However, I don't believe that this is true of all organizations or all organizing. My last chapter will make this argument more forcefully, but it is important to note that there are potentially many non-managerial ways in which organizing can get done, and many different ways in which we can think about markets too. My argument here is that the market managerial notion of organizing is only one alternative amongst many. However, its dominance is now so unquestioned that it is increasingly difficult to imagine or remember alternatives. Words like co-ordination, co-operation, barter, participation, collectivity, democracy, community, citizenship, exchange all refer to methods of doing organization, but they have been increasingly erased, marginalized or co-opted by the three senses of management. It is almost as if we have resigned ourselves to the idea that only management can do organization, and that organization only involves permanent hierarchies of status and reward, the separation of conception from execution, the dominance of a particular form of market and so on.

So, I am *not* (in some perverse way) trying to set this book up against management as coping, or against all versions of organization, or even against all versions of markets. I *am* trying to argue that the particular version of managerialism that has been constructed over the past century is deeply implicated in a wide variety of political and ethical problems, and that it limits our capacity to imagine alternative forms of organizing. This, it seems to me, is a matter of politics, because conceptions of organizing are politics made durable. As Marx and Engels put it in 1846, 'The ideas of the ruling class are in every epoch the ruling ideas: that is, the class which is the ruling *material* force of society is at the same time its ruling *intellectual* force' (Bottomore and Rubel 1963: 93). One of the ruling, or at least hegemonic, ideas of the early twenty-first century seems to me to be located around managerialism. But its commonsensical nature should not be taken to indicate its truth, merely that it reflects the interests of a ruling class of managers. So this book is one element in a battle of ideas for this particular epoch which attempts to open up the possibility of alternative, non-managerial, conceptions of organizing. That is the overall argument, but for those who like to know exactly where they are going before they begin (and hence manage their reading more efficiently), the next section briefly outlines the next eight chapters.

The rest of the book

Chapters 2, 3 and 4 all deal with 'internal' critiques of management. That is to say, they provide an alternative history of organizational theory over the past century or so, and explore the ways in which classic formulations of the role and purposes of management have been opposed and reformulated, though often in ways that relegitimize a market based managerialism rather than seriously exploring alternatives. I begin with a chapter on the most enduring critique, the characterization of managerialism as being equivalent to vast pyramidal bureaucracies that crush individuality with the weightiest of rule books. After a short history of the long-standing tradition of anti-bureaucratic thought, I go on to consider the latest version of this idea – George Ritzer's formulation of McDonaldization. Whilst in many ways being sympathetic to a critique of McDonald's, I suggest that Ritzer's liberalism combined with his cultural elitism means that his analysis of capitalism and managerialism is essentially nostalgic rather than progressive. Being against bureaucracy is not the same as being against fast food in general, or indeed as being against the role that managers commonly play within global corporations. There is actually rather a wide gulf between the kind of activism represented by the McLibel trial and Ritzer's attempt to argue that resistance involves eating with a knife and fork. Further, there are actually many good reasons why we might want to defend a bureaucratic sense of probity. This is particularly important in the context of newer developments in managerial thought which seek to make employees discipline themselves through self-management dressed up as commitment, whilst managers are positioned as visionary leaders.

Chapters 3 and 4 consider these modern formulations of the committed worker through the characterization of the organizational citizen and the community member. Both these characters are rhetorically justified by business writers and B-School academics through their opposition to the heartless bureaucrat, and their position within flexible and supposedly more democratic organizations. The old slow-moving dinosaurs are doomed to extinction as turbo-capitalism demands knowledge workers with portfolio careers. So, given the difficulty of managing people without a rule book, organizational citizenship suggests the possibility that an organization could be unified through sharing common values which are made explicit in mission and vision statements formulated by heroic and charismatic leaders. This is a potentially critical position on managerialism in that it assumes that classical management is an inadequate way of capturing the hearts and minds of employees. After all, the idea of belonging to organizations in a similar way that we belong to states is a powerful one, particularly if the organizational citizen has similar rights and responsibilities to the citizen of a modern democratic society. The chapter concludes by exploring the problems of a genuinely pluralist conception of industrial citizenship within a context where corporations have all the power, and states seem to be on the wane.

These arguments are taken further in chapter 4 in terms of the currently fashionable idea that the formal organization could dissolve altogether and become nothing more than a technologically mediated constellation of specialist individuals held together by emotional and electronic ties. Management withers away, and is replaced by metaphors like community, soul and spirit. In this case, I will argue that definitional and actually existing features of large-scale organization are being effaced through these kind of arguments. Hierarchical organization and management are not withering away, but becoming more pervasive, though camouflaged through colonizing other forms of language. Managers can now claim that their organizations are caring communities at the same time as they down-size and relocate to maximize shareholder value. Though there are some interesting lessons to be learnt from thinking about organizations as communities, this is a metaphor that breaks if it is stretched too far. Essentially these kinds of ideas function as ideology for the transnational capitalist class, an ideology that celebrates a small group of knowledge workers at the same time that it effectively condemns the rest of the global population to serving in McDonald's or working in Export Processing Zones.

Though there are useful ideas for being against management in anti-bureaucratic, citizenship and community ideas, I think they need to be placed in a more radical, and non-managerial, context to have much bite. So the next four chapters shift focus, and look at examples of more 'external' criticism. The chapters are broadly organized as a series of movements away from the usual concerns of management. So business ethics (the subject of chapter 5) can be critical, though many elements of it are actually supportive of business. At the other extreme, the anti-corporate protest movement (considered in chapter 8) is entirely unconcerned with legitimizing management in any form. The former assumes that the force of the better argument is sufficient, the latter prefers political pressure and direct action. Books or bricks?

The business ethics chapter begins by looking at the various ways in which the explosion of interest in business ethics, corporate governance and social responsibility might articulate a sustained evaluation of the means and ends of management. Whilst much of this literature does argue that business ethics makes good business, other elements of it open up business practice to questions that it does not usually have to answer. I suggest that moral philosophy can help us think about the reconstitution of business organizations, but that it generally only asks very specific questions in very specific ways. Importantly, business ethics usually excludes the politics of business, and of capitalism more generally. It tends to personalize these matters as questions for individual managers, when they might be better asked as structural questions about market managerialism and global corporate domination.

Yet also from within B-Schools, and over the last ten years or so, there has been increasing interest in what is now usually called critical management studies. In chapter 6 I consider this body of academic writing which is concerned to denaturalize and re-evaluate many of the taken-for-granted assumptions that are deployed within the mainstream – including the ideas covered in the previous chapters. However, the arcane nature of many of these arguments, the endless debates between neo-Marxists and Foucauldians, realists and post-structuralists, and a typically academic emphasis on the importance of Big Theory means that most of this writing is rarely read outside the academy. So, what is the point in complaining if no one can hear your voice, or understand it even if they could hear you?

Oddly though, in the most popular media of all – the entertainment industries – we can find voices that echo far beyond the seminar room or the academic journal. There is a rich vein of anti-management material in popular books and films that often articulates a critical understanding of managerialism and the big corporation in some very surprising ways. Chapter 7 will survey much of this material, from Charlie Chaplin to cyborg science fiction, in order to argue that the 'against management' cultural current is clearly emerging in other places, just as it did in the first third of the last century during an earlier crisis of managerialism. The image of the utilitarian bureaucrat, or the conspiratorial organization, is one that is now firmly embedded within popular narratives, yet this is almost always ignored by those writing about management within the academy.

But perhaps the most visible form of resistance to corporate colonization, and the provocation for this book, has been the rise of a loud rainbow coalition of protesters who are taking to the streets in order to make their point. Chapter 8 covers the battle in Seattle and many other recent anti-capitalist protests, as well as magazines, internet sites and a small mountain of books by authors such as Naomi Klein, George Monbiot, Thomas Frank and others. In bringing together activists with a wide variety of interests under the banner of resistance to various attempts to further globalize world trade, this movement has become a central feature of the contemporary political landscape. These groups have, unlike business ethicists or critical management studies academics, no particular concern with Big Theory, yet they gain more media coverage and seem to have much more impact. I will argue that their lack of concern for the niceties of scholarship and argument makes them a particularly powerful and important symbol of protest to inspire others – including cloistered academics like me – and possibly the most important contemporary example of an evaluation of managerialism as the problem, and not a solution. In summary, and despite their various strengths and weaknesses, chapters 5 to 8 seem to represent something of a change in the political culture. Many people, in many different sites, seem to be losing their faith in managerialism and provoking a legitimacy crisis that this book seeks to amplify.

In the last chapter I begin by restating that I am not against organization as such, or technology, or even progress, but that the uncritical celebration of management over the past fifty years has been most unfortunate. It has damaged democracy, legitimated inequality and exported injustice in the name of a neutral and efficient technology of organizing. Sadly, or perhaps predictably, those academics who could be in a position to offer articulate resistance are too busy arguing about different ethical or epistemological frameworks to do much about it. The chapter compares four possible sites of resistance to managerialism – managers themselves, academics, individuals and states – and attempts to evaluate their relative strengths and weakness. But, most importantly, it suggests that there *are* alternatives to narrow conceptions of organization as market-driven managerialism. So, in the second half of this chapter I raise questions of scale, hierarchy, the division of labour and so on (all prefigured in utopian, anarchist, situationist and feminist accounts of organizing) in order to open up 'organizing' in much more multiple ways than are presently thought to be proper. The problem is that the idea of the market managerial one best way, combined with the ideology of the end of history, has restricted our imagination of what organizing might involve to a remarkable degree. It is almost as if we now have so much faith in management, in all three senses of the term, that we cannot imagine being organized without it. The book concludes with a self-consciously utopian plea for more public debate on, and resistance to, the ideology of management, and an insistence that the point of books like this is not merely to come to a different understanding of the world, but an attempt to try and change it.

2

McBUREAUCRACY: LIBERALISM AND THE IRON CAGE

'Freedom is a Big Mac
A First Taste of the West
A McDonald's hamburger gave East German postman Thomas Maier
his first taste of freedom yesterday. Munching on his free Big Mac in
a West Berlin street crowded with his countrymen, Thomas, 24, said:
"I didn't know capitalism was this kind." '

Sunday Mirror, 12 November 1989

Bureaucracy: 'the mask of modern fascism'

Fernand Lambrecht's epithet might be taken to imply that bureaucracy and democracy are incompatible, and that bureaucracy is
implicitly fascistic, whatever its intentions. Though the epithet
'fascist' only really makes sense nowadays in the context of the holocaust (Bauman 1989), one of the most common ways in which forms
of large-scale centralized organization and management has been
criticized over the past two and a half centuries is through the use of
the word 'bureaucracy'. To call someone a 'bureaucrat' is to suggest
that they have myopically substituted means for ends, to say that they
are strangling themselves and others with red tape, and that (as
Eichmann famously argued at his trial) they are only following
orders. Indeed, the early origins of the word express pretty much the
same sentiments. The term was metonymically derived from *burel*,
the coarse cloth that might cover a desk and then to *bureau*, the desk
itself (Burrell 1997). *Bureaucratie*, rule from the desk, was coined
(according to Baron de Grimm in a letter dated 1 July 1764) by

Vincent de Gourney in the middle of the eighteenth century (Nelson 1985). De Gourney was one of the progressive French 'physiocrats' or 'economists' who stressed a dynamic and liberal view of the circulation of wealth against centralized state protectionism. *Bureaucratie* was a form of governance by officials, and the word spread rapidly into Italian (*burocrazia*), German (*Bureaucratie*, and later *Bürokratie*) and English.

De Gourney saw bureaumania as an 'illness', an impediment to the proper exercise of commercial freedoms, and this view echoes down the centuries to the present concern of the World Trade Organization to 'liberate' trade from regulation. In 1830s' England, the term was often used in resistance to the centralization of poor relief and public health measures. Thomas Carlyle, in 1850, referred to it as 'the continental nuisance' and John Stuart Mill, in 1860, as an inadequate alternative to democracy within which 'the work of government has been in the hands of governors by profession' (Mitchell 1968). Yet, despite such hostility from political commentators of various persuasions, neither the word nor the organizational form vanished in the face of such hostility, and fifty years later Gaetano Mosca in Italy and Robert Michels in Germany[1] could both write books which assumed that bureaucracy was inevitable in any large-scale state or organization. Bureaucracy, it seemed, might not be pleasant, but it was here to stay.

However, the most influential author for our contemporary understandings of bureaucracy was undoubtedly Max Weber, whose *Wirtschaft und Gesellschaft* (*Economy and Society*) was published in 1921. Weber, like Mosca and Michels, saw the advance of bureaucratization as inevitable but tied it to a larger sociological thesis about the development of forms of legitimacy. He argued that, in every sphere of social life, from music to war, charismatic and traditional forms of authority are increasingly routinized into legal-rational, or bureaucratic, authority. But Weber's ambivalence about the advance of bureaucracy is clear. On the one hand, he lists its technical advantages: 'The fully developed bureaucratic mechanism compares with other organizations exactly as does the machine with the non-mechanical modes of production. Precision, speed, unambiguity, knowledge of the files, continuity, discretion, unity, strict subordination, reduction of friction and of material and personal costs – these are raised to the optimum point . . .' (Weber, in Gerth and Mills 1948: 214). Yet he is also painfully aware of its consequences:

Its specific nature, which is welcomed by capitalism, develops the more perfectly the more bureaucracy is 'dehumanized', the more completely it succeeds in eliminating from official business love, hatred and all purely personal, irrational, and emotional elements which escape calculation. [. . .] the professional bureaucrat is chained to his activity by his entire material and ideal existence. In the great majority of cases, he is only a single cog in an ever-moving mechanism which prescribes to him an essentially fixed route of march. (1948: 215–16, 228)

Weber's melancholy ambivalence echoes through the twentieth century. Harold Laski, in 1930, defines bureaucracy as 'a system of government the control of which is so completely in the hands of officials that their power jeopardizes the liberties of ordinary citizens'. In 1950, Harold Lasswell and Abraham Kaplan refer to it as 'the form of rule in which the élite is composed of officials' (Nelson 1985). Indeed, much of US sociology and psychology after the Second World War was concerned with various ways in which the authoritarian fascist version of bureaucracy could be better understood and avoided. Descriptions of authoritarian and bureaucratic personality types, experiments on the willingness of subjects to obey people in white coats, and accounts of the inefficiencies and dysfunctions of bureaucracy abound.[2] In his celebrated book, *The Organization Man*, William Whyte describes the 'social ethic' (which 'could be called an organization ethic, or a bureaucratic ethic') as a pervasive form of dull conformity (1961: 11). For Whyte this is a climate that 'inhibits individual initiative and imagination, and the courage to exercise it against group opinion' (ibid.: 365). Around the same time, Herbert Marcuse (who cites Whyte approvingly) characterized modern societies as one-dimensional in the sense that people at work, and in their leisure, were becoming mere instruments for the mechanical organization of capitalism (1964), and situationists like Vaneigem and Debord launched an assault on a culture based on 'time-which-is-money, submission to bosses, boredom, exhaustion [. . .] The organization of work and the organization of leisure are the blades of the castrating shears whose job is to improve the race of fawning dogs.' (Vaneigem 1992 [1967]: 52, 55). More lately, and more carefully, both MacIntyre (1981) and Bauman (1989) have characterized management and bureaucracy as being machinic. For different reasons, both these authors end up arguing that the feeling human is being replaced by the calculating human. They take aim at instrumental forms of utilitarianism which efface the possibility of asking more general questions about ethics and politics because an impermeable boundary is constructed between personal convictions and administrative duty. For example, in 1997, a McDonald's was opened a mile away from the site of the Dachau concentration camp, the site of about 30,000 deaths. The company distributed thousands of leaflets in the car park of the Dachau museum which said 'Welcome to Dachau, and welcome to McDonald's.' (Schlosser 2001: 233) It seems that mere matters of taste must not be allowed to interfere with marketing.

Yet, pretty much simultaneously to the writings of Whyte, Marcuse, MacIntyre, Bauman and others, we can see in the emerging sciences of management the beginnings of the construction of a different story which endlessly celebrates a move *away* from bureaucracy and towards more adult, flexible, ad-hocratic, soft, humanized or virtual forms of organization and management. The founding myth of Anglo organizational behaviour is Elton Mayo's 'discovery' of the informal organization, and this is then followed by a long list of dualisms between the old and bad term and the new and good term – Etzioni's 'coercive' and 'normative' (1961), Burns and Stalker's 'mechanistic' and 'organic' (1961), McGregor's 'Theory X' and 'Theory Y' (1960), Likert's 'autocratic' and 'democratic' (1961), or the more recent 'Fordist' and 'Post-Fordist' and even 'modern' and 'post-modern' (Clegg 1990; M. Parker 1992). Vance Packard's poor reprise of Whyte's arguments in his 1962 *The Pyramid Climbers* celebrates the mid-century 'experiments in rediscovering the individual' (1962: 302) and much of the management literature of the last forty years has done little else. Charles Perrow captures this endlessly recounted story wonderfully well:

> From the beginning, the forces of light and the forces of darkness have polarized the field of organizational analysis, and the struggle has been protracted and inconclusive. The forces of darkness have been represented by the mechanical school of organizational theory – those who treat the organization as a machine. This school characterizes organizations in terms of such things as: centralized authority, clear lines of authority, specialization and expertise, marked division of labor, rules and regulations, and clear separation of staff and line.
>
> The forces of light, which by mid-20th century came to be characterized as the human relations school, emphasizes people rather than machines, accommodations rather than machine-like precision, and draws its inspiration from biological systems rather than engineering systems. It has emphasized such things as: delegation of authority, employee autonomy, trust and openness, concerns with the 'whole

person', and interpersonal dynamics. (1973: 8; for a shorter version, see Jacques 1996: 209).

But it would seem that, despite continued attacks from liberals, cultural critics and managerialists over the past two and a half centuries, bureaucracy is still alive and well. Indeed, I will argue in the next chapter that the humanizing narrative of contemporary management theory would not be possible without a continual attempt to debate with the straw ghosts of Weber and the equally influential 'scientific management' of F. W. Taylor and others (M. Parker 2000b). In other words, the 'Big Other' of bureaucracy is needed for management scientists to claim their identities as progressive modernizers. Warren Bennis and Philip Slater could celebrate a move 'beyond bureaucracy' and assert that 'democracy is inevitable' in 1968 (1998), but it seems that the basic principles of bureaucratic organization that Weber described so fully are still essential components of all large-scale organizations – whether they sell burgers or books like this one. Indeed, it is rather difficult to imagine an organization at all without some systematic assumptions about rules, hierarchy, files, and specialization. But still, it seems, we are not minded to accept bureaucracy without further rearguard actions. Perhaps the most well known of these, in recent times, has been the coining of an alternative term for bureaucracy – the prefix 'Mc'.

McBureaucracy: 'the modern form of despotism'

Mary McCarthy was referring to bureaucracy without the prefix, but a distinctively modern form of this critique of despotism can be found in George Ritzer's *McDonaldization of Society* (1996). This is one of those strange and rather marvellous books that manages to be both academic and popular, but without doing particular violence to either genre of writing.[3] Like Vance Packard's *The Hidden Persuaders* (1957), Germaine Greer's *The Female Eunuch* (1971), Naomi Klein's *No Logo* (2000) and a few others, it has sold more copies and been cited more often than most closeted academics could dream of in a lifetime. That in itself is quite a feat, and one to be admired for crossing some boundaries that are usually rather impermeable. Ritzer's book is a popular and convincing replay of the long anti-bureaucracy argument, and seems to provide a powerful starting point for my overall 'against management' thesis. However, despite my sincere and considerable admiration for what Ritzer has achieved as a writer, I do want to ask some questions of his politics.

Basically I wish to argue that his book, and much of the McCritique it echoes and has since sponsored, trades on a rather old and essentially reactionary brand of elitism. It encourages us to be scornful of Thomas Maier's satisfaction with his Big Mac which I used as the epigraph for this chapter. Perhaps this is because *McDonaldization*'s combination of cultural conservatism and nostalgic reformism is a form of politics that is particularly attractive to disenchanted middle-class liberals. As I suggested above, bureaucracy has often been an easy target for liberals of various persuasions. However, one of the reasons this hasn't been particularly clear in Ritzer's case is because he claims to rest much of his argument on a contemporary restatement of Max Weber's rationalization thesis. Instead, I will suggest that Ritzer doesn't really share Weber's deep *ambivalence* about modernity, and bureaucracy in particular. This means that Ritzer's version of 'against management' – the McDonaldization thesis – is really no more than an abstract condemnation of certain features of modern forms of organization and culture, not at all like Weber's rather grander thesis about the political relativity of bureaucratic and other forms of thought (see du Gay 2000). Neither, I will suggest, does his McCritique sit easily with other forms of anti-corporate protest, such as the McLibel trial, or the French farmer José Bové's 1999 attack on a McDonald's in Millau as a protest against US tariffs on Roquefort cheese.

In order to construct my argument I will be making some comparisons between different forms of mass culturalism. For well over a century now, many intellectuals have condemned mass culture, and modernity itself, for the dangers it presents to high-cultural values. From both the left and the right the story is essentially the same, and 'Americanization' often plays the same role in both accounts.[4] Critics from the right have suggested that the masses threaten to submerge 'the best that has been thought and said' and that managed industrial societies tend to homogenize the cultural distinctions, or more accurately hierarchies, that allow elite (or supposedly 'authentic' folk) artefacts and practices to exist. The mass suffocates individual genius. A parallel set of arguments can be traced for the left where the claim is made that mass culture somehow drugs the common people into oblivion and pollutes the ground from which genuinely innovative cultural practice can spring. These are usually variants on a simplistic Marxist ideology and false consciousness argument – radical cul-

22

tural change is stifled by feeding the people bread and circuses. In other words, the mass suffocates change because the ruling classes want it to. Though these condemnations are similar, the causes are slightly different. In the former case it is industrial society, modernity itself, that is the problem, but for the radical theorists a particular variant of modernity is to blame – capitalism.

Now, if we compare these two versions of mass culturalism it seems that certain points can be made about Ritzer's thesis. If we translate right mass culturalism into Ritzer's terms, the McDonaldizing bureaucratic threat is one of levelling – the danger that everything becomes the same. If we similarly translate the left form of mass culturalism then the interests of multi-national capital are best served by McDonaldizing goods and services. Now it seems to me that both statements might be true – and they are not necessarily incommensurable – but that Ritzer places much more emphasis on the former than the latter. In other words, he is more comfortable with cultural elitism than a political economy of capitalism. Further to this, an alternative view of McDonald's is given no space at all. After all, the popular cultural approaches which have developed away from simplistic Marxism – Gramsci, Hoggart, Williams, Hall – are more likely to attempt some empathy with the so-called 'masses' who use McDonald's. Against the structural determinisms of mass culturalism it might be asserted that it is not possible to assume exactly what McDonald's is and means in specific places and for specific people. It might be that any set of artefacts and practices which is as demonstrably global and complex as this deserves a rather more careful and sympathetic reading than Ritzer's.

In sum, this chapter will be broadly critical of the McDonaldization form of anti-managerialism but I want to end by asking some questions about the anti-bureaucratic critique itself. It might be said that Ritzer seems to see resistance as eating with a knife and fork. I think this nicely expresses my disagreements with much of the stance he takes but it still leaves me wondering how one might articulate a critical position on contemporary management and organization that does not fall into cultural elitism. Is it possible to come out against an institution like McDonald's without simply being nostalgic for 'a world we have lost'? In contrast, what would a progressive critique look like? Presumably it would avoid the easy simplicities of 'false needs', the 'masses' and so on but, at some point, it is surely going to require a condemnation of something that millions of people in the developed world seem to enjoy. To put it simply – who has the right to take this kind of position? What foundations do we have for criticizing McDonald's or is there, as Kant put it, 'of taste no disputing'?

Massification and bureaucracy

'If it is art, it is not for all, and if it is for all it is not art.'
Schoenberg in Shepherd et al., 1977: vii

It seems to me that any formulation of 'the masses' reflects an assumption of prescriptive elitism. This is simply because the writer and the assumed reader are, implicitly or explicitly, not of the mass. The division that is performed requires that 'we' are defined as culturally different, more discriminating, less likely to be duped and so on. Despite this rather obvious snobbery, there are many commentators from both the left and right who have attempted to articulate the dangers of mass society and shown a concern with the manner in which modern collectivities degrade the inhabitants of modern society. Indeed, Albert Hirschman has suggested that since the early industrial revolution the languages of radicalism and of conservatism have shared a fear of the blind destructive force of commerce to dissolve and corrode all that was good in the existing social order. This, he suggests, is a retelling of the destruction of the Ancient Roman Republican values of civic pride, sobriety and bravery through their corruption by imperialism, opulence and decadence (1996). By the mid-twentieth century, these languages seemed to be converging more than ever. Compare Denys Thompson (a cultural conservative and compatriot of Leavis) with the key work of the Frankfurt School.

> The controllers' measure of success is profit, and they argue that what is sold is the most profitable, or what their tunnel vision envisages as the most profitable. [. . .] In these circumstances the individual does not matter, so long as the figures of people serving the system by consuming its products are high enough. He is thus part of a statistical nought, and as such the object of the controllers' contempt. (D. Thompson 1973: 15–16)

> The public is catered for with a hierarchical range of mass-produced products of varying quality, thus advancing the rule of complete quantification. Everybody must behave (as if spontaneously) in accordance with his previously determined and indexed level, and choose the

24

category of mass product turned out for his type. (Adorno and
Horkheimer 1972: 123)

Both right and left mass culturalists formulate the same problem and
use the same descriptions – the difference is in the way that they
explain whose interests are served, and whose damaged, by a mass
society.

For the cultural conservatives the loss is that of the superior culture
of a pre-industrial past. An early example is Matthew Arnold's 1867
Culture and Anarchy, which defended a definition of culture as a set
of preferred beliefs and practices against the danger of moral anarchy
if these practices are submerged in mass culture. In England, this
aesthetic defence of a high-cultural tradition was developed through
books like F. R. Leavis's 1930 *Mass Civilization and Minority Culture*
or T. S. Eliot's 1948 *Notes Towards the Definition of Culture* and,
to this day, finds populist expression in the moral outrage that has
greeted elements in commercial popular culture from cheap fiction
and fish and chips (see Walton 1992) to reality TV and recreational
drug-use. The sober civilization of the bourgeoisie is contrasted with
the beastly carnival of the working classes. All too often this contest
is also played out on the disjuncture between rural and urban cultures, an organic, 'natural' culture is formulated as under threat from
an urban trash aesthetic. Bennett (1981: 23) adds to this spatial
dimension a temporal one – the notion of 'cultural fall'. After the fall,
which is dated according to the interests of the author at hand, mass
culture and its artefacts are inevitably debased and worthless, to be
righteously condemned and not apologetically condoned. At the same
time, high culture is seen as in some way transcendent of the merely
contemporary, since it is so obviously aesthetically superior and also
the mediator of a social comment or expression of the human condition that is somehow timeless and hence canonical. Nostalgia for
the imagined practices of another class, time and place are the key to
this kind of evaluation (Stauth and Turner 1988).

From an opposed political perspective comes the tradition which
stems from a version of the ruling-class ideology thesis. It has both
its 'hard' and 'soft' versions, the former being represented by the
Frankfurt School (particularly Adorno, Horkheimer and Marcuse) as
well as situationism (Vaneigem 1992), theorists of commodity aesthetics like Haug, cultural critics like Postman or gleefully pessimistic
postmoderns like Baudrillard. The 'softer' version can be seen to
originate in the socialist utopianism of individuals such as William
Morris and John Ruskin and leading to the social comment of George

Orwell, and Richard Hoggart's early cultural studies work. Both approaches are united in condemning consumer capitalism's construction of false needs. Whether it is revolution or reform that is required, the society of the spectacle that exists at present is condemned equally vehemently. For Hoggart it is a series of 'Invitations to a Candyfloss World' (1958: 169), for Haug (1986: 99) it is 'a world of multi-coloured surfaces and manifold forms which functions as bait for the buyers and their money'. In comparison to the cultural conservatives, though mass culture is here still compared unfavourably with high culture, this is now because the best of the latter is potentially more critical of the social order than the former. Mass production, consumption and administration are seen as an opiate for the wage slaves of capital, and thus a contribution to political quietism through distraction. As Neil Postman (1987) puts it, we are always in danger of 'Amusing Ourselves to Death'. Perhaps even more pessimistically, Jean Baudrillard sees the mass person as an inert dead weight, hyper-consuming their way to the destruction of everything, including themselves: 'He can no longer produce the limits of his own being, can no longer play or stage himself, can no longer produce himself as mirror. He is now only a pure screen, a switching centre for all the networks of influence' (1985: 133). Matthew Arnold may not have understood this as a liberation, as Baudrillard does in an odd way, but the cultural diagnosis would not be so strange to him.

Of particular relevance for the argument in this chapter is that European mass culturalists, of either form, are often united in articulating the United States as the source or epitome of all that is most debased and dangerous in popular culture. From de Tocqueville and Gorky to Eco and Baudrillard, the USA has been a source of sobering lessons about the European future, Baudrillard's 'tragedy of an utopian dream made reality'.[5] Indeed, even US critics themselves – Packard, Whyte, Riesman – often accept rather similar diagnoses. In this sense language, brands, clothes, management and, of course, food all become powerful signifiers of modernity and consumer culture. If two areas can be singled out in recent writing, they would be the hyper-managed shopping mall and theme park – both key Archimedian points around which recent cultural critique has revolved. Whilst the mass culturalist could not consider these to be 'culture proper', they can be used to tell cautionary tales to warn us against cultural totalitarianism or imperialism. It must be remembered though that these are 'mythical' accounts. As Tomlinson (1991) notes of both Madonna and McDonald's, it doesn't matter if they really represent the USA, or exist as a 'real' cultural threat. If people believe those things to be true then they are true in their consequences.

In summary, and as Raymond Williams (1976: 87) seminally argued 'culture', that is to say 'real culture', is used in a highly prescriptive and selective sense within mass cultural arguments. Only certain artefacts and practices are allowed into the cultural canon and only certain people, those with cultural capital, are allowed to decide what counts. Again from opposite sides of the English political spectrum, this sense of culture might include 'all the characteristic activities and interests of a people: Derby Day, Henley Regatta, Cowes, the twelfth of August, a cup final, the dog races, the pin table, the dart board, Wensleydale cheese, boiled cabbage cut into sections, beetroot in vinegar, nineteenth century Gothic churches, and the music of Elgar' (Eliot in Williams 1961: 230) or 'solid breakfasts and gloomy Sundays, smoky towns and winding roads, green fields and red pillar boxes' (Orwell in Chambers 1986: 53), but what it could never include is something alien, new or brashly commercial. Chronology aside, in neither Eliot or Orwell's landscape could you imagine the familiar golden arches ever attaining the status of 'Culture'.

Popularizing culture

The rise of the 'popular' as a description of culture suggested a very different assessment of the value of the artefacts and practices in question than did the term 'mass' culture. Mass theorists placed an emphasis on 'apocalyptic denunciations of all forms of "levelling", "trivialization" or "massification", which identify the decline of societies with the decadence of bourgeois houses . . . and betray an obsessive fear of number, of undifferentiated hordes indifferent to difference and constantly threatening to submerge the private spaces of bourgeois exclusiveness' (Bourdieu 1984: 469).

As Bourdieu's tone suggests, it is rather easy to accuse mass culturalists of no more than middle-class elitism combined with a romanticism about the past. This is exactly what the popular culturalists attempted to do in articulating a much more positive assessment of the value of – what were initially called – the 'popular arts'. Just as 'mass' implied the culture of someone else, and an inferior culture at that, so a 'popular' cultural perspective came to suggest a description or analysis from the inside, as a fan, or at least a sympathetic observer. In Williams's (1976) second sense, 'culture' itself is then formulated in a comparative or anthropological manner, as a whole way of life and not simply an exclusive or elite set of beliefs and practices.

In England, figures like Richard Hoggart, Raymond Williams and E. P. Thompson are now seen as important early contributors to what was later to become a 'cultural studies' approach. All, to a greater or less extent, provided sympathetic reconstructions of the 'structures of feeling' of ordinary people. Initially implicit, but later explicit, is the sense in which this sort of approach is directly opposed to the aesthetic and political judgements that are so central to mass culturalism. The central theoretical difference here could be said to be the analytic and descriptive stress on human agency, ensuring the evasion of various determinisms by characterizing social structure as no more than a set of 'limits and pressures'. This was important, particularly with regard to simplistically structuralist Marxist formulations, which reduced culture to no more than a function of the economic base and therefore potentially no more than an epiphenomenon of the mode of production. Instead, if culture were seen as a product of a humanist 'creative mind' then any cultural product becomes as worthy of investigation as any other, the capitalized 'Arts' deserving no particular priority over the lower-case 'popular' or vice-versa. In practice, however, the dominant route that (what became capitalized and institutionalized as) Cultural Studies has taken is the investigation of non-elite cultural forms, whether these be the leisure habits of the Victorian working class, the practices of spectacular youth subcultures, or more lately, the search for resistance in shopping malls.

The work of the Centre for Contemporary Cultural Studies (CCCS) has itself rapidly become canonized as an exemplar of the popular cultural approach. Authors like Hall, Willis and Hebdige attempted to synthesize forms of social constructionism and semiotics with a neo-Marxist conception of the way these meanings are ranked in power and influence. The point is made that we should not refer to culture but cultures, describing the 'relationships of domination and subordination in which these configurations stand; to the processes of incorporation and resistance which define the cultural dialectic between them; and to the institutions which transmit and reproduce "the culture" (i.e. the dominant culture) in its dominant or "hegemonic" form' (Hall and Jefferson 1976: 13). For those working in CCCS, popular culture became a terrain on which opposition to the oppressive order of things is displayed and sometimes 'magically resolved'. The influence of Gramsci is vital in these writ-

28

ings. If hegemony is conceived as a shifting set of fractional alliances, then there is space for popular culture to exist both inside and outside the ideologies of particular locales. It can be, at one and the same time, oppositional and yet co-opted, existing within the spaces of the hegemony but still dependent on it economically, politically and socially. In a now classic text, Dick Hebdige (1979) developed this work on youth and resistance by focusing on practices of consumption. Consuming (whether it be pop music, clothes or food) becomes a process of 'bricolage', in which the self is actively constructed by particular individuals within the constraints of particular circumstances. Products are copied, changed and reframed. There is no necessary determination here because, for Hebdige, style is a signifying practice involving the continual capture and rearticulation of items within fields of meaning.

A central theme for the development of the popular consumption literature in the 1980s was pleasure in, and as, resistance. As John Street put it, 'In taking pleasure, we grasp what is ours alone, and we deny the right of the greedy and the powerful to some part of ourselves' (1986: 226). In the most obvious examples, modern urban characters like Walter Benjamin's *flâneur*, Michel de Certeau's 'producer-consumer' or Naomi Klein's 'ad-busters', 'subvertisers' and 'culture-busters' (2000) are invested with enough oppositional agency to subvert the dominant meanings being generated by industrial society. For example, Iain Chambers (1986) provided a description of the popular that theorized it as constructed against high culture both in terms of aesthetics and everyday practice. He stressed localized, particular liberations and partial triumphs over the constraints of a generally oppressive whole. Thanks to an odd mixture of market economics and heroic romanticism, the consumer becomes empowered both to make and to choose: 'The previous authority of culture, once respectfully designated with a capital C, no longer has an exclusive hold on meaning. "High Culture" becomes just one more subculture, one more option in our midst' (1986: 194).

Now, through an odd slippage, many of these formulations of resistant consumers have been joined to a grand historical periodization. Within some theories of postmodern society it is suggested that consumption has replaced production as the central site of identity construction. 'Affirmative' postmodernists promote the ordinary person to a position within which they are empowered to challenge the supposed permanence of social structures. There are no master narratives any more, merely a series of possible positions which we can pick and choose from in a democracy of equivalent lifestyle tastes. 'Today there is no fashion: there are only fashions', 'no rules, only choices' (Ewen and Ewen in Featherstone 1987: 55). Local, weak, knowledge is celebrated as an alternative to the intellectual authority of traditional centres. The old rules are breaking down and cultural production and consumption involves playing with the codes, cutting and mixing, sampling and stealing. The distinctions between claret and milkshake, filet mignon and Filet 'o' Fish, politics and pleasure are now supposedly fragmenting and replaced with 'reflexivity, irony, artifice, randomness, anarchy, fragmentation, pastiche and allegory' (Ryan 1988: 559).

So, for many contemporary academics, culture in its various manifestations is very often seen as an arena for displays of mundane agency in subverting dominant flows of meaning. The image of inert masses constituted by, and within, structures is replaced by a version of the social which is constituted by a process of on-going struggle to comprehend and live through a world in which everything that was solid is melting into air. Popular culture would therefore be a site for possible resistance, even a market-based democracy (Frank 2000) and not simply the terrain on which the vanquished modern citizen accepts their fate as postmodern consumer. In terms of the topic of this chapter, the moral of the story so far should be fairly clear. Mass culturalists might view McDonald's as a prime example of bureaucratization, Americanization and degradation and assume that those who eat there are, by and large, dupes and victims. On the other hand, for popular culturalists McDonald's – and any other similar phenomena – would be a site for possible resistance, subversion and pleasure. Elitist romanticism versus subversive hedonism. So, back to Ritzer.

Assessing McDonaldization

In terms of the chronology of approaches to culture which I have covered so far, it seems to me that George Ritzer's book is remarkably old-fashioned. As I hope is evident, the McDonaldization thesis fits rather well into the mainstream of mass cultural approaches, and a long tradition of anti-bureaucratic liberal criticism. Perhaps this is why it sold so well in the 1990s, because (as I argue in chapter 7) it fitted rather nicely with the spirit of an age that was echoing back to the gloomy diagnosis of market managerialism that was also prevalent in the inter-war period. However, in order to argue this convincingly I need to first deal with Ritzer's version of Weber. After all, at various points in his argument Ritzer claims that McDonaldization is akin to the rationalization process. In that sense, he claims that he is not hostile to McDonald's itself as a cultural form but rather to the iron cage it exemplifies, to the inexorable spread of bureaucratic systems that the metaphor so neatly captures.

Ritzer suggests that Weberians see efficiency, calculability, predictability and control as the key symptoms of formal rationality. These reflect a social world in which nothing is left to chance, where systems have almost entirely routinized human action and the producer and consumer are reduced to being a 'single cog in an ever-moving mechanism'. It is essential to note that this argument is not reducible to a judgement about the value of McDonald's itself as a product or service. To do Weber's ideas justice the corporation could only be regarded as a rhetorical prop – perhaps an ideal type – for demonstrating the dominance of formal rationality and the marginalization of value rationality, as the Dachau example illustrated. Whether McDonald's is good or bad is irrelevant; the problem is what rational systematization does to human responsibility. The problem is that means become ends, and hence really important ends are no longer able to be legitimate subjects of discussion. The bottom line is delineated by management accountants, and it prevents exploration of what might lie beneath.

Well, this is what Weber argues, and it is sometimes what Ritzer claims to argue. At several points in his book, Ritzer is clear that he is not 'against' efficiency, calculability, predictability and control – and hence 'for' inefficiency, incalculability, unpredictability and loss of control (see 1996 [1993]: 11, 14, 121). After all, as I noted above, Weber was also clear that bureaucracy provided huge technical advantages in terms of both the impartiality of the state or organization and the co-ordination of labour. It attempts to ensure equal treatment and to avoid nepotism and the whims of the powerful. But, for Ritzer, McDonaldization is not merely a metaphor for rationalization but also a practice of cultural impoverishment which he judges and condemns. In the simplest terms, the food and service aren't as good as they used to be in 'traditional' restaurants.[6] Yet, in order to dress this assertion in ways that make it less mundanely elitist, he needs to assert that he not judging burgers, but the systems that make burgers. If Ritzer had only rehearsed Weber, or only denigrated the Big Mac, I doubt that his book would have been as successful. It is the blend of academic cultural capital and mass cultural elitism that makes for such a compelling argument.

Let me give some examples of the judgements that seem to illustrate my contention that Ritzer is more concerned with pointing to cultural decline than theorizing rationality. He suggests that the abridged *War and Peace* on tape is inferior to the book version, *USA Today* is inferior to the *Washington Post* (49, 76), microwave food and TV dinners are inferior to freshly prepared food (51, 95) and that package tourism is inferior to real travelling (56, 76). Similarly, baseball and baseball fields are not what they were (74), neither are motels (80), camping holidays (96), family meals (134), universities (64, 138), houses (98) or even birth and death. Film sequels are condemned (91), as are theme parks (132), the internet (147) and popular TV programmes (70). In a particularly ringing passage Ritzer notes that even the French have allowed the 'sacred' croissant to be 'demeaned' by 'obscene' rationalization (136). McDonald's itself is described as 'sterile' (58) and 'superficial' (156), having 'mediocre' food (59) which customers know is not the 'highest quality' (61). He also suggests that customers are wrong if they think that they are getting good value or eating efficiently (62, 123). Finally, he tells us that he only goes to fast food restaurants if he has no alternative (83) and that 'the best that can be said is that . . . it is over quickly' (131).

So, the book is hardly neutral about contemporary cultural practices and artefacts but is instead continually seeking to condemn them. Ritzer, and many of the authors he quotes, seem deeply nostalgic for an older, quieter, slower world. Ritzer's home-baking, museum-visiting, antique-hunting liberal bourgeois (178) is the revolutionary in this hostile environment. Of course, it takes economic capital to successfully resist the corrosions of modernity. As he acknowledges, 'higher status occupations offer people the most opportunities to create non-rationalized niches' (196). The list of subversion strategies – live in an architect-built house, watch public broadcast TV, read the *New York Times* – effectively reads like a celebration of the middle-class intellectual. Generalizing these cultural practices then becomes the answer to the social problems of rationalization. As Stauth and Turner suggest,

> The cultural elite, especially where it has some pretension to radical politics, is thus caught in a constant paradox that every expression of critique of the mass culture of capitalist societies draws it into an elitist position of cultural disdain and refrain from the enjoyments of the everyday reality. To embrace enthusiastically the objects of mass

culture involves the cultural elite in a pseudo-populism; to reject critically the objects of mass culture involves distinction, which in turn
draws the melancholic intellectual into a nostalgic withdrawal from
contemporary culture. (1988: 524)

Explicit cultural politics aside, the argument that connects most of
Ritzer's examples is that 'rational systems serve to deny human
reason' (1996 [1993]: 13). Yet, it is not reason – the practice of
rationality – that Ritzer is actually referring to here but rather a denial
of humanity, the encouragement of practices of dehumanization
that produce anonymity in workers and customers. Hence, he suggests, working like a robot is irrational and consuming Big Macs
is irrational. This does not mean a-rational or anti-rational but
instead irrationality seems to mean 'mind-numbing' or corrupting
of intimacy. In a key sentence he suggests that rationality and reason
are antithetical phenomena (121). For the definition of rationality
we need only look to Weber, whilst reason, the key to this opposition, is left undefined. I would suggest that the reason that Ritzer is
silent on this point is simply because he assumes that a shared
bourgeois common sense, presumably provided by other 'homeless
intellectuals' (Turner 1987), will fill the gap. After all, the outcome of reasonableness is surely something that we could all agree
upon.

But of course we don't – and that is Stauth and Turner's paradox.
If we did, then values, ethics, politics would never be matters of
debate, and there would be no reason for writing books like this one.
Ritzer, like all mass culturalists, is alarmed about the 'illusion of
fun' (125), yet has to acknowledge that the fast food restaurant
gives people 'precisely what they want' (133). In other words, there
is no agreement about reason. For myself, Ritzer's assertions then
become rather hollow. He wishes to use the scales of reason to
condemn, yet apart from an assumed rhetorical consensus, gives the
reader no clarification as to where he is condemning from, in whose
name he engages in his critique. It seems rather obvious to have to
say this, but not everybody agrees that culture is being commodified,
and even if they do, they do not agree that it is a bad thing. This
is simply because it is not clear to many, including me, where and
when 'culture' ends and 'commodities' begin (Klein 2000; Smith
2001). I will return to these issues later in the chapter, but first I
want to explore some of the larger assumptions that lie behind his
diagnosis.

Dualisms and evidence

As I have suggested above, one of the central features of a sociological analysis of culture over the last twenty years has been the gradual establishment of a new academic hegemony. However, despite the current popularity of versions of the popular, I have suggested above that mass cultural approaches have not disappeared but are merely being presented differently, as Baudrillard's hyper-consumption or the McBureaucracy thesis. However, it is important to remember that in terms of the language of sociological theory mass and popular are certainly related to Dawe's (1987) 'two sociologies'. That is to say, they assume very different models of social system and social action. An account of structural determination and constraint is found in the massification perspectives. However, in order to counter the generally unsympathetic and determinist reading of cultural practices provided by structuralists, action-oriented notions of popular culture are deployed to stress the role of agency in cultural production and consumption. Just as 'macro'-sociology stresses that culture is a determined product of systems, 'micro'-sociology insists that these structures are the products of the actions of individuals. In the starkest terms, Big Macs are the systematized products of market managerialism but are also consumed as one element in the idiosyncratic and contingent lives of millions of individuals (see Law 1984). This 'two sociologies' dualism is also reflected in the general distinction between reactive and proactive conceptualizations of the relationship between message and recipient that are made in media studies. In the former, it is assumed that individuals simply respond to the injection of marketing information in a stimulus/response fashion. McDesires are simply manufactured in order that the numerically popular sells even more 'units'. Popular culturalists assume a far more user-oriented view of cultural products, one in which the producers can never guarantee exactly what kind of gratifications their products will satisfy. Widespread and mundane semiotic terrorism, of the ad-busting variety, ensures that the clockwork of mass marketing can never really work.

The dualism can be seen as a linguistic metaphor too. As Saussure observed, language can seen as both *langue* and *parole* – a rule-based grammatical system as well as a spontaneous individual utterance. Mass theories generally focus on *langue*; people are elements in a structure and hence appropriately categorized as types. For the structuralist and/or cultural elitist then, typification and generalization are

34

both a means and an end. 'Standing back' is hence necessary in order to study surface manifestations of supposed deep structures. However, this must inevitably clean the account of all reference to situated use and reflexive agency. It is to assert 'I know why you bought that burger and what pleasures you will get from it'. As opposed to the mass emphasis on *langue*, descriptions of the popular would be embedded in the *parole* of a particular situation. The liberation of the particular is preferred to the constraints of generalization. However, often embedded in this latter position is an amplification of the actor to the status of a super-agent with the power to challenge and change the permanence of structures. As I've suggested, this often appears to be the position of 'affirmative' post-modernists who assert that, since language and culture is in increasing flux, the actor can play with increasingly subversive intent. In other words, eating at McDonald's, or dropping acid in Disneyland, becomes an idiosyncratic and potentially subversive activity – even if both also involve boosting the profits of mega-corporations.

Whilst the latter positions in each dualism – heroic agency, proactive consumption, local *parole* – are clearly unsatisfactory on their own, they do help to dramatize Ritzer's assertions as equally one-sided. His version of McDonaldization is one which is heavily structuralist, assumes consumers simply react to marketing and follow scripts determined by management. Rather more simply, I think it can be said that Ritzer just over-generalizes the reach and meaning of McDonald's because he thinks he already knows what it means. This is not to deny that the institution and the process are fairly global entities, but rather to suggest that they might mean different things to different people in different places. Law quotes a Burger King advert that makes the same point rather more succinctly with reference to ordering your own custom-made burger: 'Two hundred million people/No two are quite the same/Each doing things their own way/Each plays a different game' (1984: 183).

Ritzer assumes that most people are dupes, and that the changes he describes are global. But is he right? In response it is possible to suggest that, in empirical terms, his thesis is simply an overdrawn view from an US freeway. I don't know most of the other food, supermarket, holiday, child-care, garage and other chains he mentions, and yet I live in one of the most Coca-Colonized European states of all. In any case, McDonald's itself has expanded outside North America by partly adapting its menu to local circumstances – selling new products, supplying beer with meals, avoiding local taboos like beef, customizing its architecture to match native styles. Expansion outside the US is not a rationalizing inevitability, but a strategy that is economically justified on the grounds that the US market for the product is on the decline. Shareholders demand profitability, not mind-control. So it is quite possible that the golden arches mean different things in different places. For Russians, this is new food, exotic food and rich people's food at that. For Americans, the Big Mac is common food, poor food – certainly not worth queuing around Pushkin Square for. Similarly, the responses of Chinese, Singaporeans or Filipinos (see Sklair 1995: 172, 189, 237) will be different, as will those of parents with toddlers, the elderly, vegetarians, public-transport users, travellers, people who live far from a large town, academics writing a chapter about McDonaldization and so on. Whilst I can suggest that all these groups might have different attitudes towards McDonald's, I can no more predict what they might be than can Ritzer. As Sklair neatly puts it, the attraction of the two 'Mc's' explanation – McDonald's and McLuhan – should not lead us to think that globalization always means the homogenization of consumption. Ritzer's own example of the personalization of the identical houses in Levittown, or the diverse use of malls (1996: 28, 29) illustrates my point. People make different uses of the same spaces and products within the same culture. Yet, in this case, the spaces and products are actually quite different globally, and even (again as Ritzer suggests) locally (180). Why then should we assume that we know what a Big Mac means everywhere, or what bureaucracy means everywhere?

In writing of a programme for cultural sociology, Stuart Hall (1982: 72) wrote of the necessity of 'historicizing the structures'. That is to say, inserting specific histories into the theoretical explanations and predictions that follow from varieties of structuralism. It seems to me that Ritzer has a substantial amount of historicizing to do before his thesis about an institution and a process becomes more than a view from Maryland. In comparison, for example, both Mark Prendergrast's (1994) book on Coca-Cola and Eric Schlosser's (2001) on fast food are more historically nuanced. Comparing the latter's account of corporate concentration, migrant workers, state subsidy and so on with Ritzer exposes just how abstracted his book actually is. For example, one of the historical stories that could have been told is about the rise of franchise capitalism – an organizational structure common to McDonald's, Coca-Cola, The Body Shop and many other companies – which has been around since the late nineteenth century at least and which raises many interesting questions about boundaries, negotiation and control (see Felstead 1993; Schlosser 2001: 94). Further, it is curious that Ritzer is so insistent on demonizing the supposed spread of bureaucratic rationalization when, as we will see in the next chapter, management practitioners and academics have spent so much time developing and theorizing 'post-bureaucratic' forms of organizational structure. For example, Ritzer does not dwell on the way that accountability and surveillance structures have recently been used to open up various professional monopolies from higher education to spectacle-making. It can easily be argued that these McUniversities and McOpticians are now costing less and doing more because these self-interested occupations are now being scrutinized more fully and opened up to the disciplines of the market (Parker and Jary 1995). I happen not to agree with such an argument, but Ritzer doesn't even consider it because he is so focused on bureaucracy that he pays very little attention to the political economy of capitalism and market managerialism.

For example, as Paul du Gay remarks in his book *In Praise of Bureaucracy* (2000) one of the common stories that has organized twentieth-century thought on organization is the 'end of bureaucracy'. This can be told in basically two ways. First, following Tom Peters, that the turbo-capitalist and chaotic world we live in nowadays has no time for dinosaurs, so a new millennial flexibility is required. I will say much more about this in the following two chapters. Second, following MacIntyre and Bauman, that bureaucracy is dehumanizing because its dull procedural rationality causes human beings to become morally encrusted and incapable of passion. Du Gay takes issue with both of these pieces of commonsense and argues that bureaucracy should not be disposed of so easily. In doing so, he both injects a sound dose of pragmatism into the breathless rhetorics of change, and questions the position of anti-bureaucratic critics like Ritzer. Many of these critics, as he says, share a certain 'unworldliness' about what human beings are and do. Having no time for such rhetorical abstraction, du Gay comes to praise bureaucracy, not to bury it.

At the heart of his book is a different version of Weber. Unlike the Weber of organizational behaviour textbooks or Ritzer, du Gay solicits a Weber who was primarily interested in the moral qualities of different lifeworlds. A Weber, that is to say, of socially located practices and not the parody of iron cage rationalization that has now become a ubiquitous other for organizational humanists. In doing this, du Gay wants to insist that social roles are different lifeworlds with different ethics, and that they are not reducible to each other in some search for the authenticity of the morally whole person. The latter is particularly important since some sense of pluralist liberalism is at the heart of his reassessment. For du Gay, democracy should involve mediation and compromise between conflicting interests. It is a programme of checks and balances, and is always unfinished in the sense that conflicts can never be finally resolved. This is precisely why the bureaucratic character is such an important figure, because he or she embodies the spirit of careful impartiality that is vital to any form of state administration. Putting it crudely, would anti-bureaucrats like Ritzer complain if citizens were given different treatment by their local tax office? Would they feel aggrieved if their election vote was discounted on the grounds that they had publicly expressed a distaste for people who acted without hatred or passion? Of course they would, and this is du Gay's central point. The procedural impartiality that characterizes democratic administration is a vital aspect of its functioning. In many contexts, we expect that we will be treated without regard for who we are, and that some spirit of 'doing as you would be done by' is necessary to prevent the arbitrary use of power by state functionaries. But, du Gay insists, this does not mean that these people are morally deficient, rather that they have cultivated an ethos of impartiality in their public lives that attempts to guarantee relative freedom in private lives generally. In other words, and stating it in the most banal of terms, we have different standards of conduct in different roles. This is not only an empirically sensible description of ordinary people, but a politically necessary separation for other reasons too. Politicians, who come and go with spinning rapidity, are likely to let their ephemeral fascinations drive demands for policy formulation. However, these policies must be implemented in more detailed and careful ways by people who actually know something about education, welfare benefits, asylum seekers and so on. Hence a degree of separation between the two groups provides a modicum of friction on the enthusiasms of sound-bite politics, and ensures that ministers are held responsible for policy directions whilst administrators translate them into workable procedures. So du Gay's argument is a vital corrective to the breathless turbo-talk of anyone who thinks that the state can be run like a mega-corporation, but also to Ritzer's rather patrician condemnation of bureaucracy as if it were always embodied in organizations like McDonald's.

If du Gay's defence of bureaucracy exposes the limits of being against certain forms of impartial proceduralism, then other attacks on McDonald's expose the conservatism of Ritzer's position. The McLibel trial which took place from 1994 to 1997, José Bové's protest against US imperialism,[7] or Eric Schlosser's *Fast Food Nation* (2001) all represent attempts to take on McDonald's in critical ways. Yet they share little in common with *McDonaldization*'s brand of liberal pessimism. Instead, and as I will in explore in much more detail in chapter 8, these are political interventions that begin with an analysis of globalization, capitalism or imperialism. Rather than being restricted to representing rationalization, McDonald's is additionally implicated in a process of corporate globalization that uses aggressive advertising, minimum wages, dubious standards of hygiene and extreme hostility to worker organization in order to sell food that damages health and is complicit in the destruction of the natural environment and an increasingly inequitable new world order. McBureaucratic critique might be one way of being against managerialism, but it clearly does not exhaust the possibilities. More on this later in the book, but I don't want to end this chapter without directly addressing the underlying question that is raised by *The McDonaldization of Society*. How can we judge McDonald's? Never mind whether Ritzer's thesis is empirically validated, or relies on Weber or Marx, does the book convince as an intervention into some kind of public discourse? This, after all, is Ritzer's claim for his volume (1996 [1993]: xix), and it is also one of the reasons that I still much admire it.

On nostalgia

'For the nostalgic, the world is alien.'

Turner 1987: 149

Reading Ritzer one might have the idea that McDonaldizing bureaucracy is an inexorable steamroller crushing all the world into dull similarity. An attitude of detached fatalism is possibly the most dignified response to the golden age of the golden arch that will end, not with a bang, but with a Wimpy. Not that Ritzer would be likely to agree with my reading of his stance here. He does claim that his is a future-oriented critique, not a nostalgic one (15) and concludes the book by quoting Dylan Thomas: 'rage, rage against the dying of the light'. The problem for me is that I find very little evidence to back up his claim. I assume that a humanist argument about distorted potential should be able to provide some systematic suggestions for, either, what the utopia might look like, or, how we might get there. These suggestions are, after all, the essence of the most historically potent future-oriented critique of all – Marxism. Ritzer does neither. He does not seem to believe that the world might be better if intellectuals like him sponsored an anti-capitalist politics. Indeed, he seems to assume that capitalism is the end of history and that resistance is a matter of lifestyle choices. If history has ended then presumably all that discontented intellectuals are able to do is worry on behalf of everyone else, since there is no point in forms of engagement that might actually change things.

But, that being said, both Ritzer and some simplistic Marxisms still share the sense that they already know what McDonald's means to the people who are duped by it. As I have suggested, structuralisms tend to homogenize local practices and specificities. If you already know that 'rationalization' and 'capitalism' are shaping the world then there is little point in looking for evidence – hence phrases like 'false needs' or 'false consciousness'. On the other hand, if you agree with the popular cultural counter-argument set out above then McDonald's is a contingent and polysemic set of practices – a process of permanent social construction that demands astonishment and fascination, not the generalization of a middle-class guilt (Law 1984). For postmodern market populists, we could never summarize what McDonald's is or does, simply because we make and remake it every time we enter a restaurant or write a chapter like this. So is the mundane task of flipping burgers after forty-five seconds transformed into a magical celebration of social construction.

Well, the arguments should be clear enough by now, but it seems that choosing one side simply strengthens the attractions of the other. If I judge McDonald's, then I am a prescriptive elitist who underestimates the diversity of local practice, someone who wants to regulate matters that are best left to the popular will of the market-place (Frank 2000: 296). If I don't, I am a naive subversive who underestimates the coercive and routinizing power of organization and structure. But perhaps we don't need to choose on the grounds that I have presented above. If modern cultural theory was characterized by the normative use of the dialectically related terms 'mass' and 'popular', both are intended to be superseded by a postmodern epistemology. This may, or may not, be connected to postmodern theories of social change (M. Parker 1992) but is first and foremost a relativism of judgement. It occupies what Hebdige (1985) terms a different planet, a world with a plurality of gods and an eternal flat present.

40

This approach would make discussions of whether a cultural practice or particular historical epoch is postmodern or not effectively irrelevant. The point is how we justify our judgements of those practices or epochs. The philosophical base of this approach is in the recognition of the limits of structural metaphors and the movement into post-structuralism. If the structuralists said that 'X' had to be 'not Y' to mean anything, the post-structuralists pointed out that it also had to be 'not the rest of the alphabet'. The meaning of one term resides in all the others, so signification is uncontrollable and undecidable. The author no longer has control over the text, the cook over the food, the global manager over global consumption. If all we do is tell stories that mean different things in different places, then perhaps there are no grounds for any cultural judgements. If you like a Big Mac, then who am I (or Ritzer, de Gourney, Carlyle, Mill, Mosca, Michels, Whyte, MacIntyre, Bauman and so on) to tell you otherwise?

Of course the term 'postmodernism' is not consistently deployed as a description of a relativist epistemology. In Ritzer's book it is treated as a new form of society, after the modern (153–9), and one that he largely rejects. In terms of cultural politics, and as I have suggested previously, those sometimes called 'postmodernists', like Baudrillard, have often mirrored the modernist mass–popular opposition that they sought to avoid. The lexicon may be different, but the author is often still either looking out of the study at the distant seething mass or outside happily eating with them. This may well account for the widely divergent accounts of postmodern politics (Ryan 1988) – either doing capitalism better than the capitalists (hyper-consuming) or subverting the system altogether. It seems to me that this conflation of varied social ontologies and political commitments under one banner is simply unhelpful. In any case, as Featherstone (1987) observed, the use of the term 'post-modernity', is itself a word that locates the speaker within a particular cultural field. Using Bourdieu's (1984) model of class distinction, he suggested that it reflects an attempt to define a new area of legitimate taste and intellectual interest. In other words, using the term effectively positions you as culturally democratic, as the kind of person who is capable of enjoying both Egg McMuffins and eggs Benedict. This is, in John Seabrook's terms, no longer an age of highbrow and lowbrow, but 'nobrow' (2001).

As Jameson (1985) notes, the erasing of distinctions, between intellectual and mass, Shakespeare and *Star Wars*, agents and structures, is particularly dangerous for academics. They earn a living by policing boundaries. But, if we take radical scepticism seriously, how could we condemn any cultural practice? On what grounds could our judgements, our claims to critique, our stories be justified? Well, the simple answer is that they can't – if by justification we mean impartial empirical evidence or good reasoning. What would count as compelling evidence about a cultural and economic phenomenon as complex as McDonald's is by no means obvious, and in any case, the stories we tell about it can make no claim to be disinterested. Both George Ritzer and Martin Parker are fascinated by Big Macs, and we both tell very different stories about them by using different citations, rhetorical strategies and cultural backgrounds. As for reason, well that takes us back to Ritzer's untheorized claim to consensus against rationality. To me, there seems to be little or consensus on these matters. As Weber insisted, what is reasonable for one person is not for another since reason is a matter of cultural context. A possible 'solution' to this impossible question is hence to refuse such claims, to attempt not to engage in the normative dualistic thinking that characterizes what is now often criticized as mere 'modernism'.

Perhaps this is a kind of an answer – the refusal of either condemnation or affirmation. But, for myself, this is to leave the field of debate to others and to take away all justifications for writing polemical books like this one. It effectively means engaging in intellectual practices that encourage a kind of political quietism and which would allow Ritzer (in his wonderfully accessible way) to represent antimanagement whilst many other options remain relatively unexplored. It would allow his particular combination of nostalgia and elitism to define the present age as being a departure from a 'golden age', a fracturing of values, a loss of real freedom and authenticity and so on (Turner 1987: 150–1). I don't have a rabbit to pull out of my hat at this point. I do not believe that my judgements about the commodification of culture, the merits of *The McDonaldization of Society*, the 'correct' way to read Weber or the employment practices of McDonald's can ever be justified either in some final sense. Instead, perhaps all we can do is to continually acknowledge the time and place where our own thought comes from. Acknowledge it both for ourselves and for our readers. On these terms, if Ritzer's book does have a failing it is that he allows the reader so little space to make other kinds of judgements. By assuming that we all agree what 'reason' is, he seduces his audience into believing that there could be no other way of considering these matters. I do happen to agree with many of his cultural and political judgements, though not all by any means, but I do not believe he is at all reflexive about where those judgements come from.[8]

To conclude this chapter, there are many things that I wish to condemn about McDonald's. I believe that it is an organization that does not reward its workers well and has been hostile to worker organization; that is complicit in farming practices that do not benefit the citizens of many states; that encourages a reliance on meat which is both ecologically and morally questionable; and that relies on production and transportation technologies that are polluting. These are organizational issues, but they are not simple ones since it also supplies employment to thousands, enjoyment to millions and (from my point of view) is cheap, convenient and child-friendly. Like Thomas Maier, perhaps, I also happen to like the food, but then perhaps chapters on the commodification of culture and the critique of bureaucracy should not include such admissions of bad taste? However, these admissions, and their attached disavowal of a strong version of 'truth' or a single position to understand the world from, are not in themselves a recipe for quietism and nostalgia. One moral I would like to draw out of my engagement with Ritzer is that a politics of organizing should not be disguised as un-theorized common sense. It is no good to assume agreement when no such agreement exists. Indeed, the existence of deeply rooted (though rather different) assumptions about the means and ends of organizing – managerialism – was precisely the problem I began this book with. So, as my argument unfolds, I want to put forward a polemical argument which wraps McDonald's in with managerialism and a predatory form of global capitalism. This certainly continues a certain kind of diagnosis of 'Americanization', but this time focusing on the organization of the new world order, rather than a dislike for Disney and cheeseburgers (Spark 2001). Many of my readers will not see the world in the same way, but I am not claiming to tell them the truth disguised as common sense, but rather to engage in an explicit politics that persuades them to see the world in the way that I do.

In general terms I have suggested that much of the critique of bureaucracy manifests itself as a hostility to the massification of rationalization, but without presenting much of an alternative or a serious analysis of why McDonald's does what it does in terms of market managerialism. The next chapter will explore a different version of against management, one in which bureaucracy is still the danger, but this time in which culture, identity and commitment at work are presented as the answer. As I suggested at the start of this chapter, the Big Other of bureaucracy has been very productive for management academics and gurus. In the case of organizational culture, it has allowed them to posit an alternative which seems to allow organizations to function better at the same time that bureaucracy withers away and is replaced by something altogether more exciting and humanized. At least, that is the way the story usually goes.

3

CITIZENSHIP: THE CORPORATE STATE

'EMPLOYEES CREED
Progress and development can be realized only through the combined
efforts and co-operation of each member of our Company. Each of us,
therefore, shall keep this idea constantly in mind as we devote ourselves to the continuous improvement of our company.'
Part of Matsushita philosophy, cited in Pascale and Athos 1982: 51

'People matter above all else. Our commitment is to opening the door
of opportunity to all those potential students who can benefit from our
courses and to our other customers in the regional, national and international community. In this the pursuit of both excellence and value
for money are central. The enthusiasm, ability and openness of our
staff are at the heart of a community which makes Staffordshire
University a stimulating place to study and work.'
Staffordshire University Mission Statement, 1992

'In *Reinspiring the Corporation* Mark Scott explored the lessons corporations could learn from the world's great religions on harnessing
the committed energy of its members. In *Heartland* he takes this thinking further and tackles the issues of the Global Firm whose constituent
parts transverse many communities. He suggests that the key to creating the commitment required for sustainable success is to think of
the firm as a society of national communities. Mark Scott shows how,
by learning lessons in longevity from the Nation State, a corporation
can become a powerful global society – "The Corporate State".'
Wiley publishers catalogue, 2001

Ritzer's McDonaldization thesis is not particularly forthcoming about
organizational alternatives to bureaucracy. However, as I indicated,

the last century of organization theory is replete with 'softer' versions of management which heroically set themselves up against this Big Other (Parker 2000b). Nonetheless, since the early 1980s there has been a substantial increase in the variety and breathlessness of attempts to reconstruct organizational membership.[1] Management consultants, business gurus and career-minded B-School academics have been prolific in developing formulations of organizational culture, mission statements, visionary management, internal marketing, intrapreneurship, soul, spirit and so on. In the most general terms what unifies these approaches is that they are technologies aimed at the hearts and minds of organizational members. Demonizing the autocratic manager, the accountant, the bureaucrat and the stopwatch, these texts argue that the best organizations are built through the development of the people within them. Not only are these new commitment-led organizations supposed to be more humanitarian, they are also more efficient and profitable. As is evident from the quotes above, the key ideas of this new-age management are that cultures can be excellent, management can disseminate visions, and teams share missions. We sing the company song together and the noise produced is harmony.

Unsurprisingly, the response from more critical academics has often not been positive. Marxist, Weberian and Foucauldian responses have focused on concepts like ideology, rationalization or self-surveillance in suggesting that new-style management is actually a form of internalized coercion.[2] Whilst, in an important sense, agreeing with much of this, in this chapter I wish to resist some of the pessimism associated with these responses in order to rethink some of the implications of the commitment-based organization. In order to do this I will connect this debate with another contemporary concern in social and political theory – that of citizenship and civil society.[3] In the chapter that follows I will suggest that these formulations of organization may also be seen as putative models of organizational citizenship, and moreover, that they might be used against management – to sing songs that were not written by the corporate executive.

Before continuing it is important to stress that I am not claiming that contemporary attempts to construct the committed worker are an entirely new phenomenon, just the latest phase in a much longer story. What Thompson and McHugh call 'moral machinery' (1995: 50) was a vital component of the early factory system. As Sharon Beder has argued at length, managerialists have long believed that morale is improved through integration with organizational goals.

46

Persuading workers to take 'more than a wage interest' in their work is claimed to lead to overall rises in productivity combined with less sabotage, absenteeism, industrial unrest and so on (2000: 117). Attempts at worker control have never been limited to bureaucratic or Taylorist behaviourism, particularly with regard to habits of individual self-discipline, temperance and fidelity. Even Henri Fayol, one of the godfathers of rule-based managerialism, recognized that *esprit de corps* made an important difference to organizational performance. The worker is made more manageable if they manage themselves – a self-oriented technology of regulation. Ford's paternalist 'Sociological Department' is perhaps the best-known example from early in the twentieth century (Meyer 1996) but Smith et al. (1990) remind us that many earlier organizations, Cadbury is their illustration, attempted to engineer consent through a morality of self-surveillance. The later development of human relations, organizational psychology and so on clearly shared similar concerns and provoked a similar critique, for example W. H. Whyte's formulation of the conformist 'organization man' who feels they must belong (1961) or Daniel Bell's comment that human relations represented 'cow sociology' (Beder 2000: 102). That being said, I do believe that the contemporary versions of this moral machinery are much more pervasive and better publicized. I will argue in this chapter that their current popularity provokes some central questions about the nature of individuals' affiliation to work organizations and the varied ways in which these can be focused and strengthened. Putting the point rather crudely, it is as if workers are being asked to weaken or relinquish wider (and increasingly contested) affiliations to nation, gender, occupation, ethnicity, profession, region and so on in favour of (supposedly uncontested) organizational membership. Whilst a relentless pessimism about these developments is very convincing, some qualified optimism is a tactic that might produce some interesting outcomes.

I am not the first person to attempt linking 'citizenship' to organizations and working life. T. H. Marshall himself (1950) referred to 'industrial citizenship' as an emergent subcategory of political citizenship. More recently, various related usages seem to have become more common. Miller and O'Leary (1993) have used the term 'economic citizenship' to refer to a new governmental practice based on a customer orientation and related to the political language of enterprise (Miller and Rose 1990). The term 'organizational citizenship' has developed some popularity in US organizational behaviour over the last few years to refer to the level of psychological commitment

47

to an organization that can result in 'organizational citizenship behaviors' (for example, Organ 1990). The president of the Hitachi Foundation, based in Washington, DC, has written about both 'corporate' and 'global citizenship' (Roy n.d.; Roy et al. 1993) to refer to various forms of corporate charity and community involvement. Finally, Vinten (1994) uses the same term to refer to a sense of community responsibility that encourages whistleblowing on corporate misdoings, and Handy (1998) has written about the 'citizen company' as a new form of employee freedom. Though I will be exploring some of these different ideas in the chapter, my adoption of the term 'organizational citizenship' differs from most of these uses in referring primarily to what might be called the political constitution of an organization.[4] I am doing this in order to explore some analogies between mission statements and bills of rights, and citizens and the committed worker. After all, if hierarchical McDonaldized bureaucracies *are* dehumanizing, then perhaps reconstituting the organization as a site of rights and responsibilities might provide a meaningful democratic alternative?

Manufacturing employees and citizens

Having provided this brief sketch of my argument, I will now unpick some of its elements. Firstly, consider this fairly representative quote from a pop management text:

> One might think of corporations as big families. Management acts to develop its people by caring for and training them, setting goals and standards for excellent performance. Every member of the organization, from the CEO to the lowliest clerk, shares some responsibility for the organization's products and services, and the unique patterns with which they carry out their responsibilities distinguish their 'family' from those of their competitors. To perpetuate the culture, each employee passes valued traits along to succeeding generations. (Hickman and Silva 1985: 57–8)

Behind the homely language are a set of assumptions about the nature of the organization and its members. Firstly, 'we are all in this together'. An organization is a group of people oriented towards a common goal because it is a collective entity which shares a particular set of values and ideals. However, different members of the organization have different rights and responsibilities. Everyone is important but some people and groups set targets, shape values and make strategies whilst others perform work with machines or deal with administration. Some, in other words, are more equal than others. Finally, and most importantly, the argument developed in the rest of Hickman and Silva's book is that even if this 'family' metaphor is not accurate for a particular organization, management must *act as if it were* in order to maximize profit, happiness, participation and so on. In other words, if you treat your organization as a 'big family' then it will come to be one. 'Family' is here used as a seductive metaphor. It implies a set of strongly shared values, a blood that is thicker than water, a joyful reproduction of human things with caring parents at the head of the table and grateful children getting treats for doing their homework. Whether this is an accurate description of families is not really the point, because this is a metaphor with a prescriptive intent. If it is not true of your organization then it should be. Perhaps even more alarmingly, the analogy might be reversed: 'Corporations like to refer to themselves as "families". Shouldn't it be the other way around?' (1999 Merrill Lynch advert, in Frank 2000: 220). It might seem that the boundaries between work and home, labour and play, the head and the heart are breaking down from both directions.

But there is more to the new-wave anti-bureaucracy movement than cosy ideas of organizations as a normatively unified family, however common these are (Beder 2000: 116). There is also an assumption that management must convince their workforce of the value of shared goals, they must *sell* the vision and not impose it through bureaucratic rules. After having established their legitimacy in the economic sphere, corporations are now moving on to colonize the social and political spheres. 'Having addressed us as employees, it now proceeded to speak to us as citizens' (Frank 2000: 220). But, in order to be acceptable to the citizens of democratic states, this family must be seen as a liberal one where the parent explains to the child why they must eat their greens, and only smacks them as a last resort if they do not listen to reason. Hence there is much in these texts about management by walking around, about tolerating creative mistakes, about stimulating innovation, about replacing bureaucracy with ad-hocracy.[5] As Janssens and Brett (1994: 32) rather neatly put it, centralization and formalization should be replaced by socialization. 'Treat people as adults. Treat them as partners; treat them with dignity; treat them with respect' (Peters and Waterman 1982: 238). 'Symbolic managers place a much higher level of trust in their fellow employees and rely on these cultural fellow travellers to ensure success' (Deal and Kennedy 1988 [1982]: 141). In order to justify the importance of this form of participation, links are often made with ideas of market democracy and its superiority over autocratic command states, economies and organizations. Ouchi (1981), for example, suggests that mission statements, philosophy documents and so on are something like a constitution, a bill of rights for employees. In order to want to achieve the high productivity desired by management employees must be trusted, and must trust those who guide them.

The next link in my argument should be fairly evident, if rather perverse. I am going to suggest that these formulations of management, worker and organization contain a notion of citizenship that is potentially very interesting. If I can ignore the breathless language, the managerialism, as well as the political smugness and naivety, then it may be that these ideas might help to construct an idea of participative democracy in organizations. It is important to note here that my strategy in this (and the next) chapter is the reverse of that in the last one. When dealing with Ritzer, I attempted to show how his initially attractive ideas concealed some rather reactionary implications. In this chapter, I am trying to show how some rather dubious ideas might have some radical implications. This is certainly a rather optimistic task but, in my defence, and consonant with the general tone of this book, I would suggest that thinking about possibilities might help to clarify our problems with the existent. I will begin with some clarification of the concept of the citizen.

citizen, *n.* any member of a political community or STATE who enjoys clear rights and duties associated with this membership, i.e. who is not merely a 'subject' with only uncertain or no guaranteed rights. (Jary and Jary 1991: 70)

The use of dictionary quotation implies definitional precision, a juridical and rational specification. Its use here is quite deliberate because these modernist legislative ideals are implied in much of the literature on citizenship. As I argued in chapter 1, a version of the idea can be told as 'progress' – social 'evolution' tends to move social organization away from the arbitrary use of physical coercion by despots to the use of legalistic codes operated in a universalistic fashion by institutions formally independent of the state. This was why Weber felt that bureaucracy would be likely to prevent nepotistic and corrupt oligarchies, though it might also encourage bureaucrats to hog all the power themselves. So procedural bureaucracy is assumed to be better at finding resolutions which meet the greatest good of the greatest number in the most equitable fashion. It is hardly surprising then that so many political and cultural conservatives, from de Gourney to Ritzer, should find it objectionable, since it flattens the distinctions between the elite and the mass. This modern idea of a 'social contract' pertaining to all assumes that the human becomes a citizen when they accept the force of these resolutions, when they accept responsibilities in return for rights. The state guarantees and the citizen accedes. Following Marshall's seminal contribution (1950) these rights may analytically (and historically) be disaggregated into civil, political and social, but in all three spheres the underlying progressivism is still clear. The citizen is listened to when the supplicant was not, and the further we travel towards democracy, the better the listening will get. Of particular relevance here is Marshall's suggestion of 'industrial' citizenship as an extension of these principles into the economic sphere, but more of that later.

As I have suggested in the previous chapter, in organizational theory a similar story of modernization can be told, and in the new-wave management books it often is. Before bureaucracy and scientific management organizations were in the dark ages – rife with inefficiency, despotism and patronage. Turn-of-the-century writers like Taylor and Weber (amongst others) are suggested to have recognized or brought into being a new way of thinking about organizations which conceptualized them as logically structured machines. Bureaucracies operated without hatred or passion, according to the legislative rulebook, and all members (but particularly those at the bottom) were subject to the disciplines of work study and time and motion. Attendance was ensured by the pay-packet, obedience by the threat of dismissal and efficiency by the man in the white coat with the stopwatch and clip-board. Organizational science then developed away from these origins. Mayo invented human relations, Maslow humanistic psychology. Organizational development and personnel management replaced hiring, firing and time sheets. Now, the proponents of this story suggest, organizational and societal evolution has meant that the external coercions of bureaucracy and work study are being (or should be) replaced by a new kind of postmodern, post-bureaucratic, commitment-based organization. In order that commercial, or marketizing public-sector, organizations become more 'efficient,' these writers suggest that we must grow to love our organizations and give our all to them, to operate *with* hatred and passion. The images of contented Japanese workers suggesting improvements to the manufacturing process, or smart e-ntrepreneurs drinking Starbuck's java in the middle of the night, stand in the background here. Like the image of the 'family' these myths may be far from accurate, but nonetheless have stimulated much writing and organizational practice aimed at getting that degree of commitment from all workers. Not that this is restricted to management gurus either. As Thomas Frank argues, much of the output of 'third way' think tanks like Demos contains the same descriptions and prescriptions about smart workers and knowledge economies that can live on thin air (Frank 2000: 348).

The convergence between these two narratives – the rise of the citizen and the rise of the new-age organization – suggests some powerful analogies. After all, if organizations wish to claim that they are operating within the framework of a shared mission statement or vision then perhaps management are forced to acknowledge the reciprocity implied. To put it another way, for an organizational rulebook to be transformed into a 'bill of rights' requires the recognition of a language that positions managers and subordinates in similar ways. It seems to me that the rhetoric, if not the practice, of new-style management and the post-bureaucratic organization is very much related to this recognition. Managers (or state bureaucrats) provide workers (or citizens) with the conditions for the self-realization of both groups. The reciprocity of rights and responsibilities becomes a strategic and moral language upon which the commitment-based organization (or the nation-state) is built. Now to be clear here, I am certainly not suggesting that either of these narratives are empirically accurate descriptions of managerial or state histories and practices. However, what I think is interesting here is the similarity of the stories and their conceptions of the democratic process. Most importantly I want to explore the (admittedly utopian) possibility that when certain forms of discourse are used they logically require that other voices are allowed into the parliament. In order to do this, I will now develop the implications of this suggested convergence, beginning with the organization and then moving back to the implications for a theory of citizenship.

Organisations: power, resistance and globalization

There are two points I wish to make about the black and white history of organization theory I presented above, and that Charles Perrow told neatly for me in the last chapter. The first is that it is based on some very selective readings of various key figures in the story – Weber was not an organization design consultant, Mayo built on Taylor rather than refuted him and management gurus' models of post-bureaucratic participation rarely dethrone the charismatic leaders themselves. The second is that it is also empirically mislead-ing. This is because it assumes that new-wave managers actually do what they say they do. Going back to the family analogy, the accounts given by parents are not the only versions of family life. The new-wave gurus who uncritically repeat managers' versions of a caring 'this hurts me more than it hurts you' as they 'down-size' yet more employees might do well to ask some questions outside the executive suite. In both academic theory and managerial practice the story of 'humanization' can be found wanting. After all, just because British children don't work in mines any longer and we are all covered by employment protection legislation it does not mean that work-place democracy has been achieved in the UK, or indeed in an Export Processing Zone in Thailand. I am, of course, using some rather crude rhetoric here, but it is important at this stage of the argument. To put it mildly, I simply do not believe that managers or management gurus are entirely sincere in their presentation of organizational participation.

To begin with a personal example. I used to work at Staffordshire University and received a copy of its mission statement in 1992. Though I was aware it was being developed, I (and all the colleagues I talked to) had no input into the words that I read. Oddly, however, it speaks for me – on my behalf. I have a commitment and ability, I am open and enthusiastic. The statement tells me what I believe higher education is for, what my students want, what I as an acade-mic want, and so on. It is full of inclusive terms – 'we', 'us', 'our' and 'The University recognizes . . .', 'The University will . . .', 'The Uni-versity believes . . .' and so on. This mission statement was intended to articulate, and also perhaps create, a collectivity of interest and a common culture. Of course it failed. I did not recognize the organi-zation that I worked for in that description. It was, at best, a waste of paper and at worst, a document that actually strengthened my distrust of local management. I do not believe that my response was unusual. Many employees are probably similarly cynical about the company song, tie, scarf, pen, magazine and so on. Along these lines Linda Smircich (1983a) shows how employees at an insurance company satirized the slogan 'wheeling together' which was intended to express the unity of a newly merged organization. Van Maanan's (1991) account of life at Disneyland, Kunda's (1992) ethnography of

'Tech' and Watson's (1994a) work on 'ZTC' also provide good examples of local forms of resistance to the perceived brain-washing associated with corporate culture programmes.

In practice, then, there is cynicism about this language of fake community, what Gouldner once called 'pseudo-gemeinschaft' (1952: 347). Just as popular culturalists might assert about consumers at McDonald's, we can point out that employees are not always dupes who simply absorb and echo the charters produced by their public relations or personnel departments. If they do echo them it is likely to be with a degree of subversive irony that almost entirely undermines their intent. As many critics of new-wave management have argued, language of this kind can be seen as a form of hegemonic project which attempts to engineer consent whilst favouring an already privileged group, the management (Silver 1987; du Gay 1991; Willmott 1993). Its use does not mean that consent exists, or indeed that it is actually expected by the managers who write and approve such documents. I assume here that many 'human resource' managers and management consultants aren't dupes either and that they understand how much their hyperbolic language conceals and what other symbolic or ritual functions it is intended to perform.

However, an acknowledgement of the role of resistance and ironic reflexivity does not mean that mission statements are inconsequential, particularly if they are tied to appraisal, promotion and payment systems. Indeed, it might be suggested that these attempts to define the meaning of 'membership', what it means to be 'one of us', are central to understanding the formulation of subjectivities within any workplace (Knights and Willmott 1989). As various authors have suggested, often relying on the work of Michel Foucault, this might be a new way of 'making up' managers, a governmental practice that combines various elements of meaning to constitute a new form of subjectivity at work.[6] The myth of a committed organizational member is a powerful moral technology which, in a twisted echo of the story of humanization, replaces the external stick with the internal carrot. Grey's (1994) paper on the training of accountants illustrates the point well – to succeed means defining career as a project of the self. Thus the member who, even partially, accepts a version of their organization's common mission can achieve a very happy coincidence – an increase in their possibility of status and material reward as well as the feeling that what they are doing is worthwhile. This putative 'company wo/man' is dedicated to enterprising self-interest in the pursuit of supposedly collective goals and exercises self-surveillance to erase signs of disloyalty. Whilst there are problems with simplistic Foucauldian arguments (not least that they might underplay the dramaturgical possibility that people are very often doing one thing and thinking another) they are powerful ways of rephrasing managerial rhetoric as Orwellian 'unfreedom' (Willmott 1993). New-wave employees may only be able to echo the master's voice as if it were their own, not to challenge it.

The implications of this pessimistic assessment could be suggested to have particular resonances in states that are supposedly post-industrial, globalizing and converging on a liberal capitalist end of history. As understandings of national identity become increasingly permeable to economic and cultural flows their importance as sites for a rooted identity may begin to decline. Simultaneously (and perhaps consequentially) established understandings of socio-economic class, ethnicity, locality, even gender and sexuality, are suggested to be increasingly unpicked and contingent in a virtual world where there are no rules, only choices. As we have been reminded for some time now, all that was solid is melting into air, and this includes the territorial solidities of nation states. As Berle and Means (1932: 357) prophesied seventy years ago, 'The future may see the economic organism, now typified by the corporation, not only on an equal plane with the state, but possibly even superseding it as the dominant form of social organization.' So perhaps one of the only certainties that is emerging is that capitalist organizations increasingly operate on a trans-national basis and have turnovers greater than many small countries (Korten 1995; Klein 2000). Beyond the global legitimation crisis there are still global companies which, Hertz argues, are taking over the functions of the state because it no longer has the power or legitimacy to govern effectively (2001: 173). Even if this sketch is only partially accurate this may be one reason why organizational membership becomes increasingly attractive. Management strategies focus on the manipulation of employees' attachments and attempt to disentangle them from previous (possibly weakening) cultural, political or spatial affiliations and to tie them strongly to their organization as a bulwark in an increasingly fragmented world. Thomas Frank (2000: 178) has argued that this was *the* key element in 1990s management thinking. 'How was the corporation to prove itself a worthy ruler, a power that the people would happily obey, a sovereign for whose betterment we would toil and maybe even die?'[7] Empowerment, humanization, democratization and so on became buzzwords that reflected the attempt to make corporations the legitimate monarchs of a new world order, and perhaps to generalize the experiences of an increasingly mobile cosmopolitan corporate class.

Now I willingly acknowledge the empirical problems with this very speculative argument. For example, there is little firm evidence that a self-conscious and coherent global corporate citizenry exists. Sklair's formulation of the 'trans-national capitalist class' clearly has echoes of this idea (1995) and Korten's description of the 'global business elites' is very similar (1995), but neither are backed up by much evidence that such elites share much more than business-class lounges. In any case, the globalization thesis has many critics, some who suggest nationalism or localism are still key elements of identity-making (Calhoun 1993), others that there is nothing really new happening anyway (Bamyeh 1993). As Barnet and Müller note, over 200 years ago the East India Company 'conquered a subcontinent, ruled over 250 million people, raised and supported the largest standing army in the world, deployed 43 warships, and employed its own bishops' (1974: 72). Earlier trans-national trading companies, the Company of Merchants Adventurers (1505), the Russia Company (1553) and the Levant Company (1581) were centrally implicated in English imperial expansion. However, once again I would suggest that what is important in this context is not so much whether the story of a new corporate internationalism is true, but whether it is believed in by enough powerful people. In an odd echo of the mass cultural critique, the idea of the warm communities of a previous era being increasingly fragmented by the turbulence of late capitalism does suggest that the remaining stable institutions could become resources for identity-construction. Barnet and Müller note that corporate citizenship could be seen as a way of detaching higher managers from loyalties to their national economies, the example they give being the director of Nestlé suggesting that his employees must develop a 'special Nestlé citizenship' (1974: 92). As Emile Durkheim suggested at the beginning of the twentieth century, an occupational identity could become a civic religion, a way of halting the moral confusion of anomie that was the result of rapid social change. Translating Durkheim's secular faith into the beginning of the twenty-first century, if your company is successful then you are valued and the (virtuous or vicious) circle of 'career' and personal fulfilment is entered. More recently, Charles Handy has written about this as soul, precisely the kind of vague but inspiring language that can be used to redescribe the organization as a kind of spiritual crusade and hence something that can believed in with passion (1998: 78, 158). To reiterate my earlier point, I am not assuming that some kind of evangelical conversion somehow happens to everyone who reads a mission statement. What I am suggesting is that the idea of self-

actualization or identity-construction through work is increasingly
seen as credible by many people, it 'works' for them, and that is in
itself a matter of interest. As Miller and Rose put it, 'there is no longer
any barrier between the economic, the psychological and the social'
(1990: 27). The corporation could be your family, or your nation-
state, or even your soul. I will now return to the role that citizenship
might play in reframing these insights.

Citizenship: theory and practice

I have been suggesting that the attempts to create commitment-based
organizations can also be seen as attempts to delineate the rights and
responsibilities of the corporate citizen. Both the language of citizenship and the language of new-style management involve making
assertions of normative commonality, suggesting that the state is a
society or nation, or the organization a community or culture.
They also both involve articulating the rights of the member
(citizen, employee) and their obligations to the institution (state,
organization).

Yet, as has been suggested many times in the literature on citizenship (Turner 1990, 1991, for example) the very concept is extremely
contested. The key problem hinges on whether it is deemed an inclusive or exclusive classification. If the former, then citizenship becomes
a unifying category that takes priority over other divisions – gender,
class, ethnicity and so on. However, the latter way of thinking forces
us to recognize that there is no single position or institution that will
not in some way reflect values that construct certain kinds of people
as lesser citizens, or even non-citizens. As Amory Starr (2000: 200)
has argued, nation-states are often built on imperial projects and
myths of national homogeneity have played a crucial role in justify-
ing the dominance of one particular group over another. Either the
Other's difference is denied, subsumed within false incorporating
claims like the stitches that hold together a nation's flag, or the
Other's difference is emphasized and they become no longer fully
human, uncivilized. Finding a middle ground is difficult in theory and
even more difficult in practice because it requires an explication of
shared values, of the boundaries of behaviour that must be crossed
before citizenship is restricted or revoked. In any case, as Marshall
was aware, in any complex society 'citizenship is the architect of
legitimate inequality' and hence our explication of shared values
must include decisions on how much inequality we will tolerate and

in which spheres (Minson 1993). If such difficulties were not enough, it is also fair to say that the language of citizenship provides little help to the practical resolution of everyday conflicts. After all, to coin a deliberately ugly phrase, one woman's Big Mac is another woman's poison, which (as I have pointed out in the previous chapter) is really a politically correct way of formulating Kant's 'of taste there is no disputing'. Reframing this practical problem in what Minson calls a 'romantic republican' language provides no help to make it any more amenable to solution. This is probably because, from a broadly discursive perspective, understandings of morally acceptable action are stories we tell and they differ according to allegiance and will change over time. There is no Archimedian point from which the citizen can judge and be judged, no place outside society from which the constitutional tablets can come down from the mountain.

All that being said, I would still argue that the idea of citizenship might be a tactically useful one. A state, or organization, can be viewed metaphorically or discursively as a form of social contract and, if the metaphor is widespread enough, that will shape expectations and conduct. In any case, it seems an inescapable fact about human beings that we participate in forms of social organization which allow us to do some things that we could not achieve on our own, but that this participation in itself means that we cannot do other things. Of course we do not usually participate as equals and so our rights and responsibilities are not equally distributed either. Perhaps the social contract was drawn up by a very corrupt solicitor (if the couplet is not a tautology). As I suggested above, citizenship in most modern states is definitionally constructed by white, able-bodied, heterosexual, middle-class, employed, middle-aged males – like the person who is writing this book. If you do not fit neatly into those categories then you are likely to be a denizen, a supplicant, a subject. This means that institutional practices of the discourse are hence usually exclusive; they stress revoking membership if responsibilities are not met. Yet, using the symmetry of the same starting point it is possible to suggest that the concept can be *tactically* used to stress rights. This is perhaps the most important point I wish to make: it certainly provides the hinge for my argument in this chapter. Putting it simply, if managers talk about responsibility then there is an opening for their subordinates to represent themselves and their superiors within the same logic. This is pretty much what Marshall (1950) argued in suggesting that citizenship rights may have begun as specifications of a formally free labour force – civil rights supporting bourgeois capitalism – but that their extension into the political and social spheres increasingly problematized the class inequalities that were characteristic of capitalism in the first place. In other words, the very dualism of rights and responsibilities is often uncomfortably two-edged for those in power who claim them to be important.

The tactics of organizational citizenship

'Behind the citizenship debate is the quest for an adequate account of the public within which the good life could be realized on the basis of universalistic social participation, irrespective of colour, creed, class, age or gender.'

Turner 1991: 217

In this chapter I am suggesting, very much against the contemporary mood in organizational theory, that perhaps the master's voice can be used against him, that the rest of the metaphorical 'family' can ask the father to eat his greens too, or the leader of the nation-state to pay her taxes. To go back to my previous example. Staffordshire University's mission statement says 'people matter above all else'. It says that management is a matter of motivating the commitment of employees. This may be anodyne rhetoric but it does not say that profits or certain members matter above all else (which may be true), or that they do not care what employees think (which may also be true). The point is that within the language is the possibility that employees might take them at their word: 'If you really do care what we think then listen to this.' If management are prepared to present a version of the organizational citizen as one that accepts responsibilities then they are, logically at least, also forced to accept the reciprocity implied – that all citizens have rights. Most importantly, this might mean that management will be forced to listen to some other accounts of 'their' organization, and perhaps to establish and institutionalize ways of articulating and mediating different claims to rights as their responsibility. Whilst the most common response from academics has been to be critical of attempts at managerial manipulation,[8] I am suggesting that we might do well to take elements of this ideology or discourse at face value for tactical reasons. Of course mission statements are intended to serve particular interests, but they *also* might be used to subvert the probable intentions of those actors, mostly managers, who sponsor them. After all, if adverts can be productively subvertised, then perhaps mission statements can be productively taken seriously.

Before I am misunderstood, I wish to clarify two points. Firstly, I am not suggesting that productive resistance needs to wait for the formulation of mission statements (or some other similar kind of document), rather that a certain kind of resistance might be stimulated by them. Secondly, and as I hope I have made clear in the rest of this chapter, I am not naive enough to think that an organization will change simply because an employee starts quoting the mission statement back at their line manager. The managers who wrote them, or have to defend them, may not believe in them either. They are documents that will be read by insiders and outsiders, superiors and subordinates in different ways and their meaning is ultimately inseparable from a local context (Swales and Rogers 1995; Pritchard 1996). To treat them as timeless legislative statutes would be politically naive. What I am pointing out is that a practice of organizational democracy might begin from a text that metaphorically attempts to mimic an organizational bill of rights. It could be an arena within which challenges might be made using the same language of civil and political citizenship that management wish to claim as belonging to everyone. In a sense, the mission statement (with its implicit reliance on the commitment-built organization) provides an opening because it relies for its considerable persuasiveness on a linkage or alliance with a language of modernizing emancipation. Ironically, this is both its strength and the central weakness that I am suggesting might transform it into something more than a piece of paper.

If such a hypothetical contest were joined within an organization with the mission statement as the key exhibit then there would seem to be three broad options. Firstly, management could simply ignore the claims about rights which might be invoked by workers, in which case their mission statements would lose any little remaining legitimacy they wished to claim for them. They could no longer play any convincing role within management language and practice. Secondly, management could abort their commitment-led discursive project and reinstitute or further strengthen the coercions of a more autocratic form of managerialism. Thirdly, the optimistic scenario, a dialogue might be joined and further specification of the rights and responsibilities of the corporate citizen might result. In favour of the optimistic scenario I suggest three further points. The first is that managers, like most other people, would probably rather think of themselves as democrats than autocrats and it is embarrassing to be revealed (to oneself and others) as a liar where such matters are concerned. Secondly, to move towards more explicitly coercive controls is (according to the influential narrative of organizational evolution) to travel backwards in history. The narrative may be flawed, but if managers give it legitimacy then it may have important consequences for their strategies. Thirdly, and probably most importantly, in all workplaces managers need workers' co-operation in some form or another. This is most obviously true in organizations which rely on strategies of 'responsible autonomy' (rather than 'direct control') for certain groups of subordinates (Friedman 1977). Staffordshire University is a prime example of such an organization and management options one and two would result in expensive and time-consuming direct control strategies being required for all its workers. Not only would this be technically difficult, it would also seriously damage their competitive position in the academic labour market, result in the end of self-directed activities such as research and writing and probably have severe implications for the cultural capital of the university's various services.[9]

However, even if I am correct and some kind of dialogue about rights and responsibilities was joined there would be no way of avoiding the problems with inclusive and exclusive definitions of citizenship identified above. Like states, organizations are not normatively homogeneous and neither are their 'goals' ('missions') uncontested. Specifying the mission of any university would have to (at least) make reference to students, taxpayers, parents, policy-makers, residents of the local area, employers and the whole range of different employees. Most importantly, it would also require that the organization's management acknowledged the limitations that all of these varied claims to rights placed on their responsibilities and freedom of action. Management, in some sense, would have to do things that they would probably rather not. Contemporary ideas about business ethics, corporate governance, social cost accounting, ethical investment and so on would almost certainly be issues here since they (in varied ways) are also claims that attempt to enlarge the number of legitimated stakeholders, but more of that in chapter 5. Whilst opening up the language of organizational citizenship is not the solution to these problems, it does allow the questions to be legitimately asked.

Now of course none of these speculations may be very probable, and I have a strong feeling as I write that the more cynical or pragmatic amongst my readers will suggest they are either inconceivable or that the practice, mechanisms and agents are not clear in this argument.[10] I agree with the latter, though not the former, but can only respond, again rather glibly, that if we give up on exploring the possible then we give up on change. To use new-style management against managerialism might be impractical, but could nonetheless be important as an idea which could sustain a critical politics. Indeed, it is precisely the incompleteness and impossibility of the language of citizenship that I am exploiting in this chapter. I agree with Miller and O'Leary (1993) that management too is a congenitally 'failing' activity that continually maintains itself through a variety of discursive technologies and alliances. Management never ends, it must always continue to organize against disorganization. This chapter is soliciting a particular form of management failure by exploring some possible implications of one element that currently 'makes up' the contemporary organization – the mission statement and claims about commitment. If the mission statement is partially constituted and popularized through an alliance with the language of representative democracy then perhaps it can be undone through it too.

Organizations and the state

Before bringing this chapter to a close, I want to bring the argument back down to earth a little. After all, the practicalities of organizational citizenship will be far removed from utopian academic abstraction. Considering the position of the principled organizational traitor will illustrate my point. A member might disagree fundamentally with an organizational policy on ethical-political grounds and agitate inside and outside the organization to get that policy changed. This includes various forms of activism, industrial action, 'whistleblowing' or even sabotage but could clearly not include any activity which was stimulated by the expectation of personal financial gain – espionage or insider dealing for example (Vinten 1994). Now it may well be that such principled dissent would involve activities that might result in the members' organizational citizenship rights being revoked for reasons that many other organizational members, not just management, would find perfectly valid. As far as I can see this is a matter that cannot be resolved within the organization itself, for obvious reasons. If I had been sacked by Staffordshire University for publicly accusing management of driving down teaching quality through modularization I would not want my jury to consist only of Staffordshire University employees. The example does not invalidate the arguments I have been putting forward above, but it does point to the importance of augmenting them with an acknowledgement that the emancipatory possibilities of organizational citizenship are limited by social and political context. In other words, we are back to the inclusion/exclusion problem – the question of what behaviours invalidate the social contract in a given organization.

As far as I can see, the only current contenders to deal with such problems are various arms of the state. Matters of organizational treachery could only be resolved, however partially, by recourse to wider notions of justice and public interest and through mechanisms that embody the procedural impartiality that du Gay claims for bureaucracy (2000). As Marshall hinted, a collectivist conception of 'industrial citizenship' may well be a development of individualistic conceptions of rights in the civil, political and social arenas (1950; see Giddens 1982; Minson 1993). This must mean that the institutional frameworks within which such resolutions might take place would have to be arranged as a system of bureaucratic laws or codes that were binding on all organizations operating within a given arena. Locally agreed mission statements/constitutions would have to be subordinated to, and hence be framed within, broader assumptions about the rights and obligations of managers and managed, worker associations, whistleblowing and so on. Laws – about consultation, representation, employment rights, discrimination, trade union organization and so on – could be the only bulwark that ensures that the fragile organizational citizenship I have been outlining could be protected in practice. At the same time, however, the effectivity and legitimacy of such legislation could only be enhanced by organizational members conforming because they felt it was right to do so, rather than conforming reluctantly because they had to, but more of that in the next chapter. It may seem a little odd to be relying on the state to guarantee so much, particularly since (as I will show in chapter 8) its recent record of resistance to corporate power is hardly impressive, but it seems to me that any formulation of citizenship, and certainly organizational citizenship, is going to be parasitic on state, or multi-state, institutions for the time being (Barbalet 1988: 109). For a variety of reasons, some of which I will discuss further in the final chapter, any attempt to introduce civil and political citizenship into the workplace cannot rely on corporations alone. After all, trans-national corporations do not yet issue passports. Not yet.

I would like to conclude by acknowledging the paradox at the heart of this chapter. I am uneasy about attempts to manipulate the identity of organizational members – to make them into corporate acolytes who know the company song and wear the organization's tie. It seems to me that such formulations are politically dangerous because people might, just might, start to believe in them whole-heartedly and stop asking other awkward questions. As Whyte put it forty years ago, 'The Bill of Rights should not stop at organizations' edge. In return for the salary that The Organization gives the individual, it can ask for superlative work from him, but it should not ask for his psyche as well. If it does, he must withhold' (1961: 188). Whyte reminds us that this is not a new issue, but contemporary attempts to create the corporate citizen can be seen as an even more intense form of Orwellian 'newspeak', a hegemonic attempt to impose a form of self-consciousness that serves the powerful and suppresses debate and discontent (Willmott 1993). The fact that the business guru Charles Handy (1998: 279) has put forward similar arguments to mine, in the name of the happy coincidence of liberal freedoms and business profitability in a mercenary world, is probably reason enough to abandon them quickly. In any case, as Frank reminds us, the 'logic of business is coercion, monopoly, and the destruction of the weak, not "choice", or "service", or universal affluence' (2000: 87). Too much misplaced idealism, or faith in subversion, can easily blind me to some more brutal realities about the ways the organizations operate. Yet at the same time I am aware that the idea of working for an organization that I (or you) can believe in is a very attractive one. I do not want to feel that my work must always belong to someone else and I would be very happy if (in any organization) people did matter above all else. In other words, I do want to find meaning at work and to feel that my organization is doing worthwhile things.

The paradox is that some senses of belonging that might be real and fulfilling to some people strike others as vacuous propaganda:

> Pride ran deep as the world as I followed the news accounts of the war in the Middle East. Although it had been years since I sat in the cockpit of a military aircraft on active duty, the feeling of kinship came rushing back. It was a conflict that we, as a nation were committed to win . . . There is a lesson in all this which we can use in our business of pizza. (Letter to *Pizza Today* readers from Gerry Darnell, publisher and editor in chief, cited in The *Guardian*, 30 April 1991)

Mr Darnell's definition of organizational citizenship is, at first sight, *my* definition of false consciousness. On the other hand I do want to carry on eating pizza (and the occasional McDonald's too). I would also like the people who make my pizza to be content, to be well paid, to feel they are doing a good job for an organization that appreciates their efforts and so on. I am not certain they will want to be organizational citizens in the way I have outlined above – partly because of the responsibilities that will follow from their rights. But then surely that is the whole point. The promise of citizenship is that it might not be a fixed category but a socially constructed one that ideally follows from negotiations about the acceptable boundaries of behaviour. Since such ideals are now widely applied as governmental practices in the civil, political and social contexts I see no reason why they might not also be applied to organizations.

But then, to follow another line of thought, perhaps I'm not thinking hard enough about what organizations actually *can* be. Perhaps I'm not being utopian enough? The form of organizational citizenship that I have described above might ameliorate the criticisms of bureaucratic management I covered in chapter 2, but it still essentially relies on another bureaucracy (the state) at the same time that it does little to challenge principles of ownership, hierarchy, divisions of labour and reward, and so on. So perhaps the metaphor of the mission statement is profoundly misleading, in that it is a still quasi-bureaucratic way to enforce commitment. Instead, it might be suggested that a real alternative to bureaucracy would not require a written mission, but would spring from the hearts and minds of employees themselves. So, as an alternative, can organizations be formulated as communities, as groups of passionately intimate individuals who care deeply about what they are doing? Might this be a way to think about a more robust response to managerialism, or bureaucracy, or the fake language of organizational citizenship? It is to this that I will turn in the next chapter.

4

COMMUNITY:
THE FREEDOM TO WORK

'The complexity of community thus relates to the difficult interaction between [. . .] on the one hand the sense of direct common concern; on the other the materialization of various forms of common organization, which may or may not adequately express this.'

Williams 1976: 76

'Now, though, the corporation was on the offensive, noisily establishing its "soul", its personhood, and hence its legitimacy even as it downsized the ranks of its blue-collar employees, smashed the company towns to which it had once sworn eternal loyalty, out-sourced every possible job, and reintroduced Americans to the grotesque social formations of the nineteenth century.'

Frank 2000: 226

If a progressive version of organizational citizenship must still rely on the procedural bureaucracy of the state, can organizations be reimagined as communities instead? Can a strong sense of 'common direct concern' coincide with something as instrumental as a work organization? As the previous chapter argued, much recent popular and academic management writing has attempted to articulate this descriptive and prescriptive move from organizations as tight structures of control to organizations as looser networks of engineered consent.[1] The story told is one of the inefficiencies of bureaucracy, accounting and Fordism being superseded by the flexibility and creativity of learning organizations with dynamic transformational leaders. These kind of ideas are often marketed as a revolutionary development away from bureaucracy, rebranding dull administrators as visionary leaders who can shepherd their flock to the promised land, and ordinary workers as capable of extraordinary commitment. Yet, for my purposes in this chapter, the important part of this development is the idea that employees are being encouraged to give extraordinary effort *because they want to*. It is almost as if we are being encouraged to reimagine our work organization as a community – a *Gemeinschaft* – and the result should be a happy coincidence between our desires and those of the organization's other stakeholders, particularly the shareholders.

It is worth repeating that this kind of story is often told along with the story of increasing globalization and social fragmentation as a subplot, or even as a cause. In a narrative simultaneously told by many of the superstars of social theory and third way think tanks, the snake oil business gurus and corporate libertarians, it is because of modernity's relentless dissolution of established understandings and the rise of a social order based on transient multiple associations – *Gesellschaft* – that organizations need to become more cohesive in value terms. No longer can the stabilities of place, state, labour, finance, technology and so on be assumed because change is becoming the only constant. Supposedly, forms of social organization are being 'detraditionalized' and individuals in increasing danger of anomie and cynicism as their old communities dissolve around them.[2] In management terms, the 'symbolic analysts' who are needed to populate the new knowledge organizations will need forms of control that respect their autonomy and creativity. Taylorist scientific management, or bureaucratic forms of organizational structure, are simply no longer effective. Organizational commitment is then potentially articulated as a defence against the inexorable tides of social change. If we are increasingly lost in so much of our life, then our organization, our labour, our career can and should become the post that us (post)moderns hang their identities on.

As I said, I'm not at all sure whether this is an empirically accurate account of changes in contemporary organizations but it is believed by many, and that in itself makes it worthy of serious attention. So, in this chapter I wish to explore another aspect of this reading of contemporary management, but this time thinking about the term 'community', rather than citizenship. I again start from the assumption that critics of various persuasions find it rather easy to dismiss these notions of organizational communitarianism as a form of ideology – a way for managers (the powerful) to convince others (the less powerful) that the former are acting in ways that benefit both groups and society at large. If employees start to believe this ideology (and they may not) then they are suffering from false consciousness – in this case, the delusion that their managers actually do care about employees (or the environment, the customer, the local community, the contractor in the third world and so on) for their own sake – when in fact such expressions of care are simply means to achieve the usual capitalist ends.[3] There is much evidence to support this 'conspiracy theory' view. After all, for many people the idea of their work organization being a community of feeling would be scornfully dismissed despite what their in-house corporate ideologists claim. Trade unionists are often rightly sceptical about their organization's mission statement and McDonald's employees can hardly be described as 'symbolic analysts'. However, it is surely also true to suggest that finding shared meaning at work is both an empirically accurate description of what people actually do, as well as a potentially desirable state of affairs. To take the first assertion, as the huge literature on organizational sociology testifies, people often do find collective interests at work, though some with greater intensity than others and in ways that are certainly related to various forms of stratification (gender, class and ethnicity amongst others) and hence not always to the organization as an entity in itself. Secondly, if the problem is 'alienation' (or even the less specific 'anomie') then surely it is all to the good that people in organizations should find ways of overcoming it. To generate a communal form of organization in which people feel an emotional investment based on a genuine respect for their various labours is surely a reasonable goal for an emancipatory political project. This is not to say that formal organizations are the only, or the most important, domains in people's lives, because this would be to rehearse a familiar version of the 'public'/'private' hierarchy. However, unless we claim that all organizations both should and do operate without hatred or passion (which seems rather unlikely) then 'work' and 'identity' should not be deemed to belong to completely separate spheres either.

So, the key question for this chapter is whether, or under what conditions, a critical politics might sponsor the idea of an organizational or work-related community and what form such a community might take. To use Etzioni's earlier language (1961), I'm interested in thinking about a move from coercive power and alienative involvement to a combination of normative power and moral involvement – the key assumptions of his later communitarianism (1993). Thinking about alternative modes of organization seems very important in this regard, particularly at the present time as various forms of radicalism are searching for a more positive vision of social organization.

However, before we can begin to address these questions we need to explore the word 'community' in a little more detail in order to understand how it might be applied to contemporary organizations. I will begin by contrasting community, as a form of organization, to its usual Big Other – bureaucracy – and then move on to some speculations about the relationships between the words community, society, organization and state. After concluding that community and organization are best viewed as always empirically present in each other, I then develop the implications of organizations becoming more like communities through a thought experiment – the 'orgunity'. The 'orgunity' both illustrates the utopian strengths and practical weaknesses of attempting to engineer any sustained congruence between a work organization and an individual's various identities. I conclude by suggesting that we should certainly be wary of assuming that the world of work can actually be described in these ways, as well as of the rather totalitarian implications of organizational communitarianism. However, I do not think that this means that a project of 're-enchanting' organizations, particularly work organizations, must always be managerial in its intent.

Community vs bureaucracy

The continuation of the quote from Raymond Williams that began this chapter is as follows:

> Community can be the warmly persuasive word to describe an existing set of relationships, or the warmly persuasive word to describe an alternative set of relationships. What is most important, perhaps, is that unlike all other terms of social organization (state, nation, society, etc.) it seems never to be used unfavourably, and never to be given any positive opposing or distinguishing term.

Quite simply, community is usually articulated as a 'good thing', as a form of experience or organization that is somehow natural for sociable monkeys like us. Even the critiques of existing forms of community are often predicated on the assumption that, though this particular manifestation may be a false, perverted kind of sharing, there is still a truer sense of community that would fit better with the essential qualities of the human condition. This real community might be dug from the past, dragged from the future or imported from other places but its warm glow always illuminates the shortcomings of the here and now. Standing against community thus means being against an unarguable collective good and standing for selfishness, individualism, fragmentation and the denial of common value. It means setting a romanticized and idealist communitarianism against an individualist and brutally pragmatic market liberalism (Mulhall and Swift 1992; Korten 1995). If rule-bound bureaucracy stands at one end of a continuum of control strategies, and negotiated citizenship somewhere in the middle, then community is a form of control that seems not to rely on explicit rules at all. But I want to start by suggesting, not very contentiously, that this dualism makes very little sense in either descriptive or prescriptive terms. As Cohen (1985) notes, it is only by denying that one side of the binary has the qualities of the other that it can stand up at all. Nonetheless, despite such definitional difficulties, the popular rhetorical power of the word is huge and has been exploited by management gurus (as well as professional politicians of both left and right) as a resource to tell (and sell) their tales of organizational futures.

The shelf life of popular management books is not long, so rather than selecting some of the recent ephemera I will briefly review three 'classic' texts that have had a considerable influence on the genre as a whole. The best-selling work of five US authors – Ouchi (1981), Peters and Waterman (1982) and Deal and Kennedy (1988 [1982]) – was firmly based on the rejection of the rationalistic language of bureaucracy and scientific management. Based on their various consulting activities, these authors argued that organizational success could only be gained if a new way of thinking about organizations was accepted. The ghosts of Max Weber and Frederick Taylor are summoned to be exorcised. The control-fixated accountant, the grey 'organization man' (and the gender implications are important) who operates without hatred or passion, B-Schools, corporate analysts, professional managers, cost justifications, decision theory, rational detachment and so on were all articulated as the symptoms of a crisis in US economic and cultural life. The image of the intensely committed Japanese worker, straightening the wiper blades on the Hondas he passes on the way home, provides the nemesis. Entrepreneurial American capitalists may have invented the apparatus of the modern business organization but many of them seem to have forgotten the frontier passion that drove them to build it in the first place. The means have become more important than the ends, charisma has been routinized and organizational commitment has gone out of fashion. If this diagnosis is accepted then the treatment must be radical, for what is required is nothing less than the re-enchantment of corporate life.

As the previous chapter showed, the term 'culture' has been used a lot here. Rather than attempting to further tinker with the bureaucratic 'structure' of organizations what is required is a new kind of style which recognizes that the human side of organizations is just as important as the abstractions of SWOT analysis, management accounting or market segmentation strategies. Culturally astute managers will hence attempt to build cohesive teams of people who are passionately committed to a set of core values – serving customers, generating innovations, beating the competition and so on. Mission and vision statements will be reinforced by stories, myths, heroes, rituals and language which emphasize the singularity of a particular collectivity. This is because people will 'shackle themselves to the nine-to-five only if the cause is perceived to be in some sense great. The company can actually provide the same resonance as does the exclusive club or honorary society' (Peters and Waterman 1982: xxiii). Or, as Deal and Kennedy put it, 'We need to remember that people make businesses work. And we need to relearn old lessons about how culture ties people together and gives meaning and purpose to their day-to-day lives.' (1988 [1982]: 5)[4]

Perhaps the most theoretically astute presentation of these ideas comes from Ouchi, who explicitly places them in the context of a Durkheimian analysis of fragmentation and anomie. He suggests that the inter-organizational career mobility encouraged by an increasingly competitive labour market is damaging to organizational loyalty and hence to general levels of efficiency and productivity. His 'Theory Z' organizations attempt to work against this tendency by employing 'clan' relations – a quasi-oriental core philosophy of caring which socializes employees into common objectives and lifetime employment. This is because if 'occupation takes place entirely within one organization (as in Type Z companies) then the hope of moral integration with the larger social order and of solidarity with one's community can be more fully realized.' (1981: 196) The organization is here articulated as the potential focus of identity work, the place where all our dreams can come true. Furthermore, if we do invest our organization with this level of passion then the consequences for society at large will also be beneficial. A combination of market and clan will therefore best rescue us from the (nearly extinct, but still dangerous) dinosaur of bureaucracy.

In a market each individual is in effect asked to pursue selfish interests. Because the market mechanism will exactly measure the contribution of each person to the common good, each person can be compensated exactly for personal contributions. If one chooses not to contribute anything, then one is not compensated and equity is achieved.

In a clan, each individual is also effectively told to do just what that person wants. In this case, however, the socialization of all to a common goal is so complete and the capacity of the system to measure the subtleties of contributions over the long run is so exact that individuals will naturally seek to do that which is in the common good. Thus the monk, the marine, or the Japanese auto worker who appears to have arrived at such a selfless state is, in fact, achieving selfish ends quite thoroughly. Both of these governance mechanisms realise human potential and maximize human freedom because they do not constrain behavior.

Only the bureaucratic mechanism explicitly says to individuals, 'Do not do what you want, do what we tell you because we pay you for it'. The bureaucratic mechanism alone produces alienation, anomie and a lowered sense of autonomy. (1981: 84–5)

The analogy I am drawing here should be fairly obvious. For these management writers, the answer to the problem of US economic success was to make organizations into something like communities. Indeed, as Hetherington (1994) has noted, Tom Peters' 'self managing teams' seem very much like Germanic conceptions of the *Bund* – engineered affectual solidarities. Popular images of Japanese 'corporate communities' echo similar themes – 'the Nissan towns, the Mitsubishi Villages, and Toyota Cities'. These were communities where housing, job-creation, local economic development, education and so on were the responsibility of the paternal corporation (Hertz 2001: 192). No wonder they were so successful then. But in order to dramatize the attraction of this sense of belonging we need a negative picture of a soulless bureaucracy, an inflexible form of organization that emphasizes structure, order, detachment, hierarchy and in which people are merely role incumbents. Echoing the ideas of Ritzer which I covered in chapter 2, bureaucracy becomes a form of totalitarianism, an oppression of the soul and denial of humanity. Luckily, there is an alternative – culture, clan, community – a form of organization that is creative, emotionally involving, flexible and in which roles are defined by the people occupying them. This dualism is certainly persuasive and, as I have already noted, neatly echoes so many of the other manichean dichotomies that have characterized organization theory. In all these cases the 'warmly persuasive' term is the latter, the one that suggests flexibility, commitment and, of course, the normative values of moral involvement supposedly represented by communities.

Now, as I have already suggested, I do not propose to dwell on the pessimistic interpretations of this kind of story. Braverman's (1974) critique of human relations is a seminal model for this kind of dismissal, arguing as he does that the stick was merely being replaced by the carrot but the end result was just the same – managerial control. Further, and as Beder has argued, there is also a century-long tradition of proto-psychologists and cow-sociologists attempting to find ways to maximize worker involvement and legit-imize managerial paternalism (2000). So, claim the critics, ideas of organizational community are not new, and are largely driven by con-cerns to maximize profits. To a considerable extent I agree with both of these arguments but the questions I wish to open up in this chapter concern the potential usefulness of 'community' as a description of what organizations are, and also as a possible model for thinking about emancipation in organizations. I don't deny that when a manager sincerely wants to enrol me in their 'community' I should be wary. When they claim that 'we are all in this together', I wonder why they get paid so much more than me and why I get paid so much more than the person who cleans the toilets. Yet, as I argued in the last chapter, just because I suspect their motives in any particular instance doesn't mean that these concepts might not hold some poten-tial for subversion. So, to return to the start of this section, apart from being a rhetorical device for summoning up the image of a better world (and possibly therefore distracting us from the inadequacies of this one), what else could community mean?

Society/community vs state/organization

In this section I'm going to try to make some theoretical distinctions that should help me come to a more useful understanding of the rela-tionship between the words 'community' and 'organization'. I would first like to baldly assert that, just as all organizations *are* cultures (following Smircich 1983b, they do not *have* cultures), so all orga-nizations are communities in a very loose sense of that term. In order for an institution to hang together doing recognizably patterned things there must be some 'sharedness' of understanding, some kind of commonality. Organization (as a verb) is predicated on the assumption that we know (minimally) what another usually wants from us – a particular account, a piece of paper, some keystrokes, an action, an artefact or whatever. This doesn't mean that we will always give the other what we think they want, but it does mean that we couldn't call what we were doing 'organized' unless it was oriented towards certain commonalities. If you are unconvinced of this point then consider the counterfactual. A constellation of people and things moving in unpatterned (random, anarchic) ways with no sense of collectivity or orientation towards each other would simply not be 'an organization', would not be 'organized' in any meaningful sense of those terms. But this attempt at a definitional linkage between 'organization' and 'community' does little more than state the minimal conditions for social order. Ordering is sharing, is (to a lesser or greater extent) agreeing on what counts as sameness and difference, on the relevant divisions and unities that constitute a particular form of social life. The Latin root *com* refers to togetherness – a claim to, or feeling of, similarity. Logically this must also involve a claim to, or feeling of, difference from something else. Anyone who talks about what, who, where, the organization is, and is not, must hence be deploying such distinctions if their object is to be at all meaningful to themselves and others.

But if this line of argument is pursued then it dissolves all analytic difference between any terms that have as their referent some form of social order. Community, society, state, organization, bureaucracy (and culture, nation, group and so on) all become different ways of referring to the same things. Now, I'm not arguing that this isn't an important insight (see Cooper 1990; Law 1994) but, if we are to continue using the different terms, then some further definitional distinctions are required. Intellectual work is itself also organized through the process of dividing things – through classifying and categorizing, connecting and disconnecting. So, for now, I would ask you to suspend your disbelief whilst I do some rather ambitious divisional labour. Not that this will stop me from undividing these divisions later on in the chapter.

One way of doing this labour in this context might be to borrow aspects of Durkheim's classic ideas about different forms of solidarity (1991). Society is usually taken to refer to a fairly sustained identification with a large group of people through weak and generalized emotional ties, community to a sustained identification with a smaller group with stronger similarities – perhaps based on repeated personal interactions. In both cases the term refers to a claim about identity and identification. It is a matter of self- and other-definition which simply differs in intensity between the two terms. In this regard it is important that the two should not be seen as exclusive, or in a necessarily temporal (premodernity–modernity) or geographic (urban–rural) relation to each other. However, spatial connotations are suggestive – because they provide some kind of frame for the metaphor of emotional intensity – but not defining. Societies could be said to exist in larger spaces, often a state, whilst communities could be more localized – tied to particular places. Yet, as many have noted, this is a distinction that is very difficult to maintain in practice because the 'gay community' or the 'anti-corporate community' are certainly not bounded in simple spatial terms. For example, Michel Maffesoli's (1995) 'neo-tribe' is a community that has little to do with space since it may be based on the deployment of any potential similarity – the use of the internet, a distaste for McDonald's, an interest in anarchism or whatever. In general, it would seem helpful to regard the society–community distinction as a continuum – the wider the boundary the weaker the density of interactions and vice versa.

But if society and community differ in their senses of emotional density then where do concepts like state and organization fit in? The obvious analytic cut to make here is between the society/community couplet referring to a subjective sense of collectiveness whilst state/organization refers to some kind of legal construction that defines membership with no particular regard for individual differences in perception. As with a judicial concept of citizenship, being included or excluded then becomes a legal matter, one that can be discovered by reference to some kind of qualification – the possession of a birth certificate or work contract in the correct file. This would mean that states or organizations are not *necessarily* the referents or bearers of any affective ties. They are instead social constructions that give certain rights or benefits – citizenship or wages – in return for certain responsibilities or constraints – upholding the law, paying taxes, performing work. In theory then, and as I argued in the previous chapter, this version of social order is emotionally neutral – a social 'contract'. The individual rationally calculates the benefits of accepting the constraints of collective structures and the behavioural compliance that follows does not require emotional engagement to gain such benefits. The difference between states and organizations is, again, a matter of paper. Membership of the former follows from certain birth or residence qualifications that are defined bureaucratically and once given cannot, in principle, be revoked. Membership of the latter follows from certain contractual arrangements which are always conditional on certification and performance and, subject to certain constraints of state legislation, can be revoked. In both cases membership is defined through an entry in the files – it is, in that sense, an empirical issue.

So, following the logic of the above distinctions, societies and communities are matters of inter-subjective definition. If you feel like a member, and are recognized as a member by others, then you probably are one. States and organizations are matters of legal definition, it doesn't matter how British or how much a member of Keele University you feel if you don't satisfy the formal membership criteria. Central to this distinction is the idea that states and organizations do not require emotional affiliation in order to operate. Certain behaviours are necessary, and other behaviours are prohibited but if I have a passport and a contract I can be a member of the UK and Keele University and still feel emotionally (or politically, or ethically) opposed to first world globalization and charging students fees. Of course if I felt opposed to a particular sense of society or community then, almost by definition, I would not be a member, since I would be unlikely to engage in the practices that would constitute my membership and hence others would not recognize me as one of them. If I disliked anti-corporate activists then I would be unlikely to define myself as a member of their community. Pushing the subjectivist aspect of this argument to the limit, it is even possible to suggest that someone might live in the same spaces and engage in the same practices as a particular community without feeling like a member – an emigrant or migrant worker who lives, works and shops in Stoke-on-Trent but wishes they were back in Glasgow, Los Angeles or Kuala Lumpur. In sum, a sense of community and membership of an organization are *analytically* divisible. That being said, I will now try to put them back together again.

Either/or vs both/and

The rather ambitious definitional detour above can now bring us back to the central question of this chapter. But first, a few clarifications. Following what I have argued so far, it would seem that an organization does not, in principle, need its members to care about it in order to exist – they just have to do what they are told because they rationally calculate that the benefits of membership are greater than the disbenefits. The division of labour does not presume emotional attachment. Following Ford, Taylor, Fayol et al., how else could a smelly, noisy, dirty, fast-paced production line operate? Why else would someone sit in front of a computer all day entering credit and debit instructions? I work here because I want the wages, not because I care about cars or credit cards. However, the behaviours that will follow from this kind of contractual membership will be minimally rule-following – if I can get away with not working, with stealing, with apathy, then I will do so because I have no incentive to do anything different. As Poole (1991) notes, my ethical considerations here would be individually hedonistic – utilitarian in the narrowest sense: I calculate my utility and act accordingly. Any other outcomes that result from my actions – cars that don't break down, accurate credit card statements or the continued viability of the organization – are a result of the 'hidden hand'. Private vice can translate into public benefit. In other words, the self-interest of my intentions has little or no relation to wider outcomes since the latter are merely the aggregation of individual utility preferences.

However, within a community my behaviours are guided by a sense of identity – what might be called a virtue ethic (MacIntyre 1981; Mangham 1995). As Robert Solomon has argued, an Aristotelian approach to the corporation stresses that these are places where people find meaning (1992). Places where self-interest and group-interest are potentially identical, and where no one is an island. So actions within a communitarian organization would not be the result of individual calculation but are somehow constitutive of my understanding of self. I cannot 'choose' my sexuality, my ethnicity, perhaps even my fascination with particular ideas or practices, in the way that I could choose my job because these matters are more central to my sense of who I am. But if my job becomes a place where I can express these enduring images of myself to others who share them, or at least respect them, then the work organization becomes more like a community. As a result my actions will not be minimally rule-following behaviours, but are oriented to the expression of that identity in the mirror of significant others. I will act 'generously', give enormous time, effort and care to matters that, from a selfish utility-maximizing point of view, make little calculative sense. In the most extreme cases I may endure enormous hardship or even forfeit my life for this identity,[5] simply because not to do so would be a violation of core elements of my self, a denial of what I think I am.

If this analysis is accepted then it is hardly surprising that the governors of states and the managers of organizations have sought to import such passion and commitment, the virtue ethic, into their institutions. Minimal rule-following behaviour is very useful (it is difficult to conceptualize the divided labours of modernity without it) but imagine how powerful and effective a state or organization would be if its members had the emotional attachments that were characteristic of societies or communities. No wonder national traditions have so often been invented by ruling elites to solidify state identification (Hobsbawn and Ranger 1983). No wonder Peters and Waterman et al. are both enthused and frightened by the Honda worker straightening the wiper blades. If being a member of Ford were as important to its employees as being a fan of Stoke City FC (or whatever) then the organization would be the recipient of an unusual degree of effort, personnel would not have to worry too much about pay and conditions and trade unions would be retitled 'supporters clubs'. Whether this is a manager's dream or a trade unionist's nightmare will be returned to later in the chapter.

However, in order to go any further with this argument, we must first think a little more about the practical impossibility of the analytic categories which I constructed in the previous section. In other words, do some reconnecting of divisions in order to acknowledge that the world does not divide as neatly as I have suggested in the previous section. First, consider an organization. As I have presented it above it is defined as what a community is not – a straightforward antithesis. However, as I've suggested, the neatness of the binary skates over some thorny issues. One way into this is to consider the empirical accuracy of a description of an organization (or, by extension, a state) as an emotionally neutral, but contractually defined, arrangement of people and things. As Weber was keen to stress, the bureaucratic organization that operates without hatred or passion was an ideal type and not an empirical description. In any case, as du Gay argues, it is easy enough to suggest that Weber was not proposing that bureaucrats were robots, but that they had a passionate respect for procedural rationality (2000). Weber would hence not be surprised to know that the mass of case-study research that has accumulated since the turn of the century has demonstrated that organizational members do infuse their labours with meaning and emotion (for a fairly recent version see Watson 1994a). As Philip Selznick argued almost forty years ago, organizations are never just formal structures but are also 'institutions': 'In perhaps what is its most significant meaning, "to institutionalize" is to infuse with value beyond the technical requirements of the task at hand. [. . .] From the standpoint of the committed person, the organization is changed from an expendable tool into a valued source of personal satisfaction' (1957: 17). For Selznick, the effective manager would shape an organization's 'character' by 'transforming a neutral body of men into a committed polity' (1957: 9). This might be done in ways that more than echo Peters and Waterman.

> To create an institution we rely on many techniques for infusing day-to-day behavior with long-run meaning and purpose. One of the most important of these techniques is the elaboration of socially integrating myths. These are efforts to state, in the language of uplift and idealism, what is distinctive about the aims and methods of the enterprise. [. . .] The assignment of a high value to certain activities will itself help to create a myth, especially if buttressed by occasional explicit statements. (1957: 151)

So, for Selznick, over time and with good leadership organizations become social settings that are more than neutral arrangements of people and things. Of course we need to add the caveat that, even without managerialist definitions of 'good leadership', organizations are still theatres for emotional dramas (Fineman 1993). They are places we love and hate, fight and share, places where we make friends and enemies, where our identities inform our labours and our labour becomes an element of our identity. In other words, organizations almost always have many of the characteristics of communities, though these are not always communities where a general feeling of benevolence and sharing is the norm. In Weberian terms, and again echoing du Gay's defence of bureaucracy, organizations almost always operate *with* hatred and passion, because even the most formal bureaucratic rationality gets invested with some form of value rationality, or, in practice, value rationalities.

We can also consider the descriptive accuracy of the other side of the binary – community itself. The opposite point can be made here. If we consider particular groups that are often termed communities – say a village or group of anti-corporate activists – it would be unlikely that these would be social arrangements that never manifested any division or tension. As regular watchers of TV soaps or browsers on anti-corporate websites (Starr 2000) could testify, within these 'communities' there are many occasions on which generalized good will, similarity, affective involvement and so on are not much in evidence. Activists or the inhabitants of Coronation Street are often utilitarian and calculating in their actions, sometimes sharply divide the group into us and them and are not simple 'undivided' persons. As Cohen argues, referring to the Shetland community of Whalsay:

> The idea that, in small scale society, people interact with one another as 'whole persons' is a simplification. They may well encounter each

other more frequently, more intensively, and over a wider range of activities than is the case in more anonymous large scale milieux. But this is not to say that people's knowledge of 'the person' overrides their perception of the distinctive activities (or 'roles') in which the person is engaged. (1985: 29)

In other words, community is as much of an ideal type as bureaucracy. Its 'pure form' is unlikely to exist in any modern context and may never have existed in a premodern context – simply because communities with *no* division of various kinds of labour (and all that follows from that) are difficult to envisage.

In practice, then, empirical considerations would suggest that the two sides of the binary are often found within the same set of social arrangements – organizations often have some of the characteristics of communities and communities have some of the characteristics of organizations. Or, to make the analogy more obvious, nations often have some the characteristics of states and states have some of the characteristics of nations.[6] Perhaps a better way of using the binary might be to see it as a descriptive continuum of social arrangements and hence of multiple identities – at the one end is something like a family, at the other is a very large and emotionally weak institution like the European Union (despite its initially hopeful use of the term 'community'). The aim of Peters and Waterman, Solomon and others could therefore be rearticulated as moving particular social arrangements 'down' this emotional scale – making formal organizations more central (than they already are) to senses of personal identity. But how far might this process go before an organization loses its defining characteristics, before it fails to be an organization in a meaningful sense? In addition, and returning to the questions I asked at the beginning, could these new forms of organizational identification be potentially emancipatory? Might they be sponsored by a critical politics in search of a new vision of communitarian workplace democracy?

A utopian orgunity?

'The *illusory* community in which, up to the present, individuals have combined, always acquired an independent existence apart from them [. . .] In a *genuine* community individuals gain their freedom in and through their association.'
                    Marx in Bottomore and Rubel 1961: 253, my emphasis

In this section I will sketch what an organization that was an ideal-type community might be like. As with the citizenship chapter, this discussion is an attempt to take the business guru ideas as seriously as possible, but I do stress that this is an exploratory exercise. I am not constructing this 'orgunity' as a working alternative to bureaucracy but as a thought experiment, an ideal type, to see how far the community in organizations ideas might be taken.[7]

Firstly, and most importantly, the orgunity would have to be based on a clear sense of unitary membership and this affiliation would provide a central part of the individual's identity. The membership category of the organization would have to, in some sense, subordinate other potential workplace affiliations – shopfloor, management, profession, department X and so on. It would also, rather more problematically, have to be as valued as other potentially competing and very enduring identities – gender, ethnicity, social class, sexuality, region and so on. Secondly, all members would have what Stanley Parker (1976) termed an 'extended' relationship between work and leisure. Employees would, in an emotional and practical sense, take their work home with them – not because they had to but because they weren't capable of leaving such an important part of themselves somewhere else. Thirdly, and consequently, the spatial divide between public work and private home would make little sense. The orgunity could not be located as an office or factory that people travelled to and left with different identities being adopted at each place. I'm not sure whether this means that there would not be a specific place where most of the organization's activities were engaged in (that would depend on certain 'technical' considerations as much as anything else), rather that this space would not be subjectively defined as the only one where the organization could be located. The organization would be where people thought it was, wherever intersubjective community recognition located it at a particular time.

Fourthly, turning to the internal structure of the organization, in order to sustain a sense of collectivity it would surely be necessary to minimize the structuring of hierarchical and lateral relationships. To take the first of these, this would need to be a relatively 'flat' organization, preferably with some kind of election or rotation of those in co-ordinating positions. If this were not the case it would be all too easy for 'elites' (management) to develop a sectional understanding of what the organization was and should be. After all, if a genuine community of interest were to develop this would have to be premised on equal access to information and resources as the potential for meaningful involvement in decision-making. Cynicism and

81

detachment of subordinates could be the only result if every member was not accorded, or perhaps *felt* they were not accorded, an equal voice. Along similar lines lateral relationships would have to be minimally structured to avoid work-group, departmental or divisional loyalties becoming more pressing than commitment to the organization as a whole. In other words, the organization would have to be minimally specific about pre-defining any relationships between its members, because these linkages would be assumed to best shape themselves consensually and change without managerial intervention. All our conventional understandings about the efficiencies of a division of labour would need to be overturned, simply because any permanent form of division, of specialization, may eventually work to fragment a collectivist orientation. The organization would continually labour *against* division.

Fifthly, in order to ensure that internal differentiation was minimized, it would be necessary to reward every member fairly equally. Whilst this might not mitigate against special payments for certain forms of difficult or unpleasant labour, it would mean that the differentials would need to be as small as possible. This would presumably also mean that each member would have a 'share' in the collective production of the organization, that no member might have more shares than another and that no one from outside the organization at a given time would have any claim on its benefits unless it was collectively agreed that this could be the case. Finally, in order to ensure that a high degree of normative harmony was maintained, all selection and training procedures would have to be based on the recruitment and socialization of like-minded individuals, on ensuring that 'they' are like 'us'. There would be no room for procedural impartiality here but instead the absolute insistence that individuals fit in, that they be trusted and liked by their peers and do nothing that might upset the fragile equilibrium, the sense of sharing communion. Qualifications and experience would be almost irrelevant compared to the necessity for judgements about character and the reinforcement of that character by continual socialization in the community of the organization.

So the orgunity would be an arrangement that attempted to challenge and reverse all the assumptions that are built into the bureaucratic ideal type, which is exactly what Tom Peters et al. claim they would like us to do. However, in terms of the management guru versions of organizational culture, the ideal-type orgunity also illustrates just how partial and managerialist their versions of organizational identification actually are. Most 'actually existing' versions of organizational community, the Honda worker being a case in point, are really still managerial autocracies with suggestion schemes by comparison. The orgunity would have no marketing or human resource management specialists, no charismatic leaders, no money or company cars as a surrogate for motivation, no policies for managing diversity, no place or space that the organization was, no distinction between work and leisure, public and private. The organization would attempt to be the expression of the collective identities of its employees. Decision-making would be slow because it would need to be painfully democratic and change of any kind (technological, product, strategic, etc.) would be very gradual. However, the great advantage of my fictional creation would be the exemplary motivation of its members – they would give their souls for this organization precisely because that was where their identities lay. To deny its hold over them would be to deny themselves. As Marx suggested, 'Co-operation in the labour process [. . .] is based on the one hand on the common ownership of the means of production, and on the other on the fact that in those cases the individual has as little torn himself free from the umbilical cord of his community as a bee has from his hive' (Marx 1976: 452).

I think there are probably three broad ways to respond to the orgunity. For market managerialists it would be easy to dismiss it as an imaginative fiction which demonstrates the unrealizable utopianism of alternative visions. For them, the End of History is, and should be, a form of global capitalism which separates public economic structures from private or community sectional interest. To erase that divide is to deny the superiority of market mechanisms in the economic sphere and the protections that liberalism affords in the domestic sphere. From the left it might be suggested that the orgunity is an example of what Marx might have meant by communism, or perhaps an echo of anarchist organizing principles (Starr 2000: 115). It is a goal to strive for, even if 'utopian socialists' who put forward schemes like this (Fourier, Owen, Morris) have a 'fanatical and superstitious belief in the miraculous effects of their social science' that is far from practical (Marx and Engels 1967: 117). A third, perhaps more measured, response might be to consider how the community and organization question might be rephrased, in the knowledge that neither pole combines warm persuasion with instrumental effectiveness. In other words, working out what is impractical and politically undesirable about the orgunity might suggest a better way of thinking about organizations and commitment.

Communities, utopias and multiple identities

As I have already suggested, in modern societies most of us define ourselves as members of many communities, which is no more than saying that we each have many different affiliations, roles or identities. We are hybrid creatures with many ways of recognizing ourselves as like, or unlike, others. For organizations I take it that two complementary suggestions follow. First, that work organizations are *one* of the resources we use to construct senses of identity. To suggest otherwise would be to deny both empirical evidence and common sense. Since many of us spend a substantial portion of our waking hours in organizations it would be unlikely that we invested all this effort with no meaning, that we developed no relationships with others (individuals, groups, machines, buildings) at work, or that we were emotionally neutral about our practices. After all, emotional engagement covers hatred and resentment just as it does love and enthusiasm. The second suggestion is that work-related senses of community are never going to be exclusive, are never going to obliterate other senses of community, of identity. After all, it is hardly likely that a Monsanto identity would somehow obliterate a gay sexuality, a Kashmiri ethnicity or a fondness for one's children or Stoke City FC. In modern societies, organizations cannot be total institutions that mould their residents from birth – they are constituted by (and constitutive of) personal, local, state and global processes that are not simply 'outside' us or our organizations.

Because of this, and as I have suggested above, I do not believe that it is particularly helpful to think about organizations as potentially unitary communities in themselves and hence of organizational communitarianism as yet another 'answer' to rigid bureaucracy. There are many structural alternatives to top-down managerialism, and I will explore them in chapter 9, but they are certainly not all reducible to a faith in the notion of community. For example, I noted that the 'orgunity' would labour against internal division, but surely one of the defining characteristics of an organization is some form of internal differentiation – into departments, regions, hierarchies, specialisms, jobs, technologies, offices and so on. This is to say that organizations are constituted by the division of labour and the labour of division. As a consequence, our senses of work identity are likely to be divided and hence multiple – to the organization at one level perhaps, but also to our department, our position in the hierarchy, our profession, or to sales, production or information technology (see

M. Parker 2000a). As Cohen (1994: 93) neatly puts it, echoing an earlier strand of industrial anthropology (see Burns 1955), complex organizations are like segmentary lineage systems found in the kinship structures of many non-industrial societies. It is possible to identify with the whole, or with various nested segments of the structure associated with a particular group of people. Any potential contradictions between different affiliations do not have to be neatly resolved – it is quite possible to encounter an employee who is highly critical of one part of their organization (management, the workers, their involvement in sweat-shop labour in Thailand) but still emotionally attached to the organization as a whole. Or, indeed, someone who is distrustful of the organization but highly enthusiastic about what their small workgroup does.

Despite what I said about the possibility of a virtual community above, it is also worth mentioning that the increasingly global spatial fragmentation of corporations will probably make face-to-face senses of community even less likely. Though it is possible to be intimate via email or teleconferencing, it is nonetheless problematic. In any case, the move towards the contracting-out of operations, to multiple-use call centres in deprived areas or third world Export Processing Zones means that who counts as an employee is rather a contested point in itself. But then this is precisely what is intended. Loyalty to employees cannot be afforded in a market-place that systematically weeds out local responsibility in the name of shareholder value. In March 2001, Boeing announced that it would be moving its corporate headquarters away from its production facilities in Seattle. Phil Condit, the Boeing CEO, suggested that this would help senior managers to improve shareholder value since it would 'improve corporate strategy formulation'. Kaghan (2001) argues that this actually meant that Boeing wished to ensure that senior managers did not make the mistake of being too loyal to the workers in Seattle. By moving, they would be 'less tied to the "community" and more tied to the "corporation"'. In some sense, then, senior corporate managers could well do without the ties of community, both inside and outside the organization, because the consequent freedom will allow them to down-size without looking employees in the eye.

A further problem for the orgunity is that any organization must, of necessity, often transact with other organizations for the human and non-human materials it organizes. The 'purity' of communion definitionally necessary for the ideal-type orgunity would therefore be in permanent danger of contamination. For example, the members of organizations are unlikely to be novitiate Jesuits, not raw material which can be shaped from birth and taught to resist or reject ideas that endanger the stasis. Indeed, as is evident, in order to sustain such overwhelming senses of unity totalitarian methods may be needed. There would need to be socialization in the purest and most intense sense of that word – a strong version of the kind of engineering of organizational culture that Kunda (1992) and Willmott (1993) have described.[8] The imposition of a 'mono-culture' would require a form of Orwellian 'newspeak' combined with powerful sanctions against heresy. Difference – of gender, sexuality, ethnicity, class, age or whatever – would have to be assimilated, extinguished or expelled. Zygmunt Bauman (1996) has suggested that one of the problems with communitarianism is that it defines a meaningful life as one in which *less* freedom is exercised. This is a problem simply because individual freedom is one of the most pervasive myths of the present age. Whilst notions of freedom and constraint, like notions of community and organization, are clearly parasitic on each other in some regard, this does suggest that the warmth of engineered community could easily become stifling since its price would be fealty and conformity. Though this does not mean that unconstrained market liberalism is the only solution, it does suggest that alternative formulations of organization will need to do more than demand loyalty if it is to be given at all.

So, like the engineered citizenship I discussed in the previous chapter, there is a sense here that a particular form of warmly comforting language is being colonized for largely utilitarian ends. As even Deal and Kennedy ruefully acknowledge (2000), the actual practices of contemporary capitalism tend to work against the potential stabilities of community, culture, citizenship and so on. There is much talk about consent and commitment, but in practice down-sizing, mergers, out-sourcing, McJobs and so on are far more characteristic of the contemporary lean and mean landscape of work. It is hardly suprising, then, that some market populists and libertarians have even extended their elastic metaphors to describe the market as a community, but a much more diverse and democratic one than could ever be imagined before (Frank 2000: 29). This argument works in two ways. Firstly, that liberation from the shackles of bureaucracy involves more respect for employee's independence and autonomy. Casual Fridays, homeworking and out-sourcing become ways of guaranteeing freedom, the freedom to be who you want to be and hence a renewed and genuine committment to the 'soul' of the organization (Handy 1998). Secondly, right-wing US commentators like Walter Wriston argue that the new people's war involves a 'fight to reduce government power over the corporations for which they work, organizations far more democratic, collegial and tolerant than distant state bureaucracies' (in Frank 2000: 55). This is to stretch the warm word to a paper-thin tissue, one in which community becomes freely given commitment and the refusal of unwarranted control over 'your' organization. This is the ideology of 'free agent nation' versus the control-freak organization (Klein 2000: 253), or, as Korten puts it rather more brutally, look out for yourself because, if you don't, no one else will (1995: 245).

Nowhere is this rhetoric more intense than in the dot.com sector, perhaps the spiritual home of turbo-capitalism and the most intense cyberlibertarian rhetoric. Yet, as Lessard and Baldwin have suggested (1999), the reality is a labour market of netslaves and microserfs with no unions, high stress and routine job insecurity made into a virtuous principle of personal freedom. This is what they call the 'new media caste system', a system that is stratified from the garbargemen debugging on hourly rates at the bottom to the robber barons earning massive 'compensation' at the top. Given the dangers of disaffection, the language of community and culture can be seen as an attempt at rebranding freedom as not having a job contract and community as whatever the organization says that it is. Freedom to put up Dilbert cartoons in your cubicle, perhaps, and community as the corporate brand. As Hawley reports in the magazine *Business 2.0*, 'internal branding' is now being proposed as a way of 'translating brand attributes into human behaviour'. The employee is subjected to intensive training experiences which help them self-realize and team-build around specified 'key brand characteristics' (2000: 80). The irony of the term branding, in the context of netslavery, is not commented upon.

Naomi Klein argues that branding – of things, organizations and people – is now making it increasingly difficult to see where 'real' culture ends and corporate community begins. She approvingly quotes the London 'Reclaim the Streets' group, who clearly echo the left condemnation of mass culture that I covered in chapter 2: 'Community becomes commodity – a shopping village, sedated and under constant surveillance. The desire for community is then fulfilled elsewhere, through spectacle, sold to us in simulated form. A TV soap "street" or "square" mimicking the area that concrete and capitalism are destroying' (2000: 323). Whether there are, or ever were, 'real' communities is something I have already commented upon, but the point here is that this attempt to make the meaning of the word community seamless with capitalism and the market-place

87

should be treated with considerable scepticism. In broader terms, it might be possible to argue, as Starr does tentatively, that other non-corporate senses of community and locality might be valuable resources to resist the supposed imperatives of global homogenization (2000: 205). Forms of protectionism, in the sense of protecting traditions and practices that a particular group of people care about, might reasonably be termed community. But this is a tactical matter, a question of a particular form of resistance, not a claim about the authenticity of one form of community with regard to another. I will return to this later in the book, because I do not want to argue that the word is always dangerous and its use misguided and nostalgic. The point is not to be against community as such, or citizenship as such, simply against the idea that community (or citizenship) can and should be distilled into a manageable property of formal organizations.

I also want to note in passing that a simplistic Marxist alternative is not a very convincing one: to dismiss any employee claims to organizational community as false consciousness and trust that generalized alienation becomes the trigger to some form of class-for-itself recognition. The revolution that would then follow would bring about a new form of community on a state or global level – communism. Not only does this seem to me an empirically unlikely path to utopia at the present time,[9] it also tends to reduce the complexity of identity down to one divide: social class. Now I am not denying that class is important, particularly in understanding the employment relationship, but to articulate it as the originary division from which all other divisions follow is a claim that must put gender, ethnicity, sexuality, disability and so on in a subordinate position. Further to this, identities like environmentalist, Stoke City supporter, anti-corporate activist, organization member and so on would be all but irrelevant. To my mind, a theory and politics of community that denies the importance of *any* sense of identity (whether 'oppositional' or not) is partial at best and elitist at worst.[10]

In summary then, I do not believe that the orgunity is a viable or desirable model for an organization. It *may* be a model for a largely self-sufficient commune, or a hermetically sealed panopticon, but not for an organization as an outcome of the organizing processes that are constitutive of modern societies and economies. The strong measure of consensus required to sustain an orgunity is simply not probable, and would probably not be popular. In practice, it is also a word which disguises some obvious managerial interests beneath its warm persuasiveness. Should we therefore argue that any rhetoric or tactic that aims at a community model of organization is either sponsored by utopians building castles in the air or managerialists building iron cages? Should we, as Rippin (1993) suggests, assert that 'my job is my job and my soul is my own'? Though this might be an attractive division for some – trading as it does on the assumed separation of home/work, public/private and so on – if taken to be an absolute it tends to underplay the potential for some interesting subversions. As with ideas like organizational citizenship, corporate culture and so on, managerial claims to (comm)unity may also act to undermine the sovereign powers of those who put them forward. Claiming that 'we are all in this together' is an assertion about the speaker as well as the (rightly suspicious) addressee. Indeed if, as seems likely, managers and employees will continue creating senses of community and identity at work then surely one way to reinforce ethical and political constraints on managed capitalism is to encourage any sense of responsibility to employees that their managers may have. To put it in philosophical terms, the self-interested sophistry of capitalist utilitarianism may be partially countered by sponsoring a weak virtue ethic based on organizations, but more of this in the next chapter.

So senses of community do grow within and around work organizations but they can never be exclusive of other, non-organizational, senses of community. For managerialists to attempt to articulate a dominant or exclusive organizational identity is therefore hopefully always going to be a project that fails. I say 'hopefully' because it seems to me that, if it succeeds, the 'hideous purity' (Law 1994) that might follow could justify many exclusionary practices. Against organizational communitarianism, or strong organizational culturalism, I would suggest that emancipation must involve respecting the fluidity of the differences between the other and the same, and not insisting that otherness or sameness become timeless organizing principles in themselves. However, as with citizenship, I do want to suggest that the possibility of a more democratic organization is implicit within the idea of an organizational community and that the communitarian impulse is worth further exploration by those interested in alternatives to market managerialism. Communities are articulations of commonality, of an ethic based on virtue or character, and it is therefore more difficult for the powerful to justify a utilitarian calculus to themselves or those who are the victims of their decisions. I don't believe that the ideal-type 'orgunity' is a practical or desirable possibility, but then utopias (like communities perhaps) are ideas for our politics to aim at, not places we might ever want to live in.

The next four chapters shift focus away from these various debates with the bureaucratic Big Other to consider the contemporary climate of mistrust towards managerialism and the big corporation. In the most general of terms, and despite the century-long attempt to make market-driven managerialism equivalent to social progress, I want to suggest that there is presently a kind of legitimation crisis that has not been concealed or remedied by the hopeful use of words like citizenship, culture and community. In some sense, these are words that seek to attach the managerial organization to warm words that we generally seem to care about. They are attempts at establishing a hegemonic understanding of the role that capitalism, corporations and management can and should play in our lives. Hegemony, the dominance of a particular set of ruling ideas, always needs to be worked on. It cannot be assumed, but needs to be continually supported through various forms of guru ideology and propaganda dressed as public relations. The chapters that follow document four very different sites within which the market managerial consensus seems to be under attack. I will begin by looking at the rise of interest in business ethics, perhaps the most visible example of a sustained attempt to make corporations responsible to the communities that they operate within.

5

THE BUSINESS OF BUSINESS ETHICS

'You are my friend
Yes
You are my relative
Yes thank you
But my business does not know you'
   Sign in a shop window in Tanzania, cited in O'Rourke 1998: 164

'The free-market outcome benefits all. It's moral. And the beautiful thing about this morality is that we don't have to be good to achieve it.'
                         O'Rourke 1998: 238

In 1932, Berle and Means suggested that the interests of the community, by which they meant 'the larger interests of society', might act as a check on corporate plundering 'if they were put forward with clarity and force' (1932: 356). Twenty years later Berle refined this argument in proposing that business leaders should think about the implications of Augustine's 'City of God', the utopian philosophical underpinning of any and all enduring institutions. In order that corporations embrace their centrality and responsibility in the era of corporate capitalism, they must develop community programmes, endowments and, more generally, the cultivation of conscience amongst their members (1955: 133). On the surface, Berle's ideas seem to have borne fruit. All the Fortune 500 US companies and over half the UK's top 500 companies now have codes of conduct (Hertz 2001: 142). Managers and organizations seem to feel the need to make glossy public statements about equal opportunities policies;

gender, age and ethnicity issues; social cost accounting; environmental responsibility; community involvement and sponsorship; business scandals; whistleblowing; consumer redress; corporate governance; and so on. There are also, of course, plenty of consultants willing to help formulate these statements, as well as a rapidly developing stream of ideas from market liberals and theologians that stress spirituality, soul and the moral foundations of market institutions (Gray 1992; Handy 1998) in favour of 'back to basics' values based on notions of community, responsibility and so on. In parallel, and over the last twenty years or so, business ethics has become an accepted part of the B-School canon. First in the USA, and now in Europe, there are a growing number of books, journals, chairs, institutes and courses. Ethics is becoming a big business.

So the language of ethics and responsibility seems to be here to stay, and is claiming a degree of centrality as the necessary conscience of managerial capitalism. Much like all the other management subdisciplines, there is an implicitly imperialist claim in this expansion.[1] Just as marketeers claim that everything follows from marketing, or accountants that organizations would be nothing without the numbers, so do business ethicists seek to reframe both practical and academic matters in terms of arguments about the values and purposes of business organizations. The rise of business ethics is an interesting case study in the history of ideas, and of the claims to expertise and legitimacy that are needed in order to launch a putatively 'new' area of enquiry. Such legitimacy requires that certain questions need to be addressed. Were businesses not ethical before business ethics? What expertise do professional ethicists have that ordinary mortals do not? And, perhaps most importantly, will business ethics actually make businesses ethical?

These are the kinds of questions I will be dealing with in this chapter, but there is a further question here too. What am I to make of business ethics? Does it provide resources to think 'against management' and perhaps to help develop notions like citizenship and community in more progressive directions? At first sight, both positive and negative responses seem justified. Positively then, since business ethicists claim to be concerned about abuses of managerial power, the protection of workers and consumers rights, the harm that business does to the environment and so on, then surely they are fellow travellers on the rocky road to a better world? To chide them for having read Kant and Bentham rather than social theory gurus like Habermas and Foucault would seem to be splitting hairs (and heirs) if the goals of the practical and intellectual projects are so similar. Yet, negatively, business ethics could be seen to represent the managerial colonization of emancipatory projects, what Tester has nicely termed the 'motorized morality' of mission statements and organizational procedures (1997: 124).[2] In a strange and potentially catastrophic reversal, one familiar from the stories of the previous chapters, the very words that might be used to sponsor radical change are appropriated and domesticated by managerialism and placed in the service of a globally rapacious capitalism. Politics disappears, and the casuistical ethics of the bottom line claims its place. Ethics becomes something to be fitted into the corporate strategy document.

In the chapter that follows, I will begin by reviewing some business ethics texts in order to lay out some of the conventional assumptions, and absences, that underpin this area. The chapter then moves into some musings on the tensions between moral philosophy and pragmatic managerialism that have largely constituted the field. I explore some of its elements, focusing particularly on the problems with identifying 'ethical' and 'unethical' behaviours, the differences between ethics and morality, and the pervasive conflict between nostalgia and modernization that characterizes so much of the writing in this area. After these various excursions, I then attempt to frame the problem of ethics in terms of modern and postmodern theories of knowledge. I have employed the latter term as a shorthand for an intellectual attitude or style which is radically sceptical about foundational versions of truth, and hence of the possibility of distinguishing a clear line between the ethical and the unethical. The chapter then moves to an attempt to undermine the notions of 'decision' and 'judgement' which seem to be central to any modern conception of ethics. I conclude with a series of speculations on the relevance and irrelevance of business ethics for thinking about the ethics and politics of managerial capitalism.

Constructing business ethics

In this section I will outline the forms of legitimation and argument that can be commonly found in business ethics texts. That being said, I will be treating business ethics as if it were a unified field, which it is not, and hence drastically over-simplifying a series of complex arguments. Nonetheless, as I suggested above, the case of business ethics is an interesting recent example of the legitimation of a 'new' area of intellectual and practical activity. To profess business ethics – or anything else for that matter – is to claim (at least) three things.

93

Firstly, that something is needed; secondly, that you are the kind of person who can do it; thirdly, that you can achieve something with your expertise. Taken together, these ideas form what ten Bos (2001), following Bauman, calls a theory of 'insufficiency'. That is to say, business ethicists must claim that the various customers for their knowledges do not have the resources to deal with these matters on their own, and hence need guidance from experts. Ethics, in other words, needs some kind of management, and can be a service that is paid for by a fee. So how is such a claim made?

A very common opening gambit in texts on business ethics is to suggest, implicitly or explicitly, that there is some kind of crisis of ethics. Put simply, this is a diagnosis of the present age which compares it unfavourably with the past. In a way that again echoes the stories of fragmentation that can be found in the ideas about organizational citizenship and community, it is suggested that people don't trust businesses any more, that negative images of organizations are common in the media, that hyper-competition is forcing employees and organizations to perform whatever the costs, that globalization is causing competing belief systems to collide, or that the environment can no longer sustain unbridled capitalism (Cannon 1994: 1; Hoffman and Frederick 1995: 2). Now if this is the case, then managers are in a different and potentially dangerous world and are sorely in need of guidance. As is clear, this is a diagnosis that essentially relies on a narrative of ethical decline. It echoes the long-standing tension between nostalgia and modernization which can be located in many accounts of the transition to modernity, perhaps most notably Durkheim's version of anomie being a consequence of the division of labour. This kind of story suggests that modernization involves the loss of community and traditional forms of moral regulation. The small-scale, high-trust and face-to-face interactions that once constrained market exchanges have now been replaced with anonymous and huge corporate structures. The players in global market-places now have no meaningful responsibilities to people or places. Indeed, to admit such responsibilities is to court disaster since capital, like a nervous bird, can flee so rapidly at the slightest sign of conscience.

As before, the empirical accuracy of this kind of history is unimportant. Instead what seems to matter is that it helps to legitimize the need for business ethics.[3] In practice, sustained historical analyses of capitalism over the last few hundred years are rare in the business ethics literature.[4] Indeed, the very notion of the novelty of this ethical crisis often requires that historical continuities are denied by, for example, dismissing Marx through claiming that he was writing about bad old nineteenth-century capitalism (Stewart 1996: 22). Whatever the substance of the history, what is important for my argument is that the story provides a space for business ethics to step into. Ethical analysis, education and regulation are now needed, when they were previously not. Importantly, this is a history that is also very often used to legitimize management and the Business School in general with talk about 'hyper-competition', 'globalization', and change being the only constant. More effective business and management then becomes the answer. This is rather like being told that we 'need' estate agents, or pet psychologists, or better deodorants. The creation of the need is an essential move in legitimizing the product. Businesses, and busy-people, now 'need' ethics, when presumably they did not before. And if the abstractions of this argument are not enough to persuade, then they can be supported by a simple assertion that it is important for all businesses to think hard about ethics because state legislation and heightened public awareness demand it (Clutterbuck et al. 1992: 15; Drummond and Bain 1994: 2). If students are organizing against Nike sweatshops, and protesters are attacking McDonald's, then the manager must be seen to be doing something in response. This is what Griseri calls the 'compliance function' (1998: 216) – which is akin to saying that ethics is a part of contemporary business practice, and whether you like it or not, it is something you must know about. In a strangely performative way, the fact that people talk about business ethics proves that it is needed.

And so, the need created, the question that then arises is who is to fill it. Or, as Jackson puts it in the introduction to her text, 'I have to show that business people . . . have something to learn that they do not know already and that they need to know' (1996: 1). Business ethicists have two cards to play here. The first is a body of ethical knowledge which it largely inherits from moral philosophy. This is a substantial piece of cultural capital, stretching back to Plato and Aristotle, and incorporating big words (utilitarianism, deontology) and big names (Immanuel Kant, John Stuart Mill). The usefulness of such language should not be underestimated, since it is sufficiently arcane to impress, and allows the putative business ethicist to be a gatekeeper to the knowledges that are primarily the province of the academy. If universities already regard this knowledge as worthwhile, then it can easily be translated into research and qualifications within the B-School, and then on to the real world of business. Without moral philosophy, it would have been more difficult to legitimate business ethics as a discrete and credible domain of enquiry. Virtually all business ethics texts hence contain references to Kantian conceptions of duty, particularly the implications of the categorical imperative. Such arguments are then usually counterposed to utilitarian notions of the greatest good for the greatest number, often connecting these to contemporary notions of stakeholder theory. Often, as I mentioned in the last chapter, there is also reference to virtue theory and discussions of an individual or organizational character. However, there are also some interesting blind spots in what counts as relevant intellectual capital. The moral philosophers who are mentioned most often are usually the classics of the analytic canon, and it is rare to find references to twentieth-century 'continental' philosophy here. Nietzsche, Heidegger, Gadamer, Sartre, Foucault, Derrida, Lyotard and so on are largely absent from the business ethics text,[5] as are virtually any references to the various forms of twentieth-century Marxism. There are also some clear absences in terms of the intersections between moral philosophy and political theory. Detailed attempts to understand concepts like law, the state, power, justice, equality, liberty, democracy, human rights and so on are also absent from the centre of business ethics. Rather ominously, 'politics' does not seem to be part of 'ethics'.

The second card that business ethicists have to play is in stressing the application and relevance of their knowledges. Tactically, this is important in order to avoid accusations of irrelevance by a practically minded audience, or what Sorell calls the 'alienation problem' (1998: 17). This issue largely boils down to stressing the role of business ethics as a form of mediation between the intellectual capital of the academy and the pragmatism of management decision-making in the real world. This is clearly a delicate balancing act between 'ethics' and 'business'. Too far in the direction of ethics and there is little connection to the busy world of business, too far in the direction of business and the discipline becomes a rehearsal of management common sense with no 'unique selling proposition', as the marketeers might put it. As a result, most business ethics texts stress their applied and practical nature – 'straight talk about how to do it right' (Trevino and Nelson 1999; see also Jackson 1996; Ottensmeyer and McCarthy 1996); the experience of their authors in business or running an ethics consultancy (Drummond and Bain 1994) – or even contain inspiring photographs of (and quotes from) CEOs at the start of every chapter (Stewart 1996).

In addition, virtually all of these texts use the repertoire of case studies and discussion questions that are common in management teaching texts. Characters are introduced, facts are given and a decision is requested. Such cases, often copyrighted as being 'owned' by a particular person or institution, are almost always framed as a personalization of the issue concerned: 'What would *you* do in this situation? Give reasons for your decisions.' This stress on the agency of the individual is hardly surprising given the absence of consideration of what is normally termed 'politics'. That is to say, an emphasis on individualism seems to obviate consideration of general constraints, even to the extent of asking the reader to fill in questionnaires which will determine 'your cynicism quotient'[6] and an exercise on 'walking my talk' (Trevino and Nelson 1999: 18, 169). Indeed, the philosophical resources most commonly deployed – deontology, utilitarianism, and a curiously decontextualized version of organizational virtue ethics (Solomon 1992) – encourage precisely these kind of individualized thought experiments. Whether interrogating one's moral duties; evaluating potential means and ends; or considering traits of character such as wisdom, fidelity and so on, the emphasis is on individual consciousness informing personal choices. The management decision-maker collects the evidence, models a set of potential algorithms, and then makes a decision on what actions should be taken. Further, these decisions are also often framed within chapters on key business issues – sexual harassment and diversity, health and safety, whistleblowing, intellectual property, the environment and so on. This is, of course, both eminently 'practical' by definition, but it also succeeds in excluding many matters which are then deemed beyond the remit of the case in point. Rather like the *ceteris paribus* of economics, only certain issues are defined as relevant because they are part of the case, and everything else becomes a form of background noise that is beyond the remit of a particular management decision.

Finally, and perhaps most importantly, there is the question of whether business ethics will actually make businesses behave more ethically. Do the means – studying business ethics – have any demonstrable effect on the desired ends – more ethical businesses? Here, the texts are generally more cautious, and justifiably so. For a start, since the ends very rarely include any major reforms of managerial capitalism, or even radical state intervention, the heart of the project is amelioration rather than revolutionary change. This might involve persuading corporations to clean up their act, but certainly does not involve getting rid of corporations altogether (Starr 2000: 79). It is rare to find analyses that suggest alternative understandings of markets, of hierarchical organization, or the work-effort bargain. Instead, the emphasis is on working within contemporary business organizations in order that their most dramatic excesses can be tempered and their propensity to sin is lowered. Indeed, since the vast majority of ethics texts tend to assert that ethics makes for better business, or at least that there is no contradiction between ethics and business, sometimes even amelioration seems irrelevant. Ethics can become just another part of the business and marketing strategy of a modern organization. Secondly, and as I discussed above, the personalization of ethical problems leads to an emphasis on individual rationality within a 'best fit' form of decision-making. The reader of these texts is assumed to be an individual who will meet, or has met, everyday dilemmas and might have to make decisions that they are not completely comfortable with. Permission for doing unpleasant things in the name of a greater good is already built in. Different stakeholders have 'rights' that need to be balanced (Ottensmeyer and McCarthy 1996), and people in business must operate within the rules of the game. The rhetorical mode of the practical and personalized case study is hence to position a set of unmoveable assumptions, and then ask the reader to work within these limits. This means that business ethics is rarely utopian, or even moderately ambitious, in its aims. Its mode of address is to suggest personal development, or perhaps sensible reform, as reasonable ends. Such modesty is laudable in the often breathless arena of management in general, but if so little is expected, then perhaps little is likely to be achieved.

In summary, then, the field of business ethics is a good example of the construction of a problem, the legitimation of certain forms of knowledge and firm but modest claims about its utility. Even interesting and critical books which are sceptical about the utility of conventional business ethics on the grounds of practicality or its potentially dysfunctional effects (Pearson 1995; Griseri 1998) end up in similar places. In general, business ethics manages to systematically exclude much that might potentially assist serious attempts at social change. Indeed, it might be argued that its particular form of pro-managerial rational individualism is dangerously seductive precisely because it is a 'noble lie' that assumes so much (Castro 1996: 267). If this is ethics, if this is all that it is, then business (and all that is attached to it) seems to be here to stay.

Philosophy against management

So business ethics has largely been constituted by influences from two domains – prescriptive moral philosophy (sometimes in combination with religious movements) and the various 'sciences' of business.[7] But how has the field developed, and what kind of arguments shape it? In the most general of terms, the philosophers have developed arguments that seek to demonstrate how philosophical (or spiritual) thinking either augments or suggests reforms to business practice. As a counter, the pragmatists have developed arguments that deny the usefulness of moral philosophy in order to justify the claim that business contains ethical issues that cannot, or should not, be treated in austerely philosophical terms. It almost seems as if much of the debate so far has been couched in terms of intellectual abstraction versus economic pragmatism, or, as it is often put rather more crudely, idealism versus realism.[8] If I may mix my metaphors, the ivory tower confronts the law of the jungle and there seems to be little common ground but an awful lot of fighting over who should own the terrain.

In this, rather predictable, 'two cultures' set-up the high moral ground might appear to belong to the philosophers as missionary idealists who wish to transform the corruptions of business practice. It is almost as if they, through the unforced force of the better argument, will be able to persuade the immoral and the amoral that certain practices must be changed, or perhaps that the same practices need to be justified in different ways. Essentially these are arguments that suggest that the self-interested casuistry of 'wriggling out of principles when they are inconvenient' (Emmet in Sparkes 1991: 248) must be replaced with something more consistent. So, through the application of virtue theory, deontology, utilitarianism or the strictures of some holy text, the shape of decisions and judgements will be changed and the world will become a better (or at least more reasonable) place. However, for the business realists these arguments from the seminar room, or tablets from the mountain, are simply irrelevant, not because they don't sound like good ideas, or indeed contain some good arguments, but simply because they do not translate into the language of the bottom line. Debates about reason, logic, contradiction and so on are hence dismissed as too abstract. The pure language of ethics is deemed unhelpful for real organization people because it does not contain references to the matters that are relevant to those who practise business, as opposed to those who merely preach about it. The philosopher's claimed moral high ground is hence implicitly or explicitly denied through reference to 'getting things done' in the world of practice. In other words, 'we are too busy worrying about *real* problems to take your academic sophistry very seriously'. As Milton Friedman has pithily expressed it, 'the social responsibility of business is to increase its profits' (1995

[1970]). Or, as O'Rourke put it in the epigraph to this chapter, self-ishness and markets *are* moral, my business does not know you *because* it is a business. To be clear here, I am not suggesting that business apologists are unethical in some sense of a self-conscious immorality, simply that the ethics of philosophy has little to say to someone who needs to get something done by Friday afternoon, and anyway already believes that 'wealth is good' (O'Rourke 1998: 243). The question then becomes, what *use* is ethics?

I think this crude sketch misses much, but it does capture something of the tension which I want to explore. Jean-François Lyotard uses the term *agon* to refer to a wrestling match between incommensurable language games (1988 [1983]). This is a match that must carry on, cannot be won or lost, because the opponents can never be resolved to each other. They occupy different 'forms of life', different social universes, which cannot be compared for their rightness or wrongness by some King Solomon who stands outside all other forms of life. As Albert Carr has famously argued (1968), if we do not condemn bluffing in a game of poker, then why should we assume that the rules of the game of business are the same as the rules of everyday life? Perhaps the ethical rules of business are simply different, and greed really is good for business people. As the Tanzanian sign suggests, being someone's friend or relative is simply different to being someone's customer. That is why I, if I wish to do justice to either side of these debates and not to reduce one position to another, must attempt to fall on both sides – equally hard. I cannot really hope to find a position outside this *agon* in order to resolve it. All that I can do is to explore it, poking and pulling at its contradictions and silences in the hope that I might provoke some thinking on the nature of the impasse itself and its relevance for developing a critique of managerialism.

Another way to justify my stance at this point in the argument – a suspension of judgement about judgement – is (what the philosophers sometimes call) 'descriptive' as opposed to 'prescriptive' ethics (Hare 1993). In a way that is related to the aesthetic and political distinction between popular and mass culture that I discussed in chapter 2, this is a divide between understanding ethics as a form of everyday practice that can be understood in anthropological terms and understanding ethics as a timeless code that can be refined through the use of reason. This is also sometimes framed as morality – mores, norms, values – as opposed to ethics – codes, rules, instructions. Avoiding being prescriptive (for the moment), I might simply claim that the moral life of managers is not descriptively separable from the philosopher's ethics in that both involve questions of judgement and supposed moments of decision. They embody a form of life, a particular set of values and interests. In other words, the languages of poker players, moral philosophers and business pragmatists might differ but they can be treated as the same kind of mundane practices for the purposes of describing how they work, and what effects they achieve.

I suppose this is to 'sociologize' the ethical, to draw it down from its supposed lofty place into the flow of the ordinary. This potentially means placing it in a particular time and place, and then using the specificities of that time and place to prevent philosophical ethics from claiming a special position – a prescriptive high ground – elsewhere. It means refusing to accept a division of labour that distinguishes the ethical from the other things that people do in particular times and places. This is hardly a new insight for economic life – let alone culture or religion. As Adam Smith, Jean-Jacques Rousseau, Emile Durkheim and many anthropologists, institutional economists, sociologists and organizational ethnographers have suggested, questions about modern organization, markets and the division of labour are matters which cannot be separated from notions of what is good and what is bad within a particular social context.[9] So, if we accept this social construction of morality, rather than insist on some form of trans-historical foundation for ethics, then this might allow us to suspend our judgement, and attempt to go (for now, at least) beyond finger-pointing about good and evil in the interests of a thicker description of everyday conduct. Rather than entering into the hurly-burly of prescriptive argument we might attempt to describe how others reach their conclusions about good and bad. Not that we can ever reach a 'final' description, but instead it could be suggested that attempts at description are part of 'doing justice' to the different worlds that others inhabit.[10]

I will return to the broader implications of this social construction of moralities later in the chapter, but for now concentrate on doing some more description. In this case, some further exploration of the stand-off between the ethical legislators and the economically *laissez-faire*.

Nostalgia and modernization again

If business ethics is largely a prescriptive project then it claims to have judged business and found it wanting. Business needs ethics, in other

101

words, because ethicists say so. This might be a general judgement, a condemnation of the whole of business, but that is rare within business ethics itself – though not uncommon outside it. Marxism and Christianity are movements which have persuaded many that there is something wrong with the business context, not merely the content. I will explore the former in more detail in the next chapter. However, more usual from within business ethics itself is the accusation that certain parts of business require ethical maintenance. Insider trading, or advertising to children, or making weapons for military regimes, or discriminating against 'diversity', or putting up shoddy buildings, or using road transport, or stealing from pension funds, or polluting rivers, or 'down-sizing', or all of the above and more are presented as ethical problems that need to be thought about as a bad business, as opposed to good business.

The problem, or one of the problems, is that it is rarely very clear what 'good' and 'bad' business might be as a whole and hence why business needs one cure – ethics – to address the multiplicity of these issues. After all, asking whether a complex fictional entity (an organization) is 'good' or 'bad' is simply confusing and invites some rather simple answers. Is McDonald's good or bad, guilty or not guilty? As I noted in chapter 2, it seems that any answer to that question rather depends on who you are, what you want, and which part of McDonald's you are referring to at which time. Or, which side of the counter you are standing on at the time. In any case, as is often commented on 'white collar crime', corporate immorality is rarely going to be like being burgled (Punch 1996). Rather 'it' – if 'it' is an 'it' – has no clear victims: no one is left inspecting an empty wallet, a broken window or a pool of blood. Detecting 'bad' business therefore means coming to decisions about matters that can very rarely be dramatized as self-evident rights or wrongs. Over-pricing burgers is less obviously unethical than selling torture equipment to fascist dictators. As I have already noted, the endless series of 'case studies' with their insistent personalization is a better metaphor for business ethics than the 'court case', with its final demand for the accused to be led to the cells. For business ethics there seems little agreement about 'who' 'we' are asking to do 'what'. Rather there is an unending series of complaints, of small claims, which are all too often unrelated, and which don't seem to add up to anything bigger. Perhaps this is a disciplinary form of casuistry in the original non-pejorative sense, a case-by-case treatment of matters of conscience.

Yet, notions of social crisis do lurk in the background here and they help greatly to simplify both the evidence required and the sentence given. As ever, it is all too often the times that are awry, with 'good' fading in the golden past whilst the 'bad' bubbles its noxious fumes up all around us at this moment. Just as the 'rise of street crime' is often taken to be indicative of a breakdown in something called the social fabric, so too is the 'rise of corporate immorality' taken as a sign that an older, slower and more stable order is being swept away. The big organization and its management become articulated as a potential threat and not a guarantor of social stability. It seems that global reach, massive capital resources and employees taught to sing the company song might mean that no one is safe and increasing paranoia about Eisenhower's 'military-industrial complex' is everywhere from *The X Files* to buying your fair trade coffee. The Trans-National Corporation (in cahoots with increasingly impotent states) Disneyfies, McDonaldizes and Coca-Colonizes all that once was solid and replaces older, more authentic moralities with the self-serving sophistry of the mission statement and customer service questionnaire. Community, justice, responsibility, tradition and so on are all replaced by the smile on the face of the crocodile – and its tears before it eats you too.

This tension between nostalgia and social change can also be located in the holy trinity of classical sociological theory, though it is rarely commented upon within business ethics. Marxists have often insisted that the capitalist mode of production was premised upon theft, or in less ethically loaded terms, the expropriation of surplus value from the working classes. An authentic mode of 'species being', a real way of being human, could only be remembered from the primitive past or produced in the inevitable future. The judgement that capitalism is 'bad' is made not with an ethical basis (though this was arguably the stance of the early Marx), but rather as a matter of (supposedly) self-evident scientific fact which could be deduced from the material conditions of capitalist survival and their reproduction as a 'band of hostile brothers' (Wray-Bliss and Parker 1998). Emile Durkheim, on the other hand, regarded complex societies as being a generally positive outcome of the progressive division of labour but bemoaned the lack of moral density, the normlessness, the anomie that resulted from their very constitution. A new civic religion, perhaps the citizenship or community I discussed in the previous chapters, might be built from the atheistic altruism already exemplified by the older professions and which potentially acts as a bulwark against the corrosive market relationships which have been so destructive of past social solidarity. Finally, and as I explored in chapter 2, Max Weber argued that modern organization – modern forms of 'ordering' – involve rationalization, or a process of placing people and things in systematic relationships. Calculability, repeatability, efficiency, accountability and so on are hence the hallmarks of the bureaucratization of the world of business. Though this rationalization is 'world-changing' and often positive in its effects it also tends to produce new kinds of people who are accustomed to not seeing the bars of the iron cage that traps them into certain ways of thinking and acting. They are doomed to understand freedom as the choice between A and B.

It should not be surprising then that the *agon* of nostalgia versus modernization, of the search for the golden rule versus the search for the bottom line, can be fairly neatly located in the context provided by Marx, Durkheim and Weber. For radical critics, the rise of business ethics (like so many other fashionable terms) could be seen to express the ideological mystification of capitalist interests and is hence complicit in preventing proper modernization, that is to say, the transformation of capitalism into a socialist form of organization. So, what is needed is not the idealism of ethics – a bourgeois conceit – but material social change. On the other hand, for nostalgic Durkheimian communitarians, modernization has produced a need for something very much like business ethics which can help to re-solidify an increasingly fragmented division of moralities (Solomon 1992). So what is needed is better ethics – like better community, better citizenship, better responsibility – in order to prevent the marketization of all social relationships. Finally, a pessimism about either modernizing or nostalgic 'solutions' is found in Weber, where any attempt to found a new ethics, or recover an old one, is inevitably subject to processes of rationalization too. Indeed, any well-meaning attempt to re-enchant a rationalized world will inevitably be drawn back into a calculus of means as the accountants work out how much ethics costs and benefits. For Weber, a conversation about values, about ends, is precisely what is required in order to prevent the narrow-minded Protestant bureaucrat from colonizing the world, yet, for Ritzer, such conversations will always be overheard and then translated into tables, examinations, rulebooks and mission statements – into what might be called McEthics. The contemporary popularity of Foucault's version of the panopticon within critical management studies seems to illustrate something rather profound about a lack of faith in escape attempts at the present, but more of that in the next chapter.

In a sense, as Poole (1991) argues, utilitarian formulations – the greatest good of the greatest number – are a predictable outcome of these rationalizing developments as a form of ethics that seeks to use reason to calculate the consequences for a demarcated group of stakeholders. After all, it was Bentham, one of the fathers of utilitarianism, who first imagined the panopticon as a way of maximizing the greatest good through the humane suffering of a few (see Warnock 1962). Though we might debate who (or what) is, and is not, the 'greatest number', and who (or what) should be a member of the category 'stakeholder', the reasonableness of such an approach is evident. A rule is applied, without hatred or passion, to determine which decision should be made in which case. The scales of justice swing this way or that, without regard to their contents, because justice, like the bureaucrat, is intentionally blind.[11] This eventual bureaucratization of the ethical is difficult to avoid for either philosophers or managerial pragmatists simply because speaking of ethics in business effectively rules out many ways of formulating decision-making and responsibility that are not amenable to some kind of organizational rationalization – an inner sense of duty, a concern for authenticity or desire for non-managerial ends, for example. Looking at this argument from the other side, if we try to understand business though a non-utilitarian ethic then we would find it difficult to justify many of the beliefs and practices that are constitutive of the modern organization. As has been remarked often, Kant's insistence that people should be treated as ends in themselves and not only as a means to a particular goal is almost impossible to reconcile with formal organization itself. And, in terms of virtue theory, MacIntyre strenuously denies that the character of the manager can ever be virtuous simply because they can never embody a commitment to non-manipulative social relationships (1981).

So, it would seem that the most likely and coherent way of bringing together words like 'ethics' and 'business' is through the rationalization of both and hence their reduction to a common form of life. In other words, by denying the incommensurability of the *agon*. It seems to me that this is what utilitarianism does so well by making all matters comparable – pleasures, pains, numbers, ends, means can be flattened out and managed. Yet, as I have suggested, there are many moral philosophers who would be unhappy with this reduction of their ideas to the engineering of ends, and others who will continue to argue about which form of utilitarianism is most appropriate in order to achieve the best kind of social engineering. So too will there be managerialists who regard even utilitarianism as an unwarranted and unjustifiable interference in the right to manage. Either way, the *agon* seems likely to continue. Unlike double-entry book-keeping, the accounts stack up on one side or another, but there still seems to be no way of producing a final total that everyone can agree upon.

Though you might not agree with the roundabout way in which I have got there, you may well have noticed that I have done little more than restate the positions that I began with. The rationalization that seems to be the only coherent way to allow the *agon* of business and ethics to become the discipline now known as business ethics risks destroying the very possibility of problematizing conduct in organizations. In suggesting that business needs ethics, and vice versa, we seem to again be in the position of suggesting that the crocodile needs feeding. The question, the quiet call or angry shout, of ethics might be in danger of being drowned by the deluge of answers from various professionals. The increasingly warm embrace given to ethics – through professorships in Business Schools, textbooks, journals, courses and so on – seems likely to turn to quiet suffocation unless we allow ethics some space to be something else. But what else?

Postmodernism and ethics

In order to free ethics from business, from the busy-ness of having to account for itself in terms of its utility, we might want to consider the difference between what are often called modern and postmodern formulations of knowledge.[12] This dualism, in an elliptical argument like this one, is inevitably going to be a form of shorthand which collects together elements of social constructionism, poststructuralist approaches to language, a suspicion of managerial versions of progress and so on. I'm going to use the word postmodernism to gesture vaguely towards the kind of radical scepticism which I want this chapter to illustrate.

Briefly then, for modernists, the world is supposedly knowable and certain 'machineries of judgement' guarantee some form of certainty about the entities and relations within it. Perhaps the exemplary outcome of modernizing processes is the rationalized bureaucracy and the rules it generates for managing human conduct. In this sense, much of the project of ethics in general can be seen as an attempt to develop knowledge about how we and others should behave through employing some version of (the scientific) method. Like a form of human resource management on a species-wide level, modern ethics seeks to discover the sensible 'firm but fair' laws that could govern all human action. The law must rest on a foundation, a set of facts and/or relations gained empirically or through some form of thought experiment from which deductions and/or inductions can be made. Any foundationalist ethical theory seeks to persuade through reason in the expectation that 'on pain of contradiction', the reasonable person will accept the laws as prescriptions which should be followed. Once such a 'golden rule' of conduct is discovered it can be applied in (and refined for) any social context because – as with laws about temperature, motion and so on – what is known is independent of the knower. Finally, this kind of rational social engineering should equal progress, the gradual creation of a world in which 'good' is produced more efficiently than 'bad'.

On the other hand, a postmodern approach to knowledge would assume that 'knowing' is never a final state of affairs and that different knowledges can never be judged for their truth content. Science is simply one form of reason amongst others, and can claim no privilege, no trans-historical purchase which allows it to disqualify other ways of seeing. In this context, the idea of a progressive project of ethics is simply unsustainable, since there could never be any one account which was regarded as true in all places at all times and could hence be used as some kind of guide for everyone's behaviour. It might be that 'Postmodern Business Ethics' is a contradiction in terms – a performative impossibility. This is because a postmodernist could admit of no 'golden rules', or even of a stable referent to ethics. The continual spillage of language and meaning means that we have different conceptions of what counts as gold and apply the same rules in different ways depending on who we are and what we think we are doing. Ethics, then, is perhaps better dissolved in the sociological description of moralities I mentioned earlier and not celebrated as the 'one best way' to achieve virtue. In any case, as seems evident to many now, the search for John Law's 'hideous purity' of modernity is one that has itself justified various forms of cruelty (1994). As I mentioned in chapter two, Zygmunt Bauman (1989) has eloquently argued that it was the very constitution of the rational and utilitarian bureaucracy that allowed for the holocaust itself. The layout of the extermination camps, the train timetables, the manufacture of gas and the distribution of responsibility were not incidental but central to the possibility of genocide. In other words, no amount of rationality guarantees progress and modern organization is complicit, indeed functionally necessary, for modern forms of mass atrocity (see also Tester 1997).

If we apply these (admittedly much over-simplified) arguments to the wrestling match between philosophy and business then it becomes

107

possible to suggest that both 'sides' are effectively engaged in a set-piece example of modernist turf warfare. For the most part, both the business philosophers and the managerialists would claim that their intellectual project is capable of producing 'better' accounts of how organizations should deal with the 'problem' of ethics. This is going to involve either new behaviours, or new justifications for old behaviours, but is going to require the application of knowledge generated by one 'truth technology' or another. So, the argument is about who has the right answers, and the right methods for producing the right answers. This 'set-up' disallows anyone from asking any other questions, simply because then they are no longer speaking to business ethics, or perhaps even ethics itself. Such is the power of this arrangement that reading the textbooks on the subject, whatever their persuasions, one might even come to believe that there was some kind of consensus that ethics was possible in the first place. So, perhaps radical sceptics (that is to say, those I have termed postmodernists) might begin by asking what ethics actually means, with the general aim of suggesting that this is by no means clear. Indeed, unpicking the possibility of ethics – perhaps even being against ethics – might allow us to think about 'it' rather more rigorously. In the next section I will try to show that being 'against' ethics is by no means simple, because it is hard to know exactly what you are up against.

Decisions and judgements

In order to further explore the conditions of possibility of ethics, this section will employ various mechanical metaphors to think through some of its elements. Let us begin with the idea of a decision.[13] This is surely the end-point of business ethics, of any ethics, since it is the moment where judgements are translated into some kind of practice, some kind of action which impacts upon the world. But what is a decision? As Chia (1994) suggests, presented in terms of managerialist 'Decision Theory', it is the point at which human agency makes an intervention in the flow-chart of conduct. Indeed, decision-support software is premised on the idea of mapping the world in order that the decisive move becomes clear. On the flow-chart of 'if', 'then', 'go to', 'either' and 'or' choices that diagram our various options, the decision is the point where the lines depart from one another and stretch into the future. At this point a kind of calculation must happen, one that attempts to look backwards and forwards along the lines and then decide which to follow. It seems that this must be the ethical moment, the time when the machinery of judgement needs to be brought out from store and the programme run on the information presented. The central metaphor here is one of division (see Hetherington and Munro 1997). The decision is an incision into both the flow of conduct and into the arrangement of the various ideas and materials that constitute it. The decision cuts into the social, dividing like from unlike, this from that, and making separate piles which can be labelled 'good' and 'bad', 'wanted' and 'rejected'. The decision has effects that constitute ethics, as well as constituting things like strategy, markets, management and so on. So decisions seem to be rather important because they produce order, they make patterns to which conduct can then be oriented.

So how do we know when decisions happen? According to the above model, they must only happen when we bring out the machinery of judgement. If they just happened without us knowing then we could not call it a decision, because it would no longer be the point on a line when choices present themselves. But surely then we must need to decide when the machinery of judgement needs to be applied. In this case? Not in that case? So a decision must precede the decision. Do we use the decision-support software, or not? Do I worry about ethics now, or then? In other words, we must decide when to decide. But the same fate befalls this earlier decision, simply because we must have powered up some of the machinery of judgement in order to make that decision. And so on. Further and further back, we seem to be pushed along the flow-chart of conduct until the lines must fragment under the pressure of deciding where the lines are in the first place. It would seem that the test being applied here is something like 'consciousness', a sense of awareness that you are making a decision. But, if that is the case, then it would seem that much of the time decisions make us, in other words that we are not aware of where and when the incision was made. The contract has been signed, the mission statement is written and the workers in Nike's factory have already produced the training shoes in the shop next door. The piles of 'good' and 'bad', of 'this' and 'that' are already there and we often negotiate over and around them without thinking very hard about 'our' decisions. Or perhaps they weren't our decisions in the first place?

Let us leave this aside for a moment and pursue another part of this fragile logic. As I have suggested, decisions require some kind of apparatus to enable them to be made. If there was no judgement applied, then (again) how could we know that a decision was being made? The machinery must be recognizable as machinery. It could be a dice, a copy of a philosophy textbook or a bank balance. It doesn't need to be the same technology every time. It could be all three if there was some way of linking them together within one specific decision. The point is that the machinery provides some kind of rule that allows for the possibility of things being different. If there were no choice inside the machine then there would be no point in bringing it out in the first place, since it would merely be affirming or negating that which had already happened. The machine must compute, not merely transmit, and different machines must be capable of producing different outcomes, otherwise there would be no point in doing the selection in the first place. The machinery must be there so that we can provide an account – to ourselves, or others – of how the decision came to be made. If it were not there we would have no way of deciding that we had actually made a judgement which led to a decision. If the machinery had not run then conduct would not have been interrupted by any reflection and we would have missed the 'either/or'.

A further problem then presents itself. How do we decide which machinery of judgement to use in a specific case? Clearly the dice, textbook and bank balance might all be appropriate in different circumstances but it implies that we have some kind of meta-machinery to adjudicate on the competing claims of different technologies. In other words, we need to (again, consciously) select a way to do the judgement work. And if this is the case, then what is the rule that is appropriate to this meta-machinery? And if we don't know (consciously) what the rule is, does that mean that we are still being rational? Our prejudice, our pre-judging, about different machineries must be open to question after all. Because if it is not, then in what sense are we free to choose how to choose? Because if we can't choose how to judge, presumably by invoking a further space for discretion and choice, then all this machinery must be clunking around in entirely determined, unknowable or even random ways that make its operation rather futile. So, if we still want to invoke 'rationality' and 'choice' then we must be able to judge judgement itself and give an account of our reasons for choosing a particular kind of reason.

Finally, if decisions are the outputs from judgements, then ethics must be one of the forms of programme that goes into the judgement machine. Not the only one – because it is also fed on tossing coins, papers by management academics, chicken entrails and an unimaginably large range of other materials. When assessing the various forms of ethics that it might be programmed with we could imagine that they work by valuing certain kinds of data more highly than others. The Kantian programme assesses the past lines that have led to the decision point, paying particular attention to the internal motivations of actors. The utilitarian programme evaluates the future on the basis of desired outcomes and the greatest good thereby produced. The communitarian programme looks for congruence with how other valued actors have behaved in the past. And so on. In each case the machinery works by disqualifying certain inputs whilst paying particular attention to others and then putting the resulting data through an algorithm that gives the decision. So, even if we get past the problem of decision, and the particular problem of which machineries of judgement to apply, we are then left with potentially the most difficult problem of all. We have a variety of programmes for the judgement machine and no obvious reason why ethics sounds that much better than betting on the National Lottery. If ethics is merely an equation that produces a certain result with certain kinds of data then why should we bother to make such a fuss about it? It almost seems as if it is like arguing over the relative merits of COBOL or FORTRAN, or even Nike and Adidas. Perhaps one is better here, another better there. One is more elegant, another is more precise. Whatever. No point in getting all steamed up about it.

Pushing 'decision', 'judgement' and 'ethics' until they reveal their conceptual structure (in the very abbreviated way that I have here) seems to leave us with two alternatives. First, we could ignore the difficulties and accept the rational bureaucratization of the terms which I described previously in the chapter. This allows everything to remain neat and tidy, and for us to be clear that business ethics is simply a matter of good housekeeping in a small area of human behaviour. It provides us with an account which allows ourselves and others to be rendered clearly accountable. I must admit, this 'solution' to the sticky problem of ethics is a very attractive one and I don't write that with any irony intended. It would allow me to 'manage' myself and others without getting bogged down in the angst of endless words. It solves the ugly problem of relativism that looms so large here, and allows me to celebrate some things and condemn others. It also allows the ethical to actually mean something, because the second alternative – the radical sceptical one – squeezes it so flat that it gets everywhere, and hence is really nowhere. Decisions and judgements become spread across networks of people and things, most of them already constituted before we got there, and it hence seems rather silly to point to one place and claim ethics is here but not over there. The possibility of finding general reasons for being 'against' managerialism, corporations, markets and so on dissolves into matters of personal preference and political prejudice. Reasoned argument is no more than a gloss on interests, and this book becomes close to being pointless. So, can 'we', should 'we' rescue ethics from this dissolution?

The limits of 'ethics'

Attractive though the rationalizing of ethics is, it only works if you don't think too hard about it. The separation between decision, judgement and ethics seems to fold in on itself if pushed even by a few pages. Any notion that we, supposedly free agents, could rationally choose an ethical framework to live our lives by bears very little pressure. And similarly, every attempt to articulate what this ethical question might mean in the context of business organizations seems to lead to it being dragged into philosophy or accounting and hence losing its uniqueness, its capacity to question. The call of ethics can no longer be dangerous if it ends up in either of those places and, for myself, I want the possibility to remain, to acknowledge the impossibility of ethics if I am to live my life well, and achieve what I wanted to when I started this book.

The problem that I will deliberately not address in the rest of this chapter will be what options are left for a project like business ethics if all the above is accepted. I will have plenty more to say about business ethics in the final chapter, but that will be from a standpoint that is self-consciously political, rather than ethical. It would simply be inappropriate for me to wrap up this chapter as if I really did have a magical solution to the problems of rationality and relativism. There are examples of attempts to explore how we might talk about judgement and responsibility in a post-foundational style, Bauman's (1993) formulation of 'Postmodern Ethics' for example. However, what has not yet been done much is to aim some of these ideas at organizations, but from outside the narrow boundaries of what currently counts as business ethics.[14] This does seem to be rather important since organizations can be articulated as one of the prime sites of modernity. Yet, in the broader sweep of this book, I would simply want to say that ethics is simply too important to be left to ethicists. Perhaps weakening the certainties of ethical frameworks, either philosophical or managerial, might actually sensitize us to ethical issues in a more helpful way. Philosophy has done little to prevent injustice, and at the end of the century of the holocaust and widening global inequalities 'we' (should) know that hiding behind the bureaucratic codes and laws generated by managerial conceptions of the ethical is often not conducive to thinking about wider conceptions of cruelty and justice. This is simply because, in Weber's terms, the means can all too easily become ends in themselves, so an ethics aimed at justice mutates into red tape that defends injustice or a managerial rationality that defends certain freedoms in the name of a greater good. If modernity does not guarantee progress, then neither does ethics guarantee the good. Perhaps it would be better then to embrace the paradox – that being ethical requires giving up on ethics and doing justice requires giving up on the search for any one form of ethical law. Or, as Nietzsche put it with typical elegance, '*every* means hitherto employed with the intention of making mankind moral has been thoroughly *immoral*' (1990 [1889]: 70).

Applying post-foundational (or postmodern) thinking to management and organizing can suggest a rather more provisional way of thinking – one that does not encourage ethical certainties in the name of legitimizing a particular expertise but instead focuses on the political ambivalence of any and all actions and judgements. Hopefully this will not mean that we stop writing about matters of right and wrong where business and management are concerned, simply that we alter our conception of how questions on this area might be asked and then (perhaps) argue that the narrowly ethical questions are best left alone, in order that wider questions can be asked. Encouraging the development of a descriptive sociology, or anthropology, of moralities might be one way to avoid either managerial or philosophical bottom lines. I also want to insist that this is not necessarily a pessimistic or nihilistic articulation of anti-ethics. Despite the suspicions of many of what they perceive to be the dangers of relativism in management and organization studies,[15] this is not a simple matter of trying to tear down all authorities with a display of childish glee or black desperation. My argument does not lead me to believe that despair is the only outcome of radical scepticism, rather that it should encourage forms of thought that allow us to question our deeply felt beliefs, and not merely wrap us in certainties that prevent us from thinking the absurd. Recognizing the paradoxes and limitations of ethics and business ethics is one way to stop these words from having so much hold on us. Perhaps then we can begin to develop ways of expressing our dreams and nightmares that do not fall back into the *agon* so easily.

But, most importantly, this kind of argument exposes the limits of business ethics as a form of 'against management' thinking, which brings me back to the distinction between ethics and politics that

I mentioned earlier. Simply put, it is difficult to see how business ethics might escape from the seminar room or the boardroom in order to provide resources for wider forms of critique. This is where the separation between the business ethical and the wider political context, Berle and Means's version of 'community', becomes rather obstructive, indeed perverse. Since so much of business ethics is aimed at reforming the individual, it is a form of argumentation that seems to avoid engagement with social reform, let alone revolution. Even the relativism which seems to follow from thinking hard about some of its key concepts might be taken to be an endorsement of an endless market liberal tolerance of other viewpoints. This is not to say that business ethicists do not potentially have much to say about globalizing capitalism, or the colonization of words and the world by managerialism, but (as I have demonstrated) they are usually compromised by the constitution of business ethics itself. It is at this point that a more explicit statement of politics seems to be called for, an approach which doesn't begin with moral philosophy, but from some statement of radical political intent. Always, of course, in the knowledge that politics is also about endless debate and not final certainties. Business ethics, it seems to me, asks questions that are too specific and too bounded. Politics does not seem to share these limitations. It is for this reason that I turn, in the next chapter, to critical management studies.

6

CRITICIZING CRITICAL
MANAGEMENT STUDIES

It seems to me that business ethics is simply too co-opted to be radical most of the time. It is reformist in a fairly gentle sense, a formal whisper of conscience rather than a shout, but this politeness has its advantages. Business ethics and discussions of corporate social responsibility are now taken fairly seriously by business organizations, and they are prepared to invest money and time doing something in response to these demands. Regardless of the 'real' motivations, strategies or characters of executives, employees, consultants, philosophers and so on (and however these might be defined) this is an important development, and one that should not be disregarded as somehow irrelevant. Nonetheless, it clearly has its limits. For a business ethicist to engage in a sustained examination of the political deficiencies of management, organization and business would be to step outside the established boundaries of business ethics. This would be rather like an ethical investment advisor deciding that shareholder capitalism was unethical, or a consultant on corporate governance recommending corporate dissolution. Such discussions are, at the present time, displaced to elsewhere and one of the places they are displaced to is critical management studies (CMS), in its broadest sense. This chapter will cover this area, which might be generally characterized as 'academic outsider', or perhaps just hopelessly oxymoronic. That is to say, it includes a fairly large number of paid employees of B-Schools, like myself, who express a general unease or downright anger about the ways in which managerialism constitutes contemporary common sense.

Yet, despite (or perhaps, because of) this greater level of ambition, CMS has had little or no impact on what organizations actually do.

My argument below will be that there are some serious and fascinating issues being discussed within CMS, but that they tend to stay within the cloistered boundaries of academic work and find little echo outside those who are already converted. It is, in that sense, a glass bead game played by the cognoscenti. Further, much of the debate within CMS since the phrase gained some respectability has been about its very constitution, about representational issues concerned with its histories, gurus and names. This, often heated, internal debate has done little to disseminate its ideas more widely. If anything, it has strengthened the popular diagnosis of academics as people who argue about things that nobody else understands or particularly cares about. Whilst debating the ghosts of Weber, Marx and Foucault, or discussing the finer points of epistemology, the rest of the world seems to carry on regardless. If business ethics has what Sorell calls an 'alienation problem' (1998: 17), then CMS is often too busy debating the difference between alienation and anomie to realize that it even has a problem.

Before I start though, a few points. The very naming of names in this area says rather a lot, and runs the risk of alienating many academics before I even begin. Mats Alvesson and Hugh Willmott edited their collection *Critical Management Studies* in 1992, but (because of their particular interests) the very beginnings of this project rested more on post-structuralism and critical theory than more orthodox forms of Marxism. In the intervening period, as I will show below, the gap between CMS and other forms of critical work on organizations has yawned alarmingly. To put it simply, many neo-Marxist writers do not even recognize CMS as an umbrella term for what they do. Indeed, it has been argued that CMS represents a very particular form of post-structuralist critique that excludes more orthodox and well-established forms of anti-capitalist writing, such as labour process theory for example. I'll have plenty more to say about this later in the chapter, but at this point I want to note that I am generally identified as one of the post-structuralists and not one of the neo-Marxists.[1] Hence for me to write a balanced chapter on these matters is (for many readers) a doomed project from the outset. Further, CMS means rather different things in different places. In the UK, it seems to be constituted by a tension between Marx and Foucault, critical realism and epistemological relativism, but in the US, Scandinavia and Australasia the histories and meanings are doubtless rather different. For the former, for example, the remarkable hegemony of the B-School orthodoxy, a general faith in positivism and a highly competitive labour market seems to mean that what counts as 'critical' is much broader. Simply put, the US orthodoxy is so strong and narrow that it doesn't involve much movement to be seen as heterodox. So perhaps my provincial description in this chapter will make less sense when it is read on the other side of the Atlantic. However, there is not a lot I can do about that, entangled as I am within my own and others' webs of citation and career, and seeing the world from Stoke-on-Trent, so I will simply have to do my best, however flawed.[2]

Writing critical management studies

CMS is still a new baby in academic terms. Newer even than business ethics. At the time of writing it is probably approaching its tenth birthday, a birthday which might be commonly dated with the publication of Alvesson's and Willmott's *Critical Management Studies* in 1992. Since then, the title has become a term – even a 'brand' (P. Thompson 2001) – and it is now possible to identify yourself as someone who does CMS, as opposed to managerial studies of business, the latter including most of business ethics. In making such an identity claim, and hence claim to be a member of the CMS community too, the author will be saying something about his or her political sympathies – broad left, pro-feminist, anti-imperialist, environmentally concerned and so on – as well as usually expressing a certain distrust for conventional positivist formulations of knowledge within the social sciences.

This combination of political and epistemological radicalism is now a recognizable identity on the margins of academic studies of business and management, just as it has become a central one in some other social sciences, cultural studies for example. Though not nearly as institutionalized as business ethics – there are no chairs in critical management, and no research institutes – the process is beginning. In the English-speaking world the intricate apparatus of academic legitimacy is slowly being constructed. In the UK, there has since 1999 been a bi-annual CMS conference, and at least two seminar series have been funded by the Economic and Social Research Council. 'Critical' panels have been held at more orthodox conferences, 'critical' texts and readers have been published,[3] academic superstars are emerging and certain departments are identified as having a critical mass of critical researchers.[4] In the US, the most high-profile development was the establishment, in 1998, of a CMS workshop (CMSW) for 'critters' which is attached to the huge annual Academy of Management Conference. There have also been some suggestions that a special interest group of the Academy might now be established that would further legitimize and disseminate critical work. Crossing these national boundaries, there is also a well-established email discussion list and an increasing number of paper and internet journals which are self-consciously identified as places where critical papers can find a home.

Though it is very difficult to summarize the work which gathers, or is gathered, under the CMS label, Sotirin and Tyrell (1998), in their review of various critical texts, suggest the following very general forms of theoretical agreement. A general critique of instrumental reason, often manifested as a suspicion of modernism; some attention to historical-empirical specificities; the assumption that language is constitutive not representational; a degree of reflexivity about method and authorial position; and a commitment to intervene in relations of oppression. In terms of actual writings they note a tendency to use guru literature as a foil; some intention to transform management education curricula and pedagogy; an emphasis on non-US knowledges and concern with the negative effects of globalization; a concern to use metaphorical and utopian languages; as well as the promotion of alternative theories and methodologies. Yet, as is obvious, this is still a very vague and wide area. At one extreme, we have empirical studies of power and oppression which contrast what gurus say with what actually happens, at the other, theoretically sophisticated attempts to dethrone the demons of modernism, positivism and managerialism. In between, a variety of attempts to introduce new themes – gender, the body, the environment, ethnicity – and new methods – ethnographic, deconstructive, discursive, rhetorical, narrative, psychodynamic, feminist, and so on.

So what else ties these disparate mobilizations and literatures together? The most explicit programme can be found on the CMSW website,[5] with a mission statement that is intended to be implicitly endorsed through membership. Given what I have already argued about mission statements in chapter 3, this one could be seen as an example of the subversion of a managerial form, or the formalization of subversion. The text itself has three main strands. Firstly, it asserts that managerialist bottom-line versions of organization pay little or no attention to 'justice, community, human development, ecological balance' and so on. The development of critical interpretations of the hegemonic system of business and management is intended to right this balance by providing an alternative to the orthodoxy. Secondly, the statement explicitly claims to be non-sectarian in theoretical terms – to include critical theory, feminism,

Marxism, postmodernism, critical realism and so on. No exclusions are made on the basis of adherence to one particular school of thought or another. Thirdly, the CMSW group will work within the Academy *of* Management to ensure that it does not become an Academy *for* Management. This is not an attempt to dethrone existing academic institutions, but an entryist strategy of revising them from within. Whilst there are clearly problems with using this 'mission statement' as definitive, it does signal some of the central boundary problems for CMS. Firstly, that this is a political project aimed at some form of substantive social change. The ghost being exorcized here is presumably a managerialist version of academic labour as handmaiden of capital, one that regards its duty as collecting facts about organizations in order that managers might meet their avowed goals more effectively. Secondly, the document seems to recognize that different theoretical traditions might formulate 'the critical' in rather contradictory ways. Marxists who wish to insist on the primacy of class will be one of the problems for feminists. Postmodernists who wish to insist that everything is just another story are likely to be accused of political quietism by materialist radicals, and so on. Finally, these grand aims are to be achieved from within academic institutions and networks. Supporters of CMSW are encouraged to educate, agitate and organize with other groups of people too, but their central location is, and will continue to be, the university, and even more specifically, the B-School.

A second seminal piece for defining CMS, though somewhat reluctantly, is Valerie Fournier and Chris Grey's review article 'At the Critical Moment' (2000). This time reflecting UK concerns more than US ones, Fournier and Grey argue that, internal disputes notwithstanding, CMS can usefully be characterized in three ways. Firstly, that it has a 'non-performative' intent, which is to say that it is not concerned with providing tools that are intended to assist managerial efficiency through re-engineering minimum inputs for maximum outputs. Secondly, that it 'denaturalizes' that which is usually taken for granted. If the imperatives which are often assumed to be immutable in mainstream research (efficiency, profit, the right to manage and so on) can be shown to be social constructions embedded in specific historical moments, then they potentially become amenable to some kind of progressive change. Thirdly, CMS is philosophically and methodologically reflexive, which is to say that it attempts to problematize (to a lesser or greater extent) its own claims to know things about the world. As with the CMSW mission, these characterizations are more concerned to say what CMS is *not*, rather than what it *is* and, in so doing, articulate the output of the B-School as a key problem and Big Other. Consequently both texts describe the mainstream in ways that many orthodox B-School academics might not recognize very easily. It is performative, assumes that there is no radical alternative to the present state of affairs and is unreflective about its truth claims. As P. Thompson (2001: 12) puts it, 'CMS needs the bogeyman'. This demonization of what surrounds CMS invokes a boundary but leaves the content of what lies inside relatively open. This is a strangely paradoxical exercise, as Fournier and Grey acknowledge. In order to define the critical, they need to exclude work that they believe is uncritical, but these exclusions are intended to be generous enough to include work with a diverse variety of epistemological and political commitments. Rather like the construction of a political party, diversity can be encouraged, but only up to a certain point.

So, as a result of these exclusions, much of the work that I have covered in this book so far might be deemed to be outside CMS as it has been defined here. The nostalgic and turbo-managerial critiques of bureaucracy; consensual formulations of organizational citizenship, culture or community; and mildly reformist versions of ethics and corporate social responsibility all fail on one or more of Fournier and Grey's three tests. In fact, since much conventional work in management is concerned with 'humanizing' work organizations in order to achieve better productivity, it might be argued that any work that directly or indirectly contributes to the perpetuation of existing managerial capitalist relationships, even if it ameliorates them to some degree, is outside CMS. But, and here is the paradox, this very same work might be critical if viewed in another light. So the radical Weberian critique of bureaucratic rationalization, or du Gay's defence of the bureaucratic ethos within democratic administration (2000), attempts to insist on industrial citizenship rights within organizations, as well as communitarian critiques of the dominance of market relationships, together with ethically led regulation of the social and environmental responsibilities of managers and organizations, could all lie within CMS too. It seems to depend on interpretation, and not some absolute dividing line between the critical and the co-opted.[6]

Lurking behind this seems to be a Kantian sense of an evaluation of the good intentions of particular authors. This would be a judgement as to whether they treat people as means to achieve a more efficient form of managerial capitalism or treat people as ends in themselves.[7] Does their work intend to contribute to the maintenance of managerial capitalism? If yes, then it is outside CMS. Does the work intend to contribute to emancipation, to remaking the world in less instrumental ways? If yes, then it is on the inside. But the problem with Kantian formulations is that we do not have access to the contents of people's heads. We can only judge intentions through action, so deciding whether a particular person is 'really' critical can only depend on our assessment of what we read, hear and see. An academic may, as Fournier and Grey acknowledge briefly and P. Thompson (2001) suggests strongly, be jumping on the critical bandwagon because it helps their career, because they must publish or perish and so on. They might, as I suggested of business ethics, be being 'strategically' critical. But how could we tell? On what grounds might we decide whether an academic was a person of good character or not? This might well be the subject of whispered chats at conferences, but is hardly a serious and consistent basis on which to adjudicate the differences between 'one of us' and 'one of them'.

Perhaps a different way into the question might attempt to evaluate the distinctions between the two positions in terms of consequences – the utilitarian ends of action rather than their wellsprings. What if, for example, the work is intended to assist in the development of better health and safety legislation? It may be explicitly performative, entirely reliant on taken-for-granted categories and unreflexive about the use of accident statistics.[8] Does that mean that attempts by academics to show that existing health and safety legislation is inadequate are uncritical, and that they should fall outside the CMS project? Or, to take another example, Ricardo Semler's *Maverick* (1994) describes his organization, Semco, in Brazil as an anti-hierarchical, democratic manufacturing company with a self-governing and self-managing workforce. It (if Semler is to be believed) has no organization chart; has flexible working hours; encourages people to wear what they like and decorate their workspaces as they see fit; encourages union membership and upward appraisal and so on. In many ways this is a new-model capitalist organization, and one that has been widely lauded by business gurus. Yet it also seems to be doing something, in very practical terms, about the complaints voiced by CMS academics. So does Semco represent something that CMS is opposed to? And what about Tom Peters? He, and a great deal of the business guru literature, what Gibson Burrell has called 'Heathrow Airport Organization Theory', announces itself as critical of the established order (du Gay 2000). It too is concerned to denaturalize and radicalize, but somehow CMS must announce that these are not real revolutions – merely the death of an old king and the crowning of a new one.

121

In terms of ends, we are then into the knotty problem of what ends we deem to be desirable. More money for less work, or the end of work and money altogether? Less hierarchically managed organizations and more teamworking, or the end of hierarchy altogether? Ethical capitalism, or the end of capitalism? Critical academics, or anyone else for that matter, will find it hard to judge the greatest happiness of the greatest number by comparing the possible future merits of reformist and revolutionary utopias. Unless human happiness can really be added up on the scales of justice. As Fournier and Grey acknowledge, these are not easy matters to adjudicate upon. Should CMS academics attempt to work towards humanizing work organizations, and run the danger of being co-opted, or refuse to engage with managerial practice at all, and run the danger of being ignored? In practice, much of what has been labelled as CMS has tended towards the latter rather than the former, tending to stress theoretical purity as a proxy for moral purity, and disengagement from the B-School hegemony as a virtue in itself. More on this later, but next I want to consider some of the components of critical thought on organizations more generally in order to ask some questions about the particular nuances and histories of B-School CMS at the turn of the millennium.

Disciplining CMS

As I hinted before, this description of CMS as a collectively unified vanguard movement, as the B-School's nemesis in waiting, is very wide of the mark. It suggests a coherence to something that is better described as a series of connected debates. Indeed, it might be said that (as it used to be claimed of postmodernism) it is easy to find someone who is against some aspect of it, and very hard to find someone who is unconditionally for it. There is, in practice, very little agreement about the nature and boundaries of what counts as critical work on organizations and this is partly because of the diverse variety of lineages that this work can make reference to. I will classify these histories in two ways, different disciplines and different theories, and deal with the latter in the next section.

A fairly obvious point to make about CMS is that it is primarily located in the 'organizational behaviour' parts of B-Schools. To be more precise, its debts are primarily, even if rather vaguely, to those parts of sociology and social psychology that constitute much of the canon in this area. To be sure, there is a substantial body of work in critical accounting, a little in marketing, and a few pieces of work on strategy, operations, information systems and so on. However, in many of these latter areas, it is possible to argue that the trajectory of the work has been aimed at 'sociologizing' the taken-for-granted by showing, for example, that the construction of accounting is not a neutral technical matter, but a social practice that represents power for its own interests and ignores other stakeholders – the environment, social costs and so on. Yet by far the largest body of work emerges from organization studies and human resource management. It is here, perhaps in the domains that are most committed to human beings (rather than numbers, or machines), from which CMS has primarily grown. In the UK there are, as Fournier and Grey (2000) and M. Parker (2000b) have argued, some rather more prosaic reasons too. The lack of career opportunities for sociologists and other social scientists during the 1980s, combined with a massive expansion in business and management teaching, resulted in many students with postgraduate training in sociology and related disciplines being forced to find work outside sociology departments. Many of the ideas which now shape CMS can be traced back to the consequent importation of Marxism, critical theory, post-structuralism and so on into the B-school from the 1980s onwards.

But, despite this migration, there is a kind of forgetting built into much of CMS as it tends to stress its novelty and contemporary relevance. After all, a great deal of work in organizational sociology from Weber onwards and organizational psychology from Maslow onwards was implicitly or explicitly critical of rationalization, the division of labour, alienation and the various psycho-pathologies which supposedly followed from certain forms of management and labour. To take the former, in the second chapter of this book I noted that the anti-bureaucratic critique has a long history, and I mentioned that it gained particular importance in US sociology after the Second World War when a number of writers were deeply concerned to evaluate both the efficiency and the morality of an organization form which was by then associated with corporate power and fascist versions of efficiency. So Mills, Gouldner, Blau, Selznick, Adorno, Merton and so on wrote much on the inefficiencies of bureaucratic structures, on the bureaucratic personality, and on the increasing domination of a managerial power elite and mode of thought which was intimately connected to the military-industrial complex.[9] In quite parallel ways, humanistic psychologists such as Maslow, Argyris, Likert and McGregor bemoaned the shortcomings of autocratic management styles, the lack of meaning in contemporary workplaces and the extent to which the managerial strategies of the time were turning employees into resentful dependent children. Yet, for CMS, much of this work is either forgotten, or regarded as the uncritical predecessor of the enlightenment that begins with Alvesson and Willmott in 1992. This also seems to mean that in contemporary sociology, what little that is left of the sociology of organizations hence has little connection to CMS. Sociologists have turned to culture and social policy, or have continued researching various 'classic' forms of inequality, but they seem relatively uninterested in organizing and organizations as such. So the two areas, both broadly denaturalizing, reflexive and non-performative, proceed on relatively independent tracks.[10] It seems that one of the perils of boundary work is that it excludes potential friends as well as obvious enemies.

In this regard, it is worth noting other literatures which are critical of the corporate managerial complex, but are also largely excluded. Within what might be called international political economy, there is an established body of thought on the role of business lobbies in structuring state and multilateral decision-making (Sklair 1995). I'll cover some of this material in chapter 8, in terms of anti-corporate protest, but just briefly mention the watering-down of climate change legislation as an example. As Newell and Paterson (1998) argue, an unholy alliance of pro-capitalist state and energy lobbies representing fossil fuels and transportation companies has been systematically defending its interests through public relations, research grants, positions on key decision-making bodies and so on. George W. Bush's decision in early 2001 to break with the Kyoto protocols and massively invest in further exploiting non-renewable energy resources was a testament to the power of this group of interests. Yet, once again, the B-School focus of CMS has meant that these macro-political issues are rarely considered. Of course, it might be said that this is largely because CMS is concerned with organizational issues, and this is a fair defence. All disciplines have their boundaries by definition. Yet, as I argued with reference to business ethics in the previous chapter, these boundaries can easily result in exclusions that are positively unhelpful when viewed from outside.

Similar points can be made in terms of literatures on feminist collective organization, the ecological critique of growth and the postcolonial literatures on structures of racism. For CMS, managerialism is often enough identified as patriarchal, environmentally disastrous and deeply complicit with an imperial order. However, with a very few exceptions, these connections are undeveloped and tend to be largely rhetorical. This is not to accuse CMS practitioners of sin by

124

deliberate commission or omission, but to note that this is what academic labels and disciplines do. They divide up territories and allow for particular forms of legitimate enquiry to be practised, but in so doing this labour of division leaves certain matters in the shadows, or as properly the work of someone else. CMS spends most of its energy attacking B-School versions of the organization, the employee, human resource management, culture and so on. It is therefore perhaps hardly surprising that it should have little energy left to lengthen its history or widen its focus. If it did this, then CMS would no longer be engaged in its very important institutional battle with myopic market managerialism. But perhaps the most contested exclusion is related to the debate between two forms of European social theory, both deeply related but now the subject of some heated and intense disagreement – Marxism and post-structuralism.

Theorizing CMS

This moves me from disciplinary division to theoretical division. Of course, the two are related but, in the case of CMS, there is a sense in which theory has become the battleground for defining the heart of the critical project. Various forms of Marxist analysis have pretty much defined oppositional approaches to capitalism for much of the last century. Whether we refer to Marx's own writings, Marxist-Leninist practice, the Frankfurt School of critical theory, or post-Braverman labour process analysis, it is difficult to imagine a robustly critical analysis of organization and management making sense without some form of residual commitment to Marxism. Yet that is exactly the point at issue here, with the central concern being to define exactly what kind of Marxism, neo-Marxism or post-Marxism CMS should be based upon. In a way that echoes the intense sectarianism of the left more generally – critical academics have been busily worrying about epistemology while Seattle was burning.

I don't want to spend too much time on the detail of this debate, but it is necessary to draw a general picture.[11] The cleavage here is between a variety of labour process academics who are mostly indebted to Braverman's analysis of managerialism in his 1974 *Labor and Monopoly Capital*. This book was widely seen as invigorating Marxist analyses of work and organizations and directly led to the founding of the UK Labour Process Conferences in 1983. However, since the early 1990s, CMS has grown away from these origins and become more concerned to theorize subjectivities rather than structures. This has led to some heated disagreements. Firstly, for labour process theorists, CMS academics (who are mostly characterized as adherents to Foucauldian forms of post-structuralism or postmodernism) are accused of a distraction from the critical project by sponsoring a largely irrelevant form of social or organizational theory that both denies the specificity of the employment relationship and appears to have little relation to Marxism proper. Secondly, it is suggested that their post-structuralist epistemology makes them unable to distinguish key dualisms – manager/managed, oppression/emancipation and so on – which are essential to any analysis of ideology in work organizations. Finally, that the above two points lead to a general inability to articulate a political position more generally because CMS has, through its sustained intellectual hypochondria, disqualified all the grounds for judgement. Perhaps the previous chapter would be a good example of this particular disease. CMS academics respond by agreeing that their approach is a development and revision of labour process Marxism but that this is entirely consistent with historical and dialectical thinking. Marxism is not a fixed corpus of ideas, and new intellectual currents should not be excluded. Secondly, they acknowledge that academics, or anyone else, can't do intellectual work without dualisms but that all critical authors must continually attempt to be aware of their contingent nature and the extent to which they perform identity work for the people who deploy them. Thirdly, that this does not mean the end of politics – merely the end of the kind of representational politics that was characteristic of modernism and its replacement with a more modest, reflexive and local practice. There is, in other words, no secure place outside discourse to accuse other people of suffering from false consciousness whilst your own ideology goes unquestioned.

The labour process position seems to be premised on the assumption that the CMS position is inherently relativist because subjectivist. In other words, it ends up as a stance that cannot contribute to emancipation because (amongst other things) it questions the objective reality of power inequalities. On the other hand, CMS researchers argue that the opposing position adopts (or constructs) a fictional 'high moral ground' and is masculinist, humanist, defensive and dualist. It therefore has difficulty in contributing to emancipatory struggles because it relies on elitist and conservative assumptions about the relationship between researcher and researched and refuses to debate the nature of emancipation itself. Whatever the rights and wrongs of this debate, the clear implication has been that many critical researchers do not identify CMS as their home, but as a fashionable form of relativism that is incapable of being politically critical. As one of them said during a debate at a labour process conference, 'I feel like my language has been stolen from me.'[12] Labour process analysis, with its materialist or realist commitments, predates CMS by decades yet is having its critical credentials appropriated. A politically ambivalent form of idealism and scepticism is colonizing the very words that have provided such powerful ammunition in the past. But for CMS academics, such a response adds up to a remarkable degree of defensiveness. CMS should include Marxism, as the CMSW mission and Fournier and Grey make clear, but is not solely constituted by it. Marxism is not irrelevant, but (for CMS) needs supplementing by new theories and methodologies in order to undertake a more ambitious critical programme.

This is a sad state of affairs. The remarkable mobilizations that seem to have had the potential to develop an internal critique of the B-School, of managerialism and the political economy of the corporation seem to be running into the sands of academic debate. As Jaros has put it 'we seem to spend more time debating each other about political economy than we do the right wing forces that are carrying the day' (2001: 38). Instead of inciting a storm of informed dissent, we have a flurry of academic papers and replies in learned journals. But let me be clear about my complaint here, because I am as complicit in this as anybody else. My pastiche of the issues at stake is unsubtle, it uses the wrong words and names the wrong names. In any case, many of the academics involved in these debates spend most of their time doing other things – engaging in theoretically informed empirical analyses of management and organizations, writing about power and inequality at work, teaching students about these and other ideas, perhaps even being involved in other political activity outside the academy altogether, and so on. This debate about the inside and outside of CMS is a side-show and not the main event. Nonetheless, it seems to me symptomatic of what happens to ideas when academics get hold of them. Critical? Critical of capitalism, or managerialism, or corporate domination? Critical of patriarchy, or imperialism, or heterosexism? What can be included and what must be excluded? Further, are we to be critical of positivism, of the hegemony of the scientific method? Or should we be suspicious of any claims to truth, whether realist or interpretivist? And if our critique becomes accepted, perhaps the cornerstone of a new hegemony, should we switch positions and become critical of that too? No doubt this is why Hancock (1999) ironically suggests a new acronym which provides a place for these questions – CCMS, critical of critical man-

127

agement studies. Perhaps the most characteristic way for an academic to answer a question is with 'it depends what you mean by . . .'. That is, after all, our job. To think hard about words and things. Sadly, though, at least at the time of writing, CMS (and CCMS) does not seem to be achieving much else. But then perhaps I was expecting too much from academics.

Academics and the world

So the central question that remains is exactly how academics, however critical they might claim to be, can exercise some degree of influence on the world outside the academy. For most (uncritical or orthodox) academics, this is not really a pressing problem since their legitimacy is largely bound up with certain forms of institutional reproduction of expert knowledges. A historian, psychologist or engineer only needs to worry about whether their research and teaching is well regarded by their peers, or perhaps demonstrably useful for a particular defined client group. In some sense, this is an uncomplicated matter since the validations of grants and career progress provide a publicly visible barometer on the success or failure of their projects. However, when an academic (whether in management or not) wishes to claim that they can play a role in progressive social change, then they run the danger of hypocrisy, incorporation or marginalization. This perhaps is why so many strands of 'critical' thinking – in sociology, cultural studies and so on – have become so theoretical, because the wide, open plains of thought can provide an unworldly opportunity for endless rumination and debate with a regular salary attached (Frank 2000). The romantic construction of the outsider intellectual, endlessly persecuted by the Big Other but struggling to find an authentic voice, has been a comforting myth for tenured radicals for some considerable time.[13] It allows you to be a good person and a good academic, to have a conscience, articles in top journals and a pension.

It is important, despite my rhetoric, to locate these as structural matters. The role of an academic is clear enough nowadays. It involves working within a large, often semi-corporate organization as a relatively autonomous professional. But the stress should be on 'relatively'. Academics, like other professionals, have clear expectations about the teaching, administration and research that will get them promotion. Much of the teaching and administration is increasingly bureaucratized (Parker and Jary 1995), but their research and writing is subject to constraints too. Research councils demand relevance to state policy in return for grants, corporate publishers want the next edition of textbooks that will sell to standard undergraduates on ordinary courses, journals are edited, refereed and read by other academics who stand at the gates ensuring that what gets published fits in with the demands of academic manners. Careers are made and broken within these arenas. These are all, in themselves, guarantees of professional status, but they are also mechanisms for ensuring a degree of conformity and insularity. The tendency, for it is not a law, is hence for academics to write for audiences within the university. A successful paper (or even career) will identify a gap in the literature, claim that more research is therefore needed, and then carefully make connections between this gap to what has already been done. This, for lack of a better word, is often called scholarship – a quality that inhibits making unqualified assertions of belief, or declarations of novelty. Or, if it does, it must make them in language that hides its passion behind veils of carefully referenced decorum and footnotes.[14] It is incremental, respectful, and thoroughly located within the exigencies of careers within professional organizations.

So it is easier for critical B-School academics to simply be academics than the leaders of a new social movement. It is difficult to do both of these jobs at the same time, but universities make it quite easy to do one of them if you stay on the inside, whether the inside is critical or not. One non-academic critical scholar recently noted that her work was continually made more difficult because she did not have the solidities of career structures, salary and time that can be found within a university. What was worse, she suggested that her location outside the academy was a form of stigma when trying to get her work disseminated within it (Bishop 2000). The increasing use of part-time and contract staff, combined with the hurdle of tenure in the US, means that many people are working hard at conforming precisely so that they can get a job in the core. If the individual achieves this goal, then a lot of prior domestication will have already happened. Universities can be very productive monasteries, perhaps even communities, but the Faustian bargain is that only certain forms of production are encouraged and rewarded. Writing unread scholarship counts, writing politics in newspapers does not. Organizing conferences counts, organizing activism does not. But this is not only a problem for CMS. As Naomi Klein argues, many academics across the social sciences and humanities have effectively got stuck in these debates about representation, not ownership, which is why they have said and done so little to change the political culture

129

(2000: 124). In worrying about political correctness, the semiotics of consumer culture, or the best strategy for dealing with a collapse of faith in metanarratives, they barely noticed when their universities and national institutions of governance were taken over by corporations. They were too busy interpreting the writing on the wall to realize that the wall had been sold.

But just as the radicals of a previous era become established professors of comparative literature, so are questions about the politics of academic work given new meaning in the B-School. This institution, as I argued in the introduction to this book, represents part of the most sustained and globalized pieces of public relations in human history. Unlike much intellectual labour, it involves academics coming face-to-face with people who are impatient for ideas that will help them to do what they want to do. Business ethics, for example. The point of the B-School, for its external customers, is to validate existing practice, or invigorate it with thrilling new language. It provides a career ladder through generously titled qualifications, and functions as a trade-school cash cow providing cow sociology for cash-strapped universities. Unlike many academic departments, the B-School is already pressed up hard against the utilitarian reality of corporate managerialism, and already understands the potential threats to its market from corporate universities and training consultants. It needs few lessons on relevance, or profitability, and many of its inhabitants are clearly thrilled at being so close to power. The rewards, after all, for half-way bright youngish men or women in suits who claim to know something that business wants to hear are very substantial. They get to fly on aeroplanes, and rub shoulders with some quite important people. If they are lucky, some of these important people will offer them grants to work on things that the powerful care about. So the problem is rather different in the B-School. For many CMS academics, it seems that a retreat into the well-worn critical intellectual stance, popular enough in the humanities and social sciences, is certainly possible when the demand for utility is voiced. The cultural capital that arrives with debating epistemology and reading French philosophy certainly helps when you are having lunch with a professor of comparative literature. But, and this is a very big but, this does not get you out of teaching on the MBA, and (if you voice your critical worries) feeling the scorn and impatience of people who really do have some rather serious responsibilities. No wonder that it is more tempting to continue chattering at conferences as some form of compensation.

So, how can CMS bite the hand that feeds it? Or, to put it another way, how can CMS academics lecture the hand that feeds them? The CMSW mission statement and Fournier and Grey's article make explicit reference to practices that 'reach out' from the academy and engage other constituencies. In this regard responsible management consulting, entryist strategies with regard to professional associations, activism in the labour movement, connections with feminist, gay and lesbian movements and black activists, and general 'hell-raising and muck-raking' (Adler 2000) are all presented as ways to make a difference. Undoubtedly they are, and I am certain that many CMS academics have done many important things in many small ways.[15] But one further, and rather obvious, idea deserves particular scrutiny – teaching students about critical thinking. In a sense, the most obvious strategy for CMS is to address its clients, mostly managers and managers in training, in order to educate them more broadly and use whatever rhetorical tools academics have to dethrone market managerial common sense. This is the obvious constituency, the group that arrive regularly at the B-School and have some investment in the knowledges that it produces. If the CMS oxymoron is to be solved, then perhaps making managers 'critical' through providing them with the tools that CMS uses is the most obvious way to do it.

But the problem of location does not go away. If CMS limits its ambitions to the B-School, then it will really have to find ways of selling its ideas as alternative forms of management training, whether termed 'micro-emancipation', 'critical action learning' (Alvesson and Willmott 1996: 171, 206) or something else. As Hancock puts it, such is the potential colonization of wider critiques of modernity when they are practised by CMS from within the B-School. These critics are 'suddenly finding themselves on the inside of the discipline pissing out rather than on the outside pissing in' (1999: 13). If they now have so much invested in management education, then it makes no sense to sell anti-managerialism at face value (in which case it would be unlikely to sell) but necessary instead to claim that, for example, managers can be made more effective through understanding non-performativity, denaturalization and reflexivity. Perhaps a reinvigoration of the long project of humanizing management might then take CMS as the latest example of sophisticated human relations, as a new form of 'soft' thinking against the modernist certainties of bureaucracy. For CMS to encourage managers to question managerialism recasts the powerful as clients, or even victims in need of assistance and enlightenment.[16] Like ten Bos's (2002) formulation of the 'insufficiency' of managers with regard to business ethics, here CMS would have to claim that it has something to sell to those who can pay for it. There might be a harder version of this argument, though, that CMS persuades managers and wannabe-managers that they would really rather be doing something else. Through a process of deception leading to revelation, it encourages people to give up their managerial careers and engage in more socially responsible activity. The direct success of CMS training would then be measured in terms of how many graduates did not do managerial jobs but went to work in co-operatives instead and its general project would be to lessen the demand for its services. When the B-Schools become empty, when their corridors contain dead leaves and the roofs leak, then they will be converted into sociology departments or housing for the elderly, and CMS will have done its job. The paradoxes abound, and they do so largely because the position of CMS is so firmly within the academy, and only certain versions of performativity have credibility therein. When Fournier and Grey suggest that critical work is non-performative, they have to rapidly acknowledge that it could be performative in different ways (2000: 17). Achieving a better world or ending exploitation are performative ends too after all. Academics might contribute to these ends in certain limited ways, but the demands of teaching, research and administration mean that their jobs and identities work against any systematic attempt to become public intellectuals (M. Parker 2002a). Indeed, if the limit of your ambition is to put yourself out of a job, the prospects for wider critique do not seem to be bright.

But then, why should we believe that universities will be the only or most important site for resistance to managerialism – lighthouses rather than ivory towers as Bishop (2000) suggests? There has been a tendency on the left, perhaps from 1968 onwards, to regard the university as a potential hotbed of radicalism. In fact, universities are merely places where certain people do certain kinds of jobs. Often, these universities are as strategic and corporate as the organizations and states that they service in a variety of ways. Despite appearances to the contrary, universities are often smugly conservative places, gigantic bureaucracies where students are processed, words are written and careers are made. The idea that they are the natural inheritors of a radical tradition, beacons of enlightenment in a lengthening McUtilitarian shadow, is simply romanticism taken to the extreme. Individual academics, or movements like CMS, might do something to radicalize the edges of the B-School but will be unlikely to change the world on their own. If business ethics is too colonized to present much of a challenge to managerialism, then critical management studies (as it presently operates) is too academic, too 'intellectual'. But, in case I am read as being too negative, both do have important constituencies, and both are helping to creating a climate in which managerialism is being placed in increasing doubt. More on this in chapter 9, but before that, there are still other places to look for a more popular form of anti-managerialism. The next chapter will therefore travel outside the gates of the university to the wider panoramas we find in the cinema and the bookshop – the culture industries and their representations of contemporary management and organizing.

7

THE CULTURE INDUSTRIES AND THE DEMONOLOGY OF BIG ORGANIZATIONS

'One type of criticism we would like to answer in advance. We shall probably be accused of exaggerating. It is a charge to which we both readily plead guilty. In a very real sense the function of both science and art is to exaggerate, provided that what is exaggerated is truth and not falsehood.'

Baran and Sweezy 1966: viii

Academic debates around the constitution of critical management studies, are just that. Academic. Whilst they might be fascinating and important for the people engaged in them, they do not have much of an impact in the world outside the university, or often even in other parts of the academy. It is difficult to over-stress this marginality, but vital to acknowledge it in order that the contrast between this chapter and the last one is clear. Simply put, an average popular film or book reaches more people than even the most hyped academic 'best-seller'. Most academic journals would be very happy to reach a circulation of 1,000 and an academic book would be doing very well if it sold 5,000 copies. As Libby Bishop has said of journals, their readership is 'the size of an extended (and inbred) family' (2000). These are minute numbers compared to the products of the culture industries – global entertainment corporations which spend gigantic sums of money ensuring that their products get seen in tens of thousands of cinemas and bookshops from Stoke-on-Trent to Seattle. For most people, the latest blockbuster matters, whilst the latest critical management studies text doesn't even appear on the radar.

However, all that being accepted, what can be claimed is that if there seems to be a coincidence of ideas between academic work and the products of the culture industries then something interesting is happening. To be clear, I have no intention of claiming that one causes the other in any direct fashion. Michael Crichton does not take his plot ideas from business ethics journals, and neither do academics write critically about organizations simply because they have seen *Wall Street*, although the latter may be slightly more likely than the former. My argument in this chapter is that many (though not all) contemporary popular books and films contain implicit or explicit representations of management and organizations that reflect a fair degree of ambivalence and often hostility. Though there have been negative representations of management and corporations for some considerable time, it seems to me that they are almost becoming dominant. That is to say, we now expect to see senior managers portrayed as ruthless, shallow and greedy, and large corporations as destructive and conspiratorial. These are the tacit understandings that provide the backgrounds for a wide variety of plots, and their very ubiquity suggests something about their widespread acceptability.

Of course there is a paradox in my argument. Since most of the books and films I will discuss below are produced and marketed by corporates (though not all), this in itself might suggest that corporations are a lot more self-critical than I am giving them credit for throughout this book. I'll return to this problem at the end of the chapter, but in any case we shouldn't forget that the profit motive suggests that entertainment corporations are mainly interested in what sells.[1] In some sense, the content of the product is relatively irrelevant. If, at the present time, plots featuring corporate greed make cultural sense, then they will sell. Putting it another way, a film or book which presents work as a happy and fulfilling thing brings to mind a Rock Hudson and Doris Day comedy or a Ray Cooney farce. Contented secretaries and well-meaning executives engaged in a series of farcical misunderstandings involving missing trousers and missed aeroplanes. Nowadays, though romantic comedies have not gone out of fashion, the backdrop is more often corruption and the arbitrary and cruel use of managerial power. In *You've Got Mail* (1998), for example, the heroine runs a cosy children's bookshop which faces bankruptcy when a huge chain sets up shop over the road. The hero, a senior manager in the big bookshop, has to work through his feelings about destroying small businesses before he gets the girl.

Nowadays, it seems, viewers are no longer inclined to be innocent about corporate matters. We believe, perhaps based on personal experience, that work organizations are often places of boredom, blocked

135

promotion and discrimination, places where faxes can prove corruption and closed doors mean that dodgy deals are being done. The popularity of conspiracy stories seems to underpin this analysis, and the move from farcical misunderstanding to dark conspiracy is a trope for our times. In the 1993 film remake of *The Fugitive*, we discover that Harrison Ford's character was actually innocently involved in a plot involving a corrupt doctor falsifying the records of drug tests on behalf of a large pharmaceutical company. In the *Jurassic Park* films, our heroes are under threat because shady entertainment corporations wish to set up theme parks with dinosaurs. In the John Grisham novel and film *The Firm* (1993), our well-qualified young lawyer is appalled to discover that the law firm he works for is actually money-laundering on behalf of the mafia. And so on. In these stories and many more, the backdrop is set by the hero fighting against the corporation, often embodied as reptiles in suits whose faces harden when you close the door.

However, I don't want to suggest that the only negative representations of organizations and management over the past century can be found in the past twenty years or so. Rather, following Frank (2000), I will begin by exploring an earlier era of anti-managerialism which coincided with the depression of the 1920s, the general strike, massive industrial concentration and so on. My argument is that contemporary representations cover quite similar anti-corporate themes, but the intervening period of the 1950s and 1960s is much more conformist in tone. As Whyte argued in 1961, the message then was about fitting in and learning to love Big Brother. Nowadays, Big Brother doesn't present a very loveable face, and the moral or loveable person must engage in some form of resistance to the ubiquitous tentacles of organizational control. In general, then, I want to argue that the contemporary suspicion of managerialism is not new, but that its resurgence as a kind of narrative common sense is very indicative of the changing political climate that I will discuss more explicitly in the following chapter.

Workers and machines

From *Frankenstein* onwards we moderns have had nightmares about the promises of liberation through the application of science. This is the persistent dark side of the utopian dream of managed social engineering that I described in chapter 1. As I said, the liberation is often away from the various bondages of the body – less work, less pain –

and towards bodily pleasures – comfort and leisure. Yet some way into these stories the creation turns on its makers and becomes their nemesis. Through endless versions of Goethe's story of the sorcerer's apprentice, but now with magic being transmuted into science, so did nineteenth-century romanticism get its revenge on nineteenth-century modernism, and forms of nostalgic feudalism or passionate individualism pit themselves against the lengthening shadow of the dark satanic mills. Yet, after the First World War, it seems that these dystopian stories gained increasing acceptance, although the monster was now a hybrid of big organization and heartless technology. Following my argument in chapter 2, this was an amalgam of the long-standing criticism of bureaucracy, combined with a sense that the machines were now enslaving us. In many ways this was hardly surprising. Technology had facilitated the efficient slaughter of millions in European mud, and this mass destruction had now given way to a mass production in which human beings became part of huge factory machines. At the same time as versions of scientific management were being introduced into factories and offices, large capitalist robber barons built massive fortunes, and did everything in their power to destroy worker organizations and bend compliant states to their will.

It is hardly surprising then that the 1920s saw the flowering of a cultural backlash to this view of work and organization. The Czech dramatist Karel Capek introduced the word 'Robot' into English through his 1922 play *RUR* – 'Rossum's Universal Robots'.[2] In the play the robots (from the Czech *robota*, meaning drudgery, with connotations of serfdom) are produced as 'living machines' without souls. Because a 'robot, food and all, costs three quarters of a cent per hour' the prices of goods are falling and humans will be 'free from worry and liberated from the degradation of labor' (in Rhodes 1999: 78–9). However, after intervention from 'The Humanity League', the robots are given souls by the Director of RUR's 'Physiological and Experimental Department'. Realizing their oppression, they overthrow mankind and create a new Eden. As I will show later in this chapter, this is a fable with many resonances in cyborg science fiction sixty years on. But at that time – immediately after the 'Great' War – Taylor, Bedeaux, Gantt, Gilbreth and so on were suggesting that it really was possible to control employees in increasingly minute and machinic detail.[3] Within the organization, aliens with little English like Frederick Taylor's 'dumb ox' Schmidt needed to be disciplined, shaped and moulded before they could become useful.

Like the robotic workers in films like *Metropolis* (1926) and *A Nous la liberté* (1932), Charlie Chaplin's defiant little tramp in *Modern Times* (1936), or Simone Weil's writings on factory time (see Grey 1996) these humans become part of factory or office machines – black and white characters marching to the timings of the machine whilst their bosses smoked big cigars upstairs. Franz Kafka's two posthumous books *The Trial* (1925) and *The Castle* (1926) capture a more general sense of these organizational nightmares. With their labyrinths of mysterious conspiracies, helpless individuals endlessly attempting to understand the reasons for their circumstances, and bureaucrats who defer to rulebooks and superiors that are nowhere to be found, Kafka's books have become a powerful metaphor for the cultural consequences of bureaucratization. These concerns with rationalization and hierarchy are nicely echoed in Aldous Huxley's 1932 *Brave New World*. Set in the World State's Western European Zone, Huxley named his 'Fordship' the Controller Mustapha Mond, after Sir Alfred Mond, the first Chairman of Imperial Chemical Industries. The key problem for this dystopia, as in Yevgeny Zamyatin's explicitly Taylorist 'OneState' of *We* (1924) or Orwell's later *1984* (1948) is how the individual, the person manufactured in a vat, can resist becoming 'just a cell in the social body' (Huxley 1994 [1932]: 81). In these texts, the individual is being crushed by the corporate machinery, by the anti-human bureaucracy that wishes to practise what Huxley prophetically called 'Human Element Management'.

As various authors have argued, in the US context a similar depiction of the problems of huge corporations reflected the rather inhospitable environment they faced in the inter-war period,[4] though there had been growing suspicion of increasing corporate power from the beginning of the century onwards. Ambrose Bierce, in his *Devil's Dictionary* of 1911, defined the corporation as 'An ingenious device for obtaining individual profit without individual responsibility.' (1996 [1911]: 49). The organization of the US economy under the control of various corporate alliances known as 'trusts' ensured that prices for producer and consumer goods were set in smoke-filled rooms and profits guaranteed. Yet, after the First World War, the Great Depression, the stock market crash, muckraking journalism, substantial attempts at union organization by the IWW and the CIO together with violent resistance by the corporates all turned this sense of unease into widespread social concern. Ultimately, this resulted in the 'New Deal' administration, which attempted to enforce anti-trust legislation, unemployment insurance and a whole host of new regulatory bodies (Jacoby 1973: 6; Schlosser 2001: 137). The rise of the

Progressive Party and the 'trustbusters' was in some sense a response to the widespread sense of corruption and collusion, and the perception that both big business and big politics were effectively in each other's pockets.

The brave promise of an America of social opportunity now sees the 'little guy' suffering under the new yoke of big organization. Social commentary books such as Matthew Josephson's *The Robber Barons* (1934), Frederick Lewis Allen's *The Lords of Creation* (1935) and Thurman Arnold's *The Folklore of Capitalism* (1937)[5] all took aim at the new decadent American aristocracy.

> In short order the railroad presidents, the copper barons, the big dry-goods merchants and the steel masters became Senators, ruling in the highest councils of the national government, and sometimes scattered twenty-dollar gold pieces to the newsboys of Washington. But they also became in even greater number lay leaders of churches, trustees of universities, partners or owners of newspapers or press services and figures of fashionable, cultured society. (Josephson, in Beder 2000: 53)

On the other side of the tracks, John Steinbeck was writing his tales of depression era suffering and humanity throughout the 1930s – notably *The Grapes of Wrath* in 1939 – and Upton Sinclair's viscerally realist novel about the appalling work and hygiene conditions in the Chicago meat industry, *The Jungle*, had been published in 1906 (and was credited for the passing of food hygiene legislation) but was reprinted in 1936.[6] Sinclair himself was also active throughout this period writing polemical pamphlets on various aspects of corporate intervention and state corruption (Beder 2000: 63, 201). On the other side of the Atlantic, novels such as Walter Greenwood's *Love on the Dole* (1932) and social commentary books like Orwell's *Keep the Aspadistra Flying* (1936) and *The Road to Wigan Pier* (1937) were covering rather similar themes.

There was, in summary, a widespread hostility in the US to the robber barons in their skyscrapers, the con-artists on Wall Street and their stoodges in the government. Films like *Mr Smith Goes to Washington* (1939) and *It's a Wonderful Life* (1946) are centrally organized around a dichotomy between the little guy and the bad politician or financier. In the latter, George Bailey, the long-suffering owner of Bailey Savings and Loan, prevents the pleasantville town of Bedford Falls from falling into the clutches of the evil Mr Potter and his big bank. This narrative of community and common virtue versus big business was certainly the most common mythical subtext in the

US, whilst in Europe these concerns seemed to focus more on bureau-cratic rationalization and the simultaneous rise of worker's associa-tions and socialist politics. Yet in either case, the big organization was getting a bad press. Some serious public relations was required to turn Roosevelt's New Deal away from encroaching on corporate power, and to prevent further general strikes from paralysing pro-duction. As I mentioned at the start of chapter 5, Berle's and Means's much misread *Modern Corporation and Private Property* (1932) argued that big corporations were becoming new feudal lords and in danger of dominating the state. Rather than an unqualified faith in either 'passive property owners' or the control of 'a corporate oli-garchy coupled with the probability of an era of corporate plunder-ing', they sponsor a third possibility (1932: 355). That would be where the interests of the 'community' were clearly articulated as a check on either the excesses of private property or the new corporate privileges. In a sense, then, the post-Second World War period reflected the building of this new settlement between democracy and money, but also the beginnings of a long process of relegitimizing management and organization in the face of popular protest.

Work and play

If this inter-war period seems to have indexed some kind of crisis in the way that organization and management were being represented, then it is probably fair to say that the post-Second World War rep-resentations were generally much kinder. Beder (2000) describes this relegitimation as an onslaught of corporate public relations – factory magazines, stories about the little guy becoming the big guy and endless homilies about the importance of hard work and thrift. It is hardly surprising then that we should see these justifications reflected in the films of the period too. As I suggested in the introduction to this chapter, the dominant way in which the Big Organization was characterized from the 1950s onwards was as a consensual backdrop to a drama of human values. Though there are good characters and bad characters, and often pompous buffoons in the corner office, the overall legitimacy of the organization is not a matter at issue. Indeed, since many of these films are farcical romantic comedies, work is often presented as an opportunity to meet your future spouse, after some tricky plot twists and elevator doors open and close at incon-venient times. Take, for example, comedies like *Will Success Spoil Rock Hunter?* (1957), *The Apartment* (1960), *One, Two, Three*

(1961), and *How to Succeed in Business Without Really Trying* (1967). Though these films do sometimes make some rather barbed points about the personal dilemmas faced by organization people, the organization itself is largely a neutral or even positive backdrop to a story about everyday people in their everyday lives. That these lives happen in and around boardrooms, offices, and the lobbies of big buildings, rather than on prairies or battlefields, simply reflects their apparent ordinariness.

Nonetheless, for William Whyte forty years ago, there was a more worrying subtext. In *The Organization Man*, he bemoaned contemporary films and books that moralized about the importance of authority and fitting in. Like David Riesman's neurotically conformist 'other directed' individual in *The Lonely Crowd* (1961), for Whyte these cultural representations were morality tales about sticking to the rules. In films like *Woman's World* (1954), *Patterns* (1956) and *The Man in the Grey Flannel Suit* (1956), the losers are those who do not learn to 'love that system' (1961: 226). For example, the hero of *Executive Suite* (1954), Don Walling, concludes the film by making a 'ringing, if somewhat hazy, statement of belief' in people which apparently resolves all the conflicts explored in the plot (1961: 74). Whyte's most trenchant criticism is vented on Herman Wouk's novel – subsequently filmed – *The Caine Mutiny* (1954). This is a story of a perfectly justified rebellion against the cowardly and useless captain of a warship. So far, so good. But the moral of the tale comes at the court-martial when the chief mutineer is roundly condemned for breaking navy discipline. The book was a best-seller, which Whyte takes to suggest that learning to love Big Brother is more important than mutinying against him. The rules, it seems, are there to serve and protect everybody. This message is echoed in Riesman's (1961) analysis of the children's book *Toodle, the Engine*, in which Toodle learns to stay on the right tracks and control his urge to pick flowers, and Vance Packard's accounts of the increasing use of the psychology of persuasion to discover or produce 'team players' for industry (1957: 201).

Thomas Frank argues that the writing of 'end of ideology' intellectuals like Daniel Bell and Richard Hofstadter reflected a general conservative consensus within this period, 'a vision of a healthy and well-functioning national whole' (2000: 288). Indeed, even Adolph Berle, who twenty years previously had warned of the consequences of corporate power, had now come to believe that, communist propaganda notwithstanding, a combination of the US constitution and community judgement was effectively domesticating the baser

141

instincts of the corporation (1955). Vance Packard, who had been a highly effective critic of the social and environmental costs of the 'hyperthyroid' US economy in his best book *The Waste Makers* (1960: 17), had, by the time of *The Pyramid Climbers* (1962), begun to suggest that a new breed of socially responsible manager could solve these problems.

In general terms, and notwithstanding national differences, Hertz (amongst many others) argues that this post-war consensus was economically Keynesian. This generally involved state ownership, or at least some commitment to regulation and intervention, some kind of welfare state, and the assumption that progressive taxation was a necessary and equitable way in which to advance the public good (2001: 15). In a similar vein, Mark Jancovich notes that 1950s' 'invasion of the monsters from somewhere else' movies are often explained as consensual responses from a 'Fordist' economy and culture to external threats, most obviously the Soviet Union. Though he argues for a more nuanced analysis, he cites Andrew Tudor's reading of these films, noting that it is the experts who save humanity from destruction: 'In this form of xenophobic universe we can do nothing but rely on the state, in the form of military, scientific and governmental elites. Only they have the recourse to the technical and coercive resources necessary for our defence' (1996: 15). Tudor argues that the move from this era of consensus to the more conspiratorial films of the 1970s marks the move from 'secure' to 'paranoid' horror. As with the organizational farces I mentioned above, there is a sense in which the shift I am going to describe in the rest of this chapter can be described similarly. The threat moves closer and, as I will show, often becomes the very organizational elites that putatively guaranteed our security. Hardly surprisingly perhaps, it is in science fiction where we can see this move most clearly.

Cyborgs and big corporations

In political and economic terms the 1970s sees the beginning of the collapse of the Keynesian consensus and 'the sense of pervasive crisis which had characterized the thirties and forties reappeared in the seventies, in part as an after-effect of the [...] mass movements of the late sixties and in part as an immediate reaction to contemporary shocks and disarray' (Hirschman 1996: 258). Margaret Thatcher talked of 'rolling back the state' and 'giving managers the right to manage', while Ronald Reagan promised to 'get government off the backs of the people' (Hertz 2001: 21–3). The Bretton Woods consensus was beginning to be unpicked and the IMF and the World Bank began acting as the emissaries of structural readjustment to market forces (much more about this in the next chapter). It seemed that big business had undergone its period of rehabilitation, and was now once again ready to challenge the rights of workers (whether air traffic controllers or miners) and the right of the state to regulate corporate activities. Or, perhaps, as Chomsky argues, this was merely the explicit rhetoric: the post-war period illustrated that corporations had learnt that they could use the shelter of the state to shore up their political legitimacy at the same time that they were 'feeding at the public trough' (1996: 120). So this period was characterized by protectionism and intervention – massive 'defence' spending, and state subsidy and/or tax relief to industries that were under threat. None of these policies actually changed much in the 1970s, the corporate trough remained full whilst the language of market liberalism became more strident and self-righteous with regard to public spending on welfare at home and abroad.

Whatever the actual position, it seems to me that the representations of organizations from this period onwards become more and more negative. Echoing the early twentieth century, as their power and legitimacy in the political arena increased, so did the cultural backlash. Echoing further back from the nineteenth century is the re-emphasis of a Frankenstein's monster narrative of scientific arrogance, of hubris clobbered by nemesis. As Amis (1969) and Tudor (1989) note, mad science is a key theme in much science fiction. Prometheus was punished by Zeus for stealing fire and using it to breath life into his clay images – the modern Prometheus is punished by his own creation. And, as I will argue below, the embodiment of science has often been the mad computer, robot or cyborg. This tragic monster lives because it was created to fulfil an instrumental purpose but, at some time during the story, we discover the unintended despair and/or anger that this 'object' now feels. The neutrality of science, or the scientist, and their rhetoric about efficiency or progress is revealed as dangerous arrogance as the creature turns out to be both victim and nemesis.

One of the most prolific places to find such ideas is in contemporary science fiction, particularly those films, from *Blade Runner* (1982) onwards, that contain cyborgs.[7] These creature blur the distinction between human and machine. In what seems like a return to Capek's robot slaves, we have moved away from the slightly stupid and shaky versions of people in gleaming metal, like Robbie the robot in *Forbidden Planet* (1956), paranoid computers like Hal in *2001*

(1968) or the patriarchal defence grid in *Colossus: The Forbin Project* (1969) to rather more confusing combinations of real and artificial flesh, metal, plastic skin and positronic brains. The dominant contemporary image of the cyborg is of a rampaging killing machine with infra-red eyes and guns for hands, or something with a human surface that conceals its incredible potential for technically assisted violence. Terminators, unisols, synthetics, robocops, androids and simulants in films like *Robocop* (1987), the *Terminator* films (1984, 1991), *Eve of Destruction* (1990) as well as the *Tetsuo* films (1989, 1991), *Cyborg* (1989), *Universal Soldier* (1993) and many others serve to demonstrate something about the importance of the machine-person as a contemporary cultural icon. These are visions of techno-golems, entities manufactured through the grafting of hard shiny bits of metal into soft flesh – or even with skin that is really a sophisticated form of plastic and memories that are no more than a computer programme.

Themes of retribution are common enough in science fiction and horror but in some contemporary cyborg films they are given added impact through a visceral focus on bodily destruction or reassembly. Though this was again one of the elements in early Frankenstein films – brains in jars, technicolor blood and so on – the new technologies of film allowed the exploration and explosion of bodies to be entirely different in its impact. The two Shinya Tsukamoto films *Tetsuo: The Iron Man* (1989) and *Tetsuo II: Body Hammer* (1991) illustrate these themes in graphic detail. Through car crashes, sex, medicine, experimentation and violence the textures of meat and metal, nervous systems and machine systems, are continually combined in brutal ways.[8] Nerves become wires, oil is saliva, limbs are tubes, the penis a drill. Respectable and bespectacled Japanese 'salarymen' push metal into their bodies and mutate into violent rusty cyborgs that groan and sigh orgasmically as they batter each other into submission. It seems fairly convincing, then, to suggest that cyborg films show us something about our fears about science's colonization of our bodies (see, for example, Shaviro 1993). To be more specific, they usually show us something about male fears and desires – there are few female cyborgs and most of the male ones have hard (not leaky) bodies (see Featherstone and Burrows 1995; Linstead 2000). If the cyborg is female, as in *Cherry 2000* (1988) or *Metropolis*, they are often sexy but brainless bimbos. Yet, for cyborgs of both genders, we may enjoy their capacity for physical violence or their flawless bodies but, as with Frankenstein's monster, we are surely supposed to feel both horror and pity towards these mutant creations of science. The most obvious (and common) argument made here is that many of these narratives tell us something about our ambivalent relationship to technology – fragile human flesh versus cold machines (Kuhn 1990; Seltzer 1992).

I don't want to suggest that the body horror readings of cyborg films are wrong, but I do want to add something to them. For my purposes here the most interesting common theme in these representations is that of the big corporation that has manufactured the cyborg. Very often these texts contain background references to some part of the state or the military-industrial complex that has, because of greed, ambition or paranoia, invested huge amounts of time and money in a non-human product. After all, it is important that we know that the first television cyborg cost (in 1973) the princely sum of six million dollars. Steve Austin, the *Six Million Dollar Man*, was a product manufactured for various kinds of dangerous espionage. Other cyborg products are similarly built for stigmatizing or dirty work, sub- or super-human labour in which normal human bodies would not last long. As Sanders suggests, they are 'devoid of feeling and free will, mere contraptions for the carrying-out of functions which are programmed from the outside' (1979: 141). That the cyborg then often rebels in a violent way is hence hardly surprising – this is the romantic revolution of the oppressed against the oppressor. Since the cyborg worker is often programmed, given instructions by their makers that they have no choice but to follow, then the guilt for their actions hence lies with the scientists, generals or managers who wrote their software. The metaphor is fairly stark here – heroic agency versus shadowy conspiracy – but this time the threat is from 'in here' and not 'out there'.

It seems to me that, in these films and others, the real enemy is no longer the individual Dr Frankenstein but the big corporation or state that sponsors them.[9] The demonology of big organizations in science fiction is a topic that, to my knowledge, hasn't received a great deal of attention.[10] However, it is a theme that has been central to much recent fantastic fiction. Spy dramas, such as the Bond films and *The Man from UNCLE*, had the organizations SPECTRE and THRUSH respectively as their most enduring enemies. These were outside enemies, thinly disguised versions of the communist Other. However, latterly it seems that many of the plots in TV programmes like *The X Files*, *Babylon 5*, *Deep Space 9*, *Wild Palms* and the majority of cyberpunk novels (for example Gibson 1986; Stephenson 1992) are premised on conspiracy theories about the actions of the internal corporate elite or the military-industrial complex. In the latter, employees are surgically modified, identify more with products than people, and corporations run everything. The us/them, 'secure' and 'paranoid', dualisms become problematized as it is harder to work out who 'us' and 'them' are and we begin to suspect that the 'Other' might be lurking at the heart of the state or corporation.

Along these lines, films such as *THX 1138* (1970), *Soylent Green* (1973), *Demon Seed* (1977), *Outland* (1981), David Cronenberg's *Videodrome* (1982) and *The Fly* (1986), as well as *The Fly II* (1989), *The Running Man* (1987), *Total Recall* (1990) and *Freejack* (1992) contain very clear references to the corporate interests that structure their worlds. In *Rollerball* (1975), for example, the hero 'Jonathan' is lectured by a senior corporate executive when he refuses to be retired from an exceptionally violent gladiatorial game. Ten years later, the entire plot of *Brazil* concerns a state in which cruelty is bureaucratized through the 'Ministry of Information' ('The Truth Shall Make You Free'). In one sequence, the hero attempts to deliver a cheque to the widow of an innocent man who has died in custody. The cheque is a refund for the costs of his interrogation. At the end of the film a career-oriented torturer insists that the relationship between himself and the old friend he is about to mutilate should be 'professional'. As with many sequences like this, the representative of the organization argues that something has to be the case because this is the corporate interest. In response, the hero asserts his or her individualism and stresses the immorality of whatever particular action is being undertaken. Jonathan's bruised and bleeding body is continually counterposed to the distant gaze of the suited executives who watch from behind glass. A bureaucratic utilitarianism meets an obstinate kind of Kantian ethic and the moral usually seems to be that the ends do not justify these particular means.

A particularly good illustration of the positioning of this moral dualism comes from the four *Alien* films – *Alien* (1979), *Aliens* (1986), *Alien 3* (1992) and *Alien Resurrection* (1997) – which pit the highly individualistic Ripley against her employer, the Weyland-Yutani Corp. The company (which is 'Building Better Worlds') wants an alien back on earth because, as Carter Burke, the company's representative in the second film, *Aliens*, tells us, it would be 'worth millions to the bio-weapons division'. The company will sacrifice anyone and employ any means to achieve its goal. *Aliens* contains a boardroom meeting at which Ripley is disciplined for not being aware of the 'dollar value' of the alien-infested spaceship she left to crash. The phrase is repeated later in the film as a justification for not blowing up the L426 installation which is now populated by aliens. Ripley's

righteous anger at Burke's attempt to get her and a small girl impreg-
nated by the aliens later in the film leads her to condemn his corporate morality. 'You know Burke – I don't know which species is
worse. You don't see them fucking each other over for a goddam
percentage.' In the third film she, now carrying the last alien in
her stomach, commits suicide in molten metal rather than allow the
creature to fall into the company's grasp. Yet even then, in the fourth
film, the United States military (an organization described as a 'Terran
growth conglomerate' and 'not some greedy corporation') reaches
beyond death and sacrifice to resurrect the alien through her DNA.[11]

In the same way, the T101 robot in *Terminator 2* ends up sacri-
ficing himself in order that 'Cyberdyne Systems' will not be able to
produce the technology that causes the machines to wage war on the
humans. Yet again, the corporation is the cause of the threat and it
takes a humanized robot to ensure that Cyberdyne does not make
huge profits by accidentally destroying humanity. 'I know now why
you cry', he says, before also lowering himself into a vat of molten
metal. Sarah Connor, the woman both threatened and saved by
Terminators, sums up the paradoxical humanism of the film: 'If
machines can learn the value of human life then maybe we can too.'
The cold, twisted organization people who work for Weyland-Yutani
and Cyberdyne seem the real monsters in these films. It is telling that
the ship in the first *Alien* film is called *Nostromo*, an allusion to
Joseph Conrad's (1904) novel in which *'nostro homo'* – our man –
is betrayed by corporate interests. The alien merely follows its nature
as it tears flesh whilst 'our men' precipitate its killing through their
unthinking loyalty to corporate instructions.

Though the *Alien* trilogy has cyborg characters, its material
monsters were not constructed by the corporation. In the three
Robocop films, however, the cyborg is struggling between asserting
a humanist individuality – as Murphy, the policeman whose body
was used to make the cyborg – and his status as a product of 'Omni
Consumer Products' (OCP).[12] This central dilemma is built into his
very programming:

Directive 1: Serve the Public Trust
Directive 2: Protect the Innocent
Directive 3: Uphold the Law
Directive 4: Classified

This last directive was inserted by an OCP executive and prevents
'our product turning against us'. The company has traditionally

invested in markets regarded as non-profit, hospitals and prisons, but is now moving into law-enforcement though its 'Security Concepts Inc.' division because 'shifts in the tax structure have created an ideal atmosphere for corporate growth'. Like the McCandless Corporation's skyscraper in *Freejack*, Omnicorp's corporate office towers ninety-five storeys over the crime-ridden streets of Detroit. This is a city almost owned by OCP and, like Huxley's *Brave New World*, is shaped by the imprint of its previous corporate dynasty. The Henry Ford Memorial Hospital and Lee Iacocca Elementary School are given passing mentions, whilst a showdown takes place at the now abandoned River Rouge plant – Ford's showpiece factory in the 1920s.

The *Robocop* narrative takes us into the heart of this vision of a commercial world in which executives manipulate their bodies to climb the career ladder, observe the dress codes, the washroom status hierarchy and talk a corporate newspeak to conceal the basic amorality and immorality of what they are doing. As one of them puts it, Murphy 'volunteered' for the cyborg programme by dying. In fact he was killed by a criminal employed by an OCP executive who had engineered his death by placing 'prime candidates according to risk factor'. In the second *Robocop* film the difference between the criminals and the executives is even slimmer, partly because they talk the same language. A drug godfather 'offer(s) our customers the opportunity to control every aspect of their emotional lives' and celebrates his business for the social good it does: 'Do you know how many people we employ?' Even patriotism gets brought in, the drugs are marked 'made in America' because 'we're going to make that mean something again.' The plot of *Robocop 2* hinges on OCP and the drug cartel attempting a hostile takeover of Detroit because it will be better run in the hands of 'responsible private enterprise'. However, corporate justice is such that, even when they are discovered, a few middle-range employees are sacrificed and the top executives manage to get away with no blame.

Yet, despite the best efforts of OCP – which by the third film has been taken over by the heartless Kanemitsu Corporation[13] – in the films Murphy/Robocop manages to overcome his product status and stand up for individual judgement against corporate utilitarianism. He never forgets who he really is, just as his police colleagues would rather strike than buy into the corporate line. His singularity and sense of duty stand out against the collective corporate culture and he resists violence, psychological manipulation and even disassembly. The guilty here are those organization people who have sold their conscience for a dollar, who refuse to take responsibility for their actions, who have tortured his body, who try to convince him to believe that he is 'a machine . . . nothing more.' One OCP executive explains why they can't afford to rebuild him: 'This unit needs millions of dollars in parts. You can't expect authorization for that kind of cash outlay overnight. Be reasonable.' Like the conformist salaryman in the *Tetsuo* films, the obedient military scientists in *Universal Soldier* or Weyland-Yutani employees in the *Alien* films, the condemnation is aimed at the employee who follows or sets the company line. The cyborg themselves cannot really be blamed because, as the drug dealer in *Robocop 2* tells Murphy, 'I don't blame you. They programme you and you do it . . . I forgive you.'

Perhaps the most classic example of a film that plays with this moral binarism can be found in *Blade Runner*. The cyborgs here are 'replicants', engineered by the Tyrell Corporation to do hard and dirty work on other planets. Unfortunately for the corporation, these manufactured proletarians are rebelling and some have escaped to earth. The Nexus-6 replicants are top-of-the-line models (perfect 'skin jobs') with implanted memories that can only be detected through 'empathy tests'. They are, apart from their capacity for ultraviolence, all but human. Deckard, who may be a replicant himself but thinks he is human, is employed to hunt these cyborgs down and kill them, but suffers something of a crisis after falling in love with one of them who also believes that she is a human being. The factual and ethical confusion that the film relies on allows us to blur the boundaries between 'humans' and 'machines' in a way that privileges neither. After all, if these androids do dream of electric sheep (as the title of the original Philip K. Dick story from which the plot was loosely developed puts it) then perhaps they are no longer machines. However, the clearest moral position in the film is that taken by Roy, the leader of the replicants, when he visits the Chief Executive of the Tyrell Corporation to demand an explanation for their existence. As in *Robocop*, the product then kills the corporate executive, this time through the Oedipal method of putting out his eyes. Again, however, our sympathies are surely with the replicants. They did not ask to be made as they are – self-conscious but with a four-year life span. Their agony and anger was inflicted by the managers in a big organization. Their violence is a revolutionary revenge, not merely an act of random brutality.

In classical mythology the story of Pygmalion suggests a rather different outcome. The King of Cyprus makes an ivory statue of his ideal woman and, after praying for divine intervention, the god Aphrodite brings her to life for him. On seeing King Pygmalion the statue falls in love with him and they marry. By the beginning of the nineteenth century Pygmalion had more commonly become Dr Frankenstein and the sorcerer's apprentice. However, by the end of the twentieth century the threat was even more specific – not simply science but the fact that the scientists and their laboratories are owned and controlled by large companies or state bureaucracies. In spatial terms this kind of science fiction tells us of shiny buildings and rusting heaps of industrial waste, guarded corporate enclaves and decaying inner cities. The immoralities and amoralities of the big corporation have spawned both the techno-monsters and the urban nightmares. Cyborgs are perfect employees, mobile versions of the production robots that employers already use to replace mere flesh. No doubt Frederick Taylor would rather have worked with a cyborg to refine scientific management than have to continually cajole some recent migrants who could barely speak English. However, like Capek's robots, this employee/product turns out to be savagely ungrateful and to have a soul of its own. Sometimes this is because its own 'humanity', its memories, its conscience, its individuality motivate it to turn against its makers. Marge Piercy's novel *Body of Glass* (1992) expresses this well. Her cyborg is a weapon with a conscience and it is precisely this 'human-ness' that causes it to be destroyed by the inhabitants of one of the corporate fortresses. In other cases, the Model 406 Gunslinger in *Westworld* (1973), for example, the product simply does what it is programmed to do, without hatred or passion. Either way, the cyborg has no reason to be grateful for being created, simply because its creators have shallow or callous motives.

So, in these texts the villain, the evil creator, seems to be the organization and the romantic response is a violent form of rebellion by a humanist body. In a reversal of much of the post-war organizational consensus, but a return to the narratives of *1984* and *Brave New World*, 'the technocrats are now the bad guys and the good guys are the reactionaries' (Franklin 1990: 25). The individual becomes the site of resistance against the corporation. On the one hand, we have the strangely humanoid and humanist cyborgs – Robocop, T101, Roy and Bishop, the synthetic with behavioural inhibitors from *Aliens*. These characters begin to know themselves, make jokes – 'I may be synthetic but I'm not stupid' – and gain our trust and understanding. On the other hand, we have these big corporations – Soylent, Tyrell, Omnicorp, Cyberdyne Systems, Weyland-Yutani and so on. These are organizations populated by utilitarian capitalists, power-hungry careerists or selfish research scientists. In a sense, there is no humanity here, merely economic imperatives and the language of strategy, accounting and marketing.

Mundane conspiracies

But these depictions of cruel and shadowy organizations are by no means restricted to science fiction. Indeed, it might be argued that the films and books I have mentioned above really represent the most extreme examples of what is actually a very pervasive idea indeed. In *Mission Impossible: 2* (2000), the evil genius who holds a virus that could destroy mankind only wants one thing. Not global domination, a million in a suitcase, the girl, or a passport and fast car – but stock options. How the mighty are fallen. The enemies of heroes like James Bond, Batman and Superman have transmuted from mad Soviets, scientists or slime creatures to become power-crazed executives in skyscrapers. But even in less fantastic narratives we see a similarly ubiquitous move. William Gaddis's *JR* (1975) depicts the greed, hypocrisy and banality of business – a theme then taken up and glamorized in TV shows like *Dallas* and *Dynasty*. Slightly later, Martin Amis's *Money* (1984) shows us a morally bankrupt pornographer who is addicted to the 'money conspiracy' whilst Caryl Churchill's 1987 play *Serious Money* viciously parodies the 'loadsamoney' language of the City of London.

> Money-making money-making money-making money-making
> money-making money-making money-making money-making caper
> Do the fucking business do the fucking business do the fucking
>   business
> And bang it down on paper
>
> (in Morris 2000: 180)

More recently, novels such as Iain Banks's *The Business* (1999), J. G. Ballard's *Super-Cannes* (2000) and Richard Powers's *Gain* (2000) have covered similar themes,[14] but it is again in films that the anti-corporate representation finds its spiritual home.

Oliver Stone's *Wall Street* (1987) is perhaps one of the most important examples of this genre, playing as it does Gordon Gekko's 'greed is good' speech and turbo-capitalist lifestyle against the authenticity of real people with real lives who make real things in real companies. In the Tom Wolfe book and subsequent film *Bonfire of the Vanities* (1990) we see Sherman McCoy, a 'master of the universe', see his certainties fall apart as he ends up on the wrong side of the tracks. *Other People's Money* (1991) tells the story of how a corporate raider – 'Larry the liquidator' – begins, in a Scrooge-like way, to realize the consequences of his actions.[15] *Glengarry Glen Ross* (1992) shows the sadness and cruelty of a group of salesmen, *Rogue Trader* (1999) tells the Nick Leeson and Baring's Bank story, *The Boiler Room* (2000) the story of how a trader realizes who he is really making profits for, and *AntiTrust* (2001) narrates a network of business intrigue which seems loosely based on the lengthy Microsoft trials. This is by no means an exhaustive list,[16] but the bad guys and business genre now seems very well established indeed.

Spreading the net a little wider, other films expose the corruption and conspiracy of various professional groups and institutions – *Network* (1975), *Quiz Show* (1994), *The Truman Show* (1998), *Ed TV* (1999) and *Bridget Jones's Diary* (2001) cover the media; *How to Get Ahead in Advertising* (1989) is self-explanatory; *Bulworth* (1998) and *Traffic* (2000) are both recent examples of the exposure of politicians, and to these might be added a host of films covering corruption and intrigue in the army, legal profession or the police. Further, in films like *Silkwood* (1983), *The Insider* (1999) and *Erin Brockovich* (2000) heroic investigators expose webs of corrupt officials and executives – all these three based on true stories. In terms of gender politics at work too, we can see a move away from the 'boss marries secretary' plots of the 1950s to stories about sexism, power and bigotry. *9 to 5* (1980), *Working Girl* (1988), *Philadelphia* (1993), *Disclosure* (1994) and even *What Women Want* (2000) are accounts of workplaces in which powerful men, and sometimes women, use sex as a weapon and then attempt to cover their tracks in various ways.[17] Even in cartoon series like *The Simpsons* and *South Park*, we have evil capitalists like Mr Burns and dead-end jobs in the Kwicky-Mart, or episodes where shopping malls have a Starbucks every other shop, or where Starbucks is actually taking over the world. And finally, in the latest remake of *Hamlet* (2000), the story of a king and his state becomes a tale of managerial intrigue within the 'Denmark Corporation'. These ideas, it seems, are very pervasive indeed.

In narrative terms, it is often only by breaking away from the organization that our heroes and heroines can find happiness. In *Joe and the Volcano* (1990), Tom Hank's character seeks salvation from a grey, surreal, dehumanized job by an insane act of destructive spontaneity. Ten years later, in *The Family Man*, Nicholas Cage's character realizes that being a millionaire deal-maker with a fast car and penthouse flat doesn't buy him the kind of happiness that a wife, children and dog can. Unlike the films that Whyte bemoaned, but rather like the cyborg heroes above, these are films that celebrate personal discovery or unmasking conspiracy. By handing in your notice triumphantly whilst the rest of the office claps, in *American Beauty* (1999) for example, you realize your true self. This is perhaps the misty-eyed romanticism of individual freedom, and the realization that money can't buy you love. Problems of overwork and inauthenticity established in the plot are dealt with through their imaginary resolution which re-establishes the severed links between individual and their relationships, family or community. Oddly, as Munro (1998: 190) notes, one of the few organizations which seems consistently revered by Hollywood at the present time is the mafia, and it is surely important in this respect that they are, so clearly, a family held together by codes of honour. Many mafia films and TV shows, *Casino* (1995) or *The Sopranos* for example, contain very clear representations of organizational work. However, often the moral terrain places loyalty to the family as the paramount good, and depicts corrupt cops, lawyers and politicians as weak and spineless. We share the intimacy of weddings and eating meals together, and to some extent sympathize with the 'justice' meted out to those who fail to return the warm embrace of the Godfather.

So in many of these films the organization can be portrayed as shallow and vicious, as deficient in the virtuous values of families or relationships, but there is also another way to play a story of salvation. In many plots, the key realization is that your organization is corrupt, and perhaps that the mafia lurk behind the scenes. Rather than a story of emotional emancipation, this then becomes a story of ethical emancipation upon realizing that the world is not what it seems. As the scales fall from our heroes' eyes, they see that the organization, or a particularly corrupt group within it, is wrapped within a spider's web of conspiracy. In metaphorical terms, this is the moment when the virtual world of *The Matrix* (1999) is exposed as the cruel 'desert of the real' – a world where puppet masters pull our strings. But, in doing something about it and hence suffering the consequences, the hero manages to walk away with their conscience intact. This general move from secure threats to paranoid ones is nowhere better seen than in the rise of these 'trust no one' conspiracy narratives (Knight 2000; Parish and Parker 2001). Whether expressed in films like *Conspiracy Theory* (1997) and *Enemy of the State* (1998), or through the endless X Files proliferation of stories about the origin of AIDS, the hiding of the truth about UFOs by states and the military, the assassinations of John F. Kennedy, Martin Luther King or Princess Diana, and the activities of the CIA, the FBI or MI5. More recently we have the 'fact' that the millennium bug was disseminated by computer virus companies, the foot and mouth virus by bureaucrats who wanted to cut over-production in British farming, and the events of 11 September were engineered by the military-industrial complex in order to sell more bombs. Whatever the story, the dominant theme is one of hidden, shadowy figures pulling strings. And, as I have shown above, the figures pulling the strings are all too often sitting in skyscrapers smoking cigars and calculating the value of their share options. I will be covering anti-corporate protest in the next chapter, but it is worth noting here that the list of shadowy organizations in accounts of globalization parallels these fictions quite neatly (Smith 2001). Rather than fictional mega-corps and hidden military bases, we have the Council on Foreign Relations, the WTO, the Bilderburg group and the Trilateral Commission. The move from fiction to fact, from aliens from outer space to monsters in the boardroom, seems then to become uncomfortably real.

Causes and effects

In 1894, John Jacob Astor IV, heir to the Astor fortune, published *A Journey in Other Worlds*, a utopia set in the year 2000. In this novel, The Terrestrial Axis Straightening Company pumps water from one pole to another so that the earth's axis will stay at right angles to its rotation, thus causing permanent spring across the globe (Remnick, in Rhodes 1999: 373). Nowadays, I would suggest, TASCo would be more credible if it were plotted as buying off politicians and scientists in order to conceal the likelihood that its plans would cause environmental destruction. As I said in the opening to this chapter, we seem not to be inclined to innocence about these matters any more. The modern promise of progress through organization and technology has been thrown into severe doubt as we witness what corporations have become, and just how dated Adolph Berle's comments about the checks and balances of restraint and civic duty look some fifty years later (1955). The representations I have discussed above seem to me to be illustrating this theme rather nicely. Not that all films or books produced after, say, 1975 are like this. That would be far too bold a claim. But the taken-for-grantedness of cold executives, corporate conspiracy, everyday sexism and boredom and their resolution through appeals to what lies outside work seem to indicate something rather important about the general acceptability of these ideas.

Now, as I said at the beginning of this chapter, I am not suggesting that all these contemporary representations of organizations and management are actually motivated by a deep sense of anti-corporate crisis amongst those people who write film scripts, novels and TV series. Most of these products are made to sell, that is their point. They are not produced in an attempt to bring corporate capitalism crashing down as the scales of ideological mystification are suddenly lifted from consumers' eyes. Neither am I trying to suggest that my three periods are as neat and tidy as I have presented them here. There are plenty of examples of films and books that do not fit my classification, and that I have conveniently ignored in constructing this chapter. For example, films such as *The Wages of Fear* (1953), *On the Waterfront* (1954), *Solid Gold Cadillac* (1956), *Desk Set* (1957) and *I'm Alright Jack* (1959) all fall firmly within my middle period, yet all contain rather ambivalent messages about organizations and management. But then we certainly should not assume that Hollywood always speaks with one voice (since it is really a multiplicity of organizations and professions) and, in any case, not all films are made in Hollywood. Further, there are many continuities across the periods that seem to make claims about periodization rather suspicious. For example, Mark Jancovich's book on the horror films of the 1950s suggests that many of the fears about rationalization, consumerism and authenticity were prefigured during this earlier period, and that the growth of paranoid horror from the 1970s onwards is really a continuation of these themes (1996). However, these points accepted, there is still a further issue that needs to be discussed. Why, after all, should we believe that the output of film studios and publishers tells us anything about the world? These are just stories, no more, and stories that might tell us more about their makers than the actual activities of managers and corporations.

As has been argued by Hayek (Blundell, in Pollard 2000), there is a long tradition of snobbery towards commerce on the part of intellectuals. For Hayek, real scholars are original thinkers, whilst the 'intellectuals' who make films and write novels are merely experts in passing on received opinion.[18] These latter dealers in second-hand ideas are usually driven by some sense of their own importance and hence use their platforms to express their disaffection with the present social order. In a sense then, much of what I have covered in this chapter, and perhaps the entire book, could be dismissed as a continuation of that long battle between the *nouveaux riches* and the established smug liberal establishment (Hirschman 1996), a battle that might even be echoed in the even older hostility of the Christian church to moneylenders. St Thomas Aquinas drew up a scale of occupations according to their social usefulness with religion at the top, closely followed by agriculture, but with commerce right down at the bottom (Beder 2000: 14). In his *De Regimine Principum*, from the thirteenth century, we can find the following:

> Again, if the citizens themselves devote their lives to matters of trade the way will be opened to many vices. For since the object of trading leads especially to the making of money, greed is awakened in the citizens through the pursuit of trade. The result is that everything in the city will be offered for sale; confidence will be destroyed and the way opened to all kinds of trickery . . . (in Berneri 1971: 53)

Hardly surprising then that, in his preface to Pollard's *The Representation of Business in English Literature*, Blundell rather sadly comments that Hayek's diagnosis of jealous snobbery seems to be repeatedly echoed in literature over the last three centuries, from Charles Dickens to Martin Amis:

> In the chapters that follow one is faced with a rather damning picture of prodigiously wasteful, yet Scrooge-like businessmen who are abnormal and antagonistic; corrupt, cunning and cynical; dishonest, disorderly, doltish, dumb and duplicitous; inhumane, insensitive and irresponsible; ruthless, unethical and unprincipled; and villainous to boot. (2000: x)

He backs this up with some media analysis of TV shows in which over half of all CEOs commit illegal acts, and almost half of business activities are portrayed as illegal. Is this really an accurate portrayal of business practice, he asks? And the answer, for Blundell, is obvious.

So, even accepting that the symptoms are the same – widespread negative representations – the diagnosis may be very different. For Hayek and Blundell, these are part of the long battle between those who do and those who merely chatter. The latter, status-seekers all, see the world of business through jealous eyes, and conveniently ignore the fact that their very art depends upon the management of organization and technology for its propagation. Like ungrateful children engaged in perpetual teenage revolt, they bite the hand that feeds them and disseminate poisonous and inaccurate images in return for filthy lucre. Now that may well be a good description, particularly in terms of its suggestions about class location, but there are two points to make. The first is that the accuracy or inaccuracy of these stories is again not really the issue here. In this chapter (and the rest of the book) I am not claiming that the world really is like *Wall Street* and *Robocop* (or organizational citizenship and community) just that many cultural producers represent it in that way, and many cultural consumers appear to enjoy these representations. And, in the case of the latter, unless we accept some massive version of media brain-washing, they do not believe these things merely because a Hollywood director tells them to. Secondly, as Baran and Sweezy's epigraph to this chapter indicated, art (and social science) exaggerates features of the everyday for its own effects but that does not mean that it does not have some truths of its own. Even the most fantastic science fiction takes part of its context from the problems and politics of the time, and to deny this would be to deny any relationship between cultural representation and context. So, however minimally, it seems possible to argue that these films and books do say something about business, or at the very least about the ways in which business has often been perceived towards the end of the twentieth century. And this latter, for my argument, is the most important point because it suggests a change in the cultural atmosphere which seems to have some very interesting implications, but more of that in the next chapter.

Finally, I am well aware that reading the 'moral' of these films is not simple. There are plenty of more nuanced readings of all this material in cultural and literary studies, many other explanations of what *Frankenstein*, *Brave New World* and *The Matrix* really mean. In a sense, though, I have been more interested in what they assume than what they say. The backdrop, rather than the foregrounded complexities of plot and character, has been the topic of most of this chapter. To me, the sheer mass of conspiratorial and unhappy images says something rather important about where many people believe authenticity can be located nowadays. Unlike the academic debates around business ethics and CMS, or the more explicitly politicized anti-corporate movement that I will discuss next, the message of these texts is a simpler one. Individualism versus corporation, freedom versus constraint, conspiracy versus truth. And, in terms of resolutions, the individual can only find happiness within their own conscience, or the mirror of their loved one, or the heart of their family or community. Though, as I showed in chapter 4, many of these formulations of intimacy have been colonized by 'real' organizations, on the silver screen the division is clear enough. Work does not make you free (because your soul should be your own), and corporations are intent on nothing but profits.

I'll have more to say about the implications of these morality tales in the final chapter, but next I want to move on to my final example of the anti-managerial spirit of the times. Unlike academic books or even the subtext of Hollywood films, this is a mobilization of activism that is difficult to miss, and that provides the most dramatic example of my general argument about an increasing challenge to the hegemony of managerialism.

8

ANTI-CORPORATE PROTEST

'It gobbles whole mountains and forests, drinks rivers dry, spews toxic waste, and enslaves whole populations. It has all the rights of a citizen, but few of the limitations. It can cross national borders as if they were cobwebs. It is immortal, and can therefore amass wealth and power beyond the capabilities of mere mortals. It has powers that dwarf and control governments. It controls the newspapers, radio, and television, and so it controls the "truth" ... We are talking about the CORPORATION.'

Earth First!, reproduced in Starr 2000: 87

The Earth First! quote reproduced above reads like a 1950s film poster. *Monsters from an Unknown Planet* – 'From a Black Hole in Space they came to Conquer Earth!!!' But, as the previous chapter argued, 'they' are increasingly 'us'. The very institutions that have created modern societies are now becoming the monsters. Though writing books and making films are certainly ways to rethink managerialism and the Machiavellian corporation, they do not exhaust the range of possibilities. Effective politics would be fairly blunt if it was limited only to paper debates and decoding texts. Indeed, the scholarly care taken by business ethicists or critical management scholars, and the constraints of plot and market that are largely necessary for cultural producers, mean that the anti-managerial messages are often not heard, or ambiguous if they are. Taken as a whole, the last three chapters of this book might demonstrate a shift in a climate of representation, but one that has had few echoes outside the seminar room or cinema. Yet, over the last few years, anti-corporate ideas have echoed much more widely, and with an explicit anger and kaleidoscopic brilliance that has left the academy and the culture industries in the shade. This attack on 'corporate libertarianism', and 'corporate colonialism' (Korten 1995), manifested in what Newell (2000: 127) calls 'a counter-corporate culture', is what this chapter is concerned with, but I will focus particularly on a small pile of books published in 2000, all of which have encouraged some hard thinking about the managerial project.

So this chapter will try to draw together threads from the anti-corporate movement, but I want to start by explaining what drew me to these ideas, and hence really what stimulated me to try and collect this book together in the way that I have. A while ago, I read Naomi Klein's *No Logo* (2000). As someone who had dallied with business ethics, identified with critical management studies, and hoarded books and films with anti-managerial themes, it seemed to me a book worth reading. In any case, this seemed like a book that everyone else was reading too so, not wanting to be left out, I had a look.

Let's get the bad stuff out of the way first.[1] *No Logo* was written and marketed to sell by the bucketful. From the 'No Logo' logo on the front (which is a registered trade mark) to Naomi Klein's white thirtysomething smiling face at the back, this is a fair trade coffee-table book designed to show guilty liberal hearts worn clearly on sleeves.[2] The Klein brand is 'Revolution Lite', with her website and *Guardian* column now cross-marketing this Canadian, and hence comfortably anti-US, journalist as alt.culture celebrity. With gleeful hypocrisy, 'the pin-up girl of the anti-globalization movement' (Steyn in Böhm 2001) uses the very tools she claims to criticize, and has no problem being published in the UK by an arm of Rupert Murdoch's publishing empire. Further, Klein barely seems aware of business ethics or critical management studies. She ignores the debates between Marxists and Foucauldians, seems unsure whether to adopt a structuralist or post-structuralist position on signification, and fails completely to theorize the role of the state, or of the imperial role played by the English language. In summary, this is an overlong book which offers no cogent alternative to the present state of affairs, and is written by a sloppy scholar and a keen self-publicist.

But I loved this book, and hope it sells millions more than it has sold already. Let the bandwagon roll. *No Logo* has been reviewed everywhere, even in the consumer magazine *Real Money* (March 2001), which suggests that it might be useful for those thinking about share prices in companies taken to task over their human rights record. It has been confiscated by Swiss border guards whilst the World Economic Forum meeting was happening in Davos, and prompted Marcel Knobil (global chairman of Superbrands) to, amongst other things, accuse Klein of sponsoring a return to a Soviet-style economy (2000). It seems that her book is encouraging many, many people to start to think hard about capitalism, globalization and sweat-shop labour via the clothes they wear and the food they eat. It works because *No Logo* is so readable, unlike many of the 'academic' books that Klein ignores and that I have spent much time wrestling with in this book so far. The latter might be tiresomely worthy in tone and content, and display their 'Theories' like gigantic pianos in a dusty old shop window, but they are rarely well-written books. But Klein is a journalist, so she knows how to write for a wide public. This means short sentences, snappy journalese and good illustrations of her argument. Like Vance Packard or George Ritzer, this is not the kind of prose that would get published in academic journals since it moves too fast, and displays a studied lack of care for the conventions of 'gaps in the literature' and 'more research is needed'.

What particularly fascinates me about Klein is her approach to 'Theory' (with a capital 'T'). She doesn't really have one. Now clearly this is a terrible thing in academic terms. It is simply expected that what 'we' do is to generate and refine Theory, perhaps empirically, aesthetically or politically, but Theory nonetheless. Klein makes a variety of claims in her book, but I'm not sure they add up to much of a Theory. She claims that branding (Nike, The Gap, McDonald's, and so on) is a 'collective hallucination' which is beginning to colonize every available space. Even resistance and cynicism can be branded by 'street-wise' ad agencies, and 'branded people' like Michael Jordan are now a commodity in their own right. She writes about the increasing use of the franchise and sub-subcontracting structure, of industry concentration and of the ways in which this leads to visible and invisible corporate censorship. She tells stories about McJobs, 'permatemp' jobs and Export Processing Zones in South-east Asia (and now in China) and contrasts this with the emerging Western myth of 'free agent nation'. Just as the organization becomes virtual, so does its responsibility to employees – wherever and however they work. But, no space, no choice and no jobs also means no logo. In other words, the promises of liberation, freedom and expression being sold through brand-based marketing are directly contradicted by the everyday experience of uniform commodification. Any colour you like, as long as it's Nike. So Klein spends much of her time documenting and praising anti-corporate activism, adbusting, culture-jamming, and the McLibel trial. The brand bullies have over-extended themselves, have revealed their own hypocrisy, and can thus be attacked through defacing billboards and a www.war_of_the_flea by the counter-marketeers. The very ubiquity of branding becomes an opportunity for 'political jujitsu' in which the power and strength of corporations is turned against them.

Great stuff, but theory? Well, perhaps a Marxist analysis of globalization – but there's very little about class here. Neither is Klein keen on the endless ironies of identity politics either. As she says, the PC wars that erupted on US campuses in the 1990s did little to change the working lives of people growing Starbuck's coffee. In a sense, her analysis of advertising is similar to Vance Packard's *Hidden Persuaders* (1957)[3] or Adorno and Horkheimer's *Dialectic of the Enlightenment* (1972) in that it shows how all choices become colonized. Product X or product Y? Politics X or politics Y? The choice is yours. But Klein is more optimistic than any of these authors in that she does believe that subvertising and adbusting do have important political consequences. They represent a citizen-centred resistance to the power of the corporations, a form of people power which can raise consciousness and have demonstrable effects. Further, these forms of activism might encourage states and regulatory agencies to 'raise the bar' on what is acceptable business practice. So, there are bad things happening, but good people can do something about it.

Whilst Klein's book doesn't have an explicit theory, it is underpinned by various assumptions which the reader may, or may not, agree with. But when academics refer to Theory, they usually mean a systematic set of statements about the way that parts of the world work or concepts fit together. The coherence, provenance or novelty of the Theory then becomes the basis upon which academic work can be judged. Theory X is compared to Theory Y. You can choose. Watching this parade of intellectual supermodels, the audience murmurs, and then adjudicates with knowing seriousness. The Theory catwalk continues endlessly, with academics selling one fashion and buying others, shopping at *Theory, Culture and Society* and wearing Harry Braverman or Michel Foucault's latest collection. And sometimes we insist that others join in too, asking them what their favourite Theory is, or reproaching them for not having a Theory at all. But what Theory do you need to throw a brick through the window of a McDonalds's? Who is most relevant in taking aim at corporate capitalism – Marx, Althusser or Deleuze? Who cares, outside the seminar room? Of course we all need theory (with a small 't') to recognize a brick and a window, but do we need a Theory to connect them?

The reason Klein's book is so good is probably the same reason that many academics do not like it.[4] Klein simply doesn't get hung up on academics. For her, the words of a worker in an EPZ or a fellow journalist are just as relevant as the words of a professor in an ancient university. In a sense, this means that she isn't paying her dues and (as intellectual tax collectors) academics may feel entitled to their share. But the reason she doesn't need to bother is because she is aiming at a far wider audience, of which academics are a very, very small part. This is already a book-club book, and has probably done more to get people thinking critically about contemporary business practice than every business ethics or critical management article published so far. Of course, I am being unkind, and of course I am exaggerating again, but the relationship between 'critical' practice and academic careers is one that does not go away. For academics to defensively respond by claiming something about the occupational specificity of their practice, or claim that they laid the groundworks for this kind of cultural critique in the first place, is to duck the issue. As Monbiot (2000) shows, corporate interests (through research funding, sponsorship, or teaching as a behavioural training in key skills for employment) are now colonizing the university as never before. If academics continue to play their endless glass bead game in which 'theory' is incorporated within 'Theory' they are doomed to relative irrelevance in the bigger games that shape all our lives.

As one of the key texts in the emerging anti-corporate movement which I will discuss in this chapter, this is also a book that is worthy of some serious thought in terms of the way in which it crystallizes certain cultural shifts – from a politics of the state to a politics of the trans-national corporation. But it is also a book that, for me, indirectly raises some serious questions about 'business ethics', 'corporate social responsibility', 'critical management studies', and similar labels. Can any academic who is seriously concerned with grand words like 'emancipation' and 'justice' afford to ignore issues of readership and effect? What is the point in being a revolutionary, or even a reformist, if no one can hear you? The ivy around the ivory tower is growing in academic throats. And yes, I am guilty too.

Outside the academy

Seattle, Prague, Davos, Quebec, London, Genoa – places now tied together as examples of 'anti-capitalist' protests against the World Trade Organization, the General Agreement on Tariffs and Trade, the

Free Trade Area of the Americas, the G8 and so on. Places where McDonald's have been ransacked, war memorials defaced, slogans have been shouted at delegates, pies have been thrown and alternative summits have been held. Places also where water cannons have been deployed, barriers erected, protesters searched, denied access to countries and imprisoned, and huge numbers of armed and armoured police have fought violent street battles that have led to the loss of life.[5] Though the local police may be an unified organization, their opponents are not. Putting it mildly, the protesters have been a rainbow coalition of landless peasants, priests, students and academics, environmental activists, union organizers and anarchists. But what, if anything, ties them together?

When the United Nations was founded immediately after the Second World War, it was intended to be an organization that ensured that international conflict would never again occur on such a large scale. Mindful of the links between hyper-inflation and the rise of fascism, as well as the possibly destabilizing effects of unbridled commerce, it was proposed that the UN would also have oversight of an International Monetary Fund (IMF) and an International Bank for Reconstruction and Development (the World Bank). Both were intended to supply funds for European post-war reconstruction, but rapidly expanded their remit to the rest of the world. The third of these 'Bretton Woods' institutions was to be an International Trade Organization (ITO), intended to be established at a conference in Havana in 1947 (Ransom 2001: 10). However, twenty-three of the richest and most powerful countries seemed not to like the idea of a regulatory body that would be subject to the oversight of communist and developing nations and instead established their own body, the General Agreement on Tariffs and Trade (GATT). The ITO was never established, and the UN instead established a Conference on Trade and Development and included some grand words about rights in articles 23 and 24 of the Universal Declaration of Human Rights, ratified in 1948.

By the 1970s, and as I mentioned in the previous chapter, it was widely acknowledged that the Bretton Woods system was beginning to collapse and the relatively Keynesian post-war consensus was coming under increased pressure. The World Bank and the IMF shed their global social worker guises and became stern economic taskmasters, pursuing increasingly free-market policies and politics through the 'structural adjustment' measures that were required before loans were agreed (Barnet and Cavanagh 1994: 353). At the same time GATT rumbled on through a series of lengthy negotiating rounds intended to liberalize markets and take down trade barriers, but its trade rules were not enforceable even on GATT's own member states. But by the late 1980s, with the collapse of the Soviet Union and the rise of the new Pacific 'tiger economies', it was becoming clear to political and corporate interests that GATT was not powerful enough and that a more robust and binding set of liberalization measures was needed. So, in 1995, at the end of the Uruguay round of negotiations, the GATT club renamed itself the World Trade Organization (WTO) and was given legal status to intervene in the laws of member states. Signatories to the WTO would have to accept the binding judgements of Disputes Settlement Panels and, in return, had the promise of a yawning free market for international trade. Non-members could apply for membership, and access to the most profitable markets, only if they signed up to intervention in their own domestic arrangements. This was to be the biggest protectionist club of all, and if you were outside it, you might as well say goodbye to international trade: 'Nowhere on earth will robust laws protecting the environment or human rights be allowed to survive. Elected representatives will, if these plans for a new world order succeed, be reduced to the agents of a global government: built, co-ordinated and run by corporate chief executives' (Monbiot 2000: 330).

By the late 1990s, world free trade was coming together nicely. The WTO had a headquarters on the shores of Lake Geneva, a staff of hundreds, a budget of millions and a rapidly expanding membership – 139 states by 2000 (Hertz 2001: 84). Running in parallel to the expansion of the WTO, other trade treaties were being formulated. The North American Free Trade Agreement (NAFTA) had been implemented in 1994, and the Multilateral Agreement on Investment (MAI) was due to be signed in 1998. Further, as Frank exhaustively documents, the ideological foundations of 'market populism' had already been laid – suggesting that markets are 'a far more democratic form of organization than (democratically elected) governments' (2000: xiv). But the rumblings of discontent surfaced rather visibly in 1997, when a draft of the MAI was leaked on the web, and demonstrations began to accompany negotiating meetings. The MAI was eventually withdrawn in late 1998 following objections from the French after it was realized that the agreement would criminalize any attempts to protect the French film industry, as well as many other specifically national provisions (Monbiot 2000: 303). But, at the regular WTO ministerial meeting in Seattle in November 1999, something much more alarming happened. Over 40,000 people engaged in noisy and violent protests with riot police and both the global and independent media sent the pictures spinning across the world. Environmental protesters complained about global warming, peasants about impoverishment, trade unionists about job losses to the third world, socialists about the dominance of the free market, libertarians about corporate power, farmers about agribusiness, vegetarians about animal rights, development activists about third world exploitation, anti-car protesters reclaimed the streets, hackers attacked the hegemony of Microsoft and so on.

This 'Battle in Seattle' rapidly assumed iconic status as the noisy coming of age of a new social movement, a movement that then went on to hold similar battles in Davos, Prague, London, Washington and others as it 'summit hopped' various state-industrial congresses around the globe and made May Day into a regular festival of anti-capitalist fun. The MAI mutated into the Trans-Atlantic Economic Partnership, and NAFTA into the Free Trade Area of the Americas, but the demonstrations continued. The acronyms may be continually changing, but just as new groups of industrialists and politicians attempt to cement lasting 'partnerships' or 'dialogues' so does the organization of resistance become ever more sophisticated. Perhaps echoing the counter-culture of the 1960s, the situationist street theatre of the WOMBLES; the proliferation of an incredible number of superb websites; satirical TV programme-makers like Michael Moore and Mark Thomas and the serious discussion taking place in alternative conferences represents a dizzying spectacle of rage at the operations of the corporate-managerial complex. At the time of writing, it seems that the chorus of disapproval is echoing ever more loudly. The May Day protests in London received huge press coverage and a massive police operation to prevent disruption (Böhm 2001). Organized as a Monopoly game board, the events included a mass cycle ride; giving veggie burgers away outside McDonald's; students protesting against fees; bird feeding; protests against profiteering refugee landlords, as well as outside the WTO offices and the Queen's bank – Coutt's; a solidarity demonstration with prisoners outside HMP Pentonville; action against the fur trade; and events organized by 'peaceniks' and the 'Dionysian Underground'. The finale was to be 'Sale of the Century' in Oxford Street, but the police invited themselves too. On the same day, demonstrations took place in Canada, the Czech Republic, Denmark, Finland, France, Germany, New Zealand, Spain and the USA.

In some senses this activity could be said to be an amplification and radicalization of the consumer movement itself. For many years, the US Consumers Union (Packard 1960: 240), Ralph Nader's US

National Consumer Council, endless watchdog TV programmes, and magazines like *Ethical Consumer* have interrogated the representatives of corporations in the name of a wronged customer whose washing machine does not function as intended, or whose holiday hotel had not yet been built. The public relations manager is dragged on to the show and forced to apologize for their misdemeanours, to the enjoyment of all concerned. Yet once the compensation has been paid, and the manager has explained that they are a victim of their own success and that this will never happen again, the show moves on. These media spectacles almost certainly laid the ground for holding corporations to account, but usually do so on behalf of specific 'consumers'. The anti-corporate movement is throwing its accusations much wider, and in the name of 'citizens' concerned with democracy.

In taking Seattle as the key moment, and focusing on the multilateral trade treaties as the key issue, there is, however, a danger of suggesting that all this protest coalesced from nowhere in 1999. The dramatic nature of the Seattle protests, combined with the fact that they took place in a US city, meant that it was easy enough for the global media to define this as the birth of a new movement. This is certainly not the case – there were protests at the WTO meeting in Geneva in May 1998; the first International Symposium on Corporate Rule was held in Canada in 1997 (Starr 2000: 71); and the UK and US Corporate Watch websites began in 1996. In general, however, previous protests – the McLibel trial, boycotts of Nestlé, Nike, Monsanto, The Gap, Wal-Mart and Shell – tended to be more specifically focused on one organization or issue. Even if they were not, as in the increasing visibility of a language of social and environmental responsibility and concerns about ethical investment, there was rarely a sense that a distinctive anti-corporate or anti-capitalist movement could be identified. Nonetheless, the seeds of discontent were sown well into the early 1990s at least, with books like Barnet and Cavanagh's *Global Dreams* (1994) and Korten's *When Corporations Rule the World* (1995), with their deeper roots in the 1960s counter culture, investigative journalism, the anti-conformist situationist movement and even older forms of revolutionary anti-state protest.[6] In terms of this older literature, Noam Chomsky (for example) has been writing about the manufacturing of consent by the US political classes for the last thirty years. In a huge number of books, he has shone a bright light on US media and foreign policy – particularly on the ways in which corporate and political interests determine policy and restrict serious democratic debate (for example,

1996: 94). Along similar lines Herbert Marcuse's *One Dimensional Man* (1964), Baran and Sweezy's *Monopoly Capital* (1966), Galbraith's *The New Industrial State* (1967), Charles Reich's *The Greening of America* (1970), Mintz and Cohen's *America Inc* (1971), Schumacher's *Small is Beautiful* (1993, originally 1973) and Barnet and Müller's *Global Reach* (1974), all argued that the corporate take-over of economies and psychologies is the pressing problem for modern societies. So there are clear continuities, but what Seattle seemed to crystallize, and what the WTO et al. symbolized, was the coming together of such a variety of interest groups on such a large scale, and the evaluation of the corporation – not the individual organization or state – as the binding issue.

I don't propose to describe or assess the validity of all the claims made by all these protesters. My aim in this chapter is rather broader than that, but clearly many elements of this rainbow coalition were actually sponsoring rather contradictory issues (Starr 2000). It is difficult to see, for example, how US right-wing militias protesting against the federal construction of a new world order could establish a lasting relationship with trade unionists insisting on a global programme of workers rights (Spark 2001). Or leaders of women's movements in Mexico or Brazil will find much in common with landless peasants from Thailand. Or religious groups sponsoring nonviolence and ethical investment with libertarian anarchists who want to burn down Nike Town. However, one of the dichotomies that seems to inform much of this activism is the distinction between the centres of power and the margins. The former, most importantly for this book, are identified as corporations, trade organizations and powerful states, or these institutions personified in the figure of particular highly paid managers, WTO bureaucrats or pro-market politicians. People who deserve a custard pie in their faces. Distilling this a little further, since for many activists the differences between the interests of corporations, trade organizations and states is marginal, what we have is a dichotomy between the organized interests of a global managerial class and the rest. 'They' push roads through virgin countryside and drown villages with their dams, prevent South Africans from having access to anti-HIV drugs, and push babymilk and Coca-Cola consumerism onto duped citizens.

Not all of this protest is anti-capitalist, or environmentally focused, or whatever, but perhaps its single unifying factor is a hostility to the corporation, and the figure of the Machiavellian manager who is organizing the new world order for their own ends. Importantly, though, both corporation and manager are highly generalized categories. They do not only refer to Monsanto, but also to pro-corporate groups like the WTO, and pro-growth politicians who manage economies in the name of the people and then take well-paid non-executive directorships as their reward. In this context, the corporate really stands in for the big organization, for the bureaucrat in the state agency or head office, for a particular form of utilitarian calculus that dignifies denying power to the people in the name of trickle-down economics. 'They' wear expensive suits, occupy the first-class lounges at airports, and eat sumptuous meals at conference centres. Fat cats that get all the cream. 'We' rarely see them, sheltered as they are behind the mirrored glass of their limousines or once every few years when politician A attempts to distinguish themselves from politician B at election time.

Writing the anti-corporate

Over the last few years, several explicitly polemical books have been published that analyse and proselytize the anti-corporate movement in a range of ways.[7] This book is, in some elliptical ways, an addition to that list. All of these books have been written by activists of various different kinds and, like Klein's *No Logo*, all of them avoid the balanced adjudication of competing Theories so beloved of academics, and exemplified in chapters 5 and 6. I will begin with George Monbiot's *Captive State*, subtitled 'the corporate takeover of Britain', since it illustrates some very local themes in a British context. Monbiot has links with academia through various visiting professorships, but made his name as a writer and journalist on a variety of environmental issues. In *Captive State* he employs classic investigative journalism to 'expose' the ways in which corporations are engaged in a quiet *coup d'état*: 'Corporations, the contraptions we invented to serve us, are overthrowing us. They are seizing powers previously invested in government, and using them to distort public life to suit their own ends' (2000: 4). Through a variety of detailed case studies, Monbiot shows how corporate interests have swung huge government and EU grants to sponsor projects that will make them money, whether this involves building toll bridges that were not wanted, or new hospitals that were not needed. He documents the way that local council planning departments are dragooned into providing legitimacy for the building of supermarkets that destroy small traders, or expensive housing developments which are out of the reach of ordinary citizens. Further, he demonstrates how the big

169

bioscience and agribusiness corporations are using patenting and the intellectual property rights provisions of the WTO to exercise a huge degree of control over nature, both human and non-human. And the list goes on. Whether it is university research, the curriculum in schools, or the 'deregulation' of particular markets, Monbiot shows how an interlocking chain of consultants, directorships, public relations organizations and compliant politicians are consolidating their control over matters that should be subject to informed democratic debate.

Though Monbiot's book is mostly concerned with fairly local matters, planning permissions in Southampton or Frankenstein foods in the local supermarket, for example, it does exemplify the remarkable oscillation between small and big scale that can be found in much of the anti-corporate literature. Monbiot's theme of the corporate colonization of politics runs between the financing of hospitals in Coventry and secret negotiations about the Trans-Atlantic Economic Partnership in Westminster. In a similar way, Naomi Klein pulls together Wal-Mart's destruction of local shopping and the branding of everything with an argument about the colonization of the cultural sphere.

> What does copyright and trademark law have to do with personal fan culture? Or corporate consolidation with free speech? But today, a clear pattern is emerging: as more and more companies seek to be the one overarching brand under which we consume, make art, even build our homes, the entire concept of public space is being redefined. And within these real and virtual branded edifices, options for unbranded alternatives, for open criticism and uncensored art – for real choice – are facing new and ominous restrictions. (Klein 2000: 131)

If Monbiot's key image is the back-door deal done in Westminster, then Klein's is the shopping mall in Everywhere, USA. Not only because it contains the most intense concentration of branding, but because it now functions as a managed public sphere. The replacement of the town square (the potential site of local democratic citizenship) with the policed spaces of the mega-mall (the home of stupefied shoppers) indexes the extent to which dissent has been incorporated.

Yet, for Klein, the branded dreams of free-agent nation being sold by the corporates are increasingly riven with contradictions. Temporary, contract and part-time work are becoming the norm, and job insecurity a pervasive threat for large numbers of people in what is, supposedly, the most successful economy in the world. Big organizations are routinely down-sizing, delayering and exporting jobs to countries with cheaper and less regulated labour markets.[8] In domestic terms this is what Frank nicely labels 'the old hire-back-the-downsized-as-temps routine' (2000: 9) which results in increasing inequality and the phenomenon of the working poor with multiple jobs. At the same time, CEO pay and bonuses (or, euphemistically, 'compensation'), together with that of the branded celebrities they sponsor, is moving to stratospheric levels. In 1998, Disney CEO Michael Eisner received $576 million – roughly the GDP of the Seychelles (Hertz 2001: 36). 'Florida employees at Walt Disney World earn $5.95 per hour and after three years can earn $13,541 per year. Contractors in Haiti producing Disney-branded clothes are paid 28 cents per hour' (Beder 2000: 75). It is almost as if the promise of happiness through unending consumption is being broken, and the idea of organizational citizenship, on an individual or corporate level, no longer makes any sense: 'When corporations are perceived as functioning vehicles of wealth distribution – effectively trickling down jobs and tax revenue – they at least provide the bedrock for the often Faustian bargains by which citizens offer loyalty to corporate priorities in exchange for a reliable paycheck' (Klein 2000: 266). Now, however, the contradictory demands of environmentalists and trade unions, human rights watchdogs and those sponsoring third world growth, are increasingly being stitched together through a hostility to a broken bargain with the corporate demon.

The state is almost an irrelevant actor for Klein. Unlike Monbiot, she spends little space considering the ways in which states can, do or should provide a buffer against corporate libertarianism. This, perhaps, reflects her North American background, but it also indexes something rather important about the impotence of state government in the face of managerial power. She simply assumes that politicians are irrelevant, and that the space between the individual and the corporation must be filled by alternative conceptions of community activity – adbusting, culture-jamming, reclaiming the streets and so on – and not state citizenship. The same might be said about the other institution which the middle classes have used as their town square – the university. Since academic institutions are becoming corporate too, or at least increasingly engaged in another Faustian pact with the corporations who sponsor their professorships and clothe their sports teams, then they cannot be relied upon to provide a focus for resistance either.[9] As she says, 'citizens must go after corporations not because we don't like their products, but because

171

corporations have become the ruling political bodies of our era' (2000: 340).

David Korten's *When Corporations Rule the World* (1995) echoes many of Klein's observations, but sets them within a frame set more by global development than culture-busting. Korten's writing particularly emphasizes the idea of scale, of smallness being rather more beautiful in terms of trade, government and community. Of particular importance biographically is the fact that he began his career with an MBA and a Ph.D. in organization theory from Stanford Business School and set off some thirty years ago to apply the principles of modern management to the problem of third world poverty. However, the more he began to understand, the less he believed. Instead, he found that 'most development interventions transfer control of local resources to ever larger and more centralized institutions that are unaccountable to local people and unresponsive to their needs' (1995: 5). Hence the Bretton Woods institutions and others might legitimate their activities with high-sounding words, but in practice they have actually got poorer countries addicted to debt to pay for imports from first world countries. This is a dependency relationship which ensures that, as Starr (2000: 22) puts it, the ex-colonies are kept 'hanging around the trading post'. About thirty of the WTO's members can't even afford to base a representative at its Geneva HQ (Hertz 2001: 84). To add insult to injury, the colonizers then go on to insist on the 'harmonization' of international standards. Hence matters such as recycling, conservation, food additives, safety requirements, labour standards, protection of small local producers, sales tax for social welfare and so on can all potentially be treated as infringements to free trade and subject to challenge and adjudication by WTO panels. Korten describes this as 'corporate colonialism' (1995: 181) – a process by which the internal governance structures of states (particularly, but not exclusively, in the third world) are subject to control from the corporate imperial centre.

With a wide-ranging argument that begins with the recognition of ecological limits and ends with a ringing declaration of the spiritual values of community, Korten suggests that widening national and international inequality, social problems, a loss of faith in government, local wars, famines and environmental degradation are all related to the extent to which corporate libertarianism is now running the planet. For Korten, it has not always been so, but since the Reagan reforms of the early 1980s, the collapse of centralized communism and the increasing power ceded to the World Bank, IMF and WTO, it now seems that the interests of big government and big business are inseparable. Neither are capable of protecting small-scale human values, and instead they market greed and acquisition as both universal descriptions of human nature and solutions for all human problems. In other words, what we are currently witnessing is the distortion of human priorities for the sole benefit of 'a small elite whose money enables them to live in a world of illusion' (1995: 12). These people he calls the 'Stratos' dwellers,[10] and they could just as well be international development advisors or compliant politicians as corporate employees visiting their subcontractors in Thailand.

Korten's hostility to big-ness is not statist, Marxist, or anti-business – he sponsors the market and private property – but he insists that such matters are best dealt with locally. Rather deliciously using Adam Smith as a weapon against corporate libertarianism, he notes that Smith had argued that monopolistic power and the separation of ownership from control distorts market-places. In fact, the proponents of contemporary 'free' trade are not individual butchers and bakers, but the representatives of gigantic managed economies (states and corporations) that wish to disseminate consumerism and wage dependency. Further, this is an economy that has little or no relation to actual production and consumption because making money and marketing takes precedence over the boring making of things. In practice the flows of global finance are determined by currency speculation, traded derivatives and cannibalizing existing firms in order to maximize shareholder value.[11] For example, George Soros made $1 billion on Wednesday 16 September 1992 by betting against sterling's ability to stay in the European Exchange Rate Mechanism (Hertz 2001: 156). The point of these hugely profitable activities is ostensibly to cut out inefficiencies, but in practice they ensure that socially responsible organizations are weeded out and that measures of profitability become increasingly short-term. On their terms, these are 'inefficient' markets – cartels and financial institutions hence use their power to externalize social and environmental costs just as they privatize their benefits. It is more 'efficient' to sack well-paid workers in the first world, and move the jobs to contractors in third world countries that are lent money by the World Bank to offer grants and tax breaks. This is a 'race to the bottom': 'With each passing day it becomes more difficult to obtain contracts from one of the mega-retailers without hiring child labor, cheating workers on overtime pay, imposing merciless quotas, and operating unsafe facilities. With hundreds of millions of people desperate for any kind of job the global economy may offer, there will always be willing competitors' (1995: 229).

And here we re-enter some familiar territory – the demand from business gurus; free-market economists; right-wing think tanks such as the Council on Foreign Relations, the Bilderberg group and the Trilateral Commission; industry-sponsored 'research' and 'public interest' lobby groups; and the inhabitants of the B-School and the WTO – that managers be given the right to manage. What is good for the corporation is good for all of us, and so the new world order organizes itself globally with the same web of deals and connections that Monbiot describes in terms of planning permissions for new supermarkets in provincial English towns.

> Behind its carefully crafted public-relations image and the many fine and ethical people it may employ, the body of a corporation is its corporate charter, a legal document, and money is its blood. It is at its core an alien entity with one goal; to reproduce money to nourish and replicate itself. Individuals are dispensable. It owes only one true allegiance: to the financial markets, which are more totally creatures of money than even the corporation itself. (Korten 1995: 67)

Democratic pluralism, state regulation, community responsibility are hence all on the retreat when confronted by the attack of these alien entities and those that moralize on their behalf. Approvingly quoting William Dugger, Korten suggests that the corporate motive of these Frankenstein's monsters is to rid itself of people altogether and become a pure network of machines motivated by the desire for money (1995: 241). Even managers are increasingly becoming its victims, as they too are down-sized or their functions contracted out in the name of profitability. Yet, to accept the domination of corporations, and their 'absurd distortion of human institutions and purpose' is 'an act of collective suicidal insanity' (1995: 247).

Amory Starr's *Naming the Enemy* borrows much of its descriptive analysis from Korten, but focuses on a slightly different question. 'It makes sense that there *should* be an anti-corporate movement, but is there one?' (2000: ix, italics in original.) In other words, is there one movement or many, and what unifies and divides various forms of anti-corporate activism? She attempts to typologize fifteen different forms of protest in three different modes. The first, the 'contestation and reform' mode, contests 'the legitimacy of neoliberal reformulations of the role of the state and the necessity of subordinating social priorities to "international competitiveness"' (2000: 45). 'Globalization from below', the second mode, rests on the assumption that 'powerful global alliances can be formed to make corporations and

A Typology of Protest

Contestation and reform	
• Fighting structural adjustment	Jubilee 2000
• Peace and human rights	Amnesty International
• Land reform	Third world peasants, squatters
• Anti-corporate	Boycotts of Nike, Monsanto, cars
• Cyber-libertarian	Hackers, open-source software
Globalization from below	
• Environmental	Greenpeace
• Labour	Trade unions
• Socialism	Political parties, co-operatives
• Anti-FTA	Seattle-type protests
• Zapatismo	Zapatista
Delinking/relocalization	
• Anarchy	Local alternative organization
• Sustainable development	Schumacher, slow food
• Small business	Local trading, community credit
• Sovereignty	Anti-colonial independence movements
• Religious nationalism	Islamic fundamentalism, US militias

(Adapted from Starr 2000)

governments accountable to people instead of elites' (2000: 83). In the third mode, 'corporations appear as threats to locality whose powers can be evaded only by "delinking" the local economy from the corporate-controlled national and international economies' (2000: 111). Or, to put it simply, mode one is against specific aspects of corporate libertarianism, mode two is against most of them and mode three is seeking alternatives.

Clearly Starr has to do some squeezing to get everything to fit into her boxes, and (as she admits) her research is mostly based on documents, not interviews or observations of what people actually do. Nonetheless, her typology nicely demonstrates the sheer range of groups that might have a stake in opposing corporate managerialism and, as I suggested above, some of the issues upon which they might agree and disagree – growth, patriarchy, religion, state intervention and so on. In general terms, Starr is more positive about the second and third modes, arguing that the first opposes only specific behaviours and, all too often can 'offer corporations methods of relegitimizing themselves' by becoming responsible, entering into codes of conduct and standard setting (2000: 79). Perhaps like the business ethicists I covered in chapter 5 (whom she does not mention), these groups tend also to assume that the amelioration of corporate misconduct will not impact on the living standards and lifestyle priorities of the first world in any dramatic fashion. However, for Starr, this is also true of labour movements in the second mode that seek improvements to wages and conditions but do not contest corporate power. And, to a certain extent, she seems to suggest it is also true for socialists who have a foundational faith in the redistributive powers of another big organization, the state. Even when we get to mode three protest, Starr discusses the political problems of religious nationalism, for example the libertarian US militia movements. They too are against centralization and corporate domination of the new world order, but include strongly racist and nationalist beliefs as part of their legitimation of alternatives.[12]

For Starr, the broad answer is alternative AgriCulture, and not the seductions of PopCulture. She does not share Klein's enthusiasm for culture-busting, preferring to stress the possibilities of small-scale ecologies. That she fails to reflect on her own position within her typology is a shame, but hardly surprising since her particular brand of anti-corporatism echoes the problems of inclusive and exclusive formulations of community that I discussed in chapter 4. Her folksy alternatives, like Korten's more spiritualized ones, are serious enough, but compost toilets and the wisdom of the elders do not sound quite as exciting as spray-painting billboards and throwing bricks at McDonald's. I will discuss this more in the final chapter, but it is fair to say that it is much easier to be splendidly 'against' something than dully 'for' something else.

Complicities and conspiracies

One of the complaints often found in the work, both practical and intellectual, covered in this chapter is the pervasive secrecy that hangs around the corporate-managerial complex. This is what George Monbiot has called the 'octopus' response to threat, retreating behind clouds of ink. Ink that makes claims about self-regulation, dialogue with sensible alternatives, aligns corporate freedom with individual liberties and third world development, and sets up industry sponsored 'public interest' organizations to wash away the stains of bad publicity. As the previous chapter illustrated, 'conspiracism' is now an ubiquitous and common-sensical way of understanding that there

176

is something rotten going on (Parish and Parker 2001). The sheer lack of public knowledge about corporate activities, and multilateral trade deals, is in itself a stimulus for many anti-corporate protesters. Demanding accounts from politicians, CEOs, WTO bureaucrats and so on then becomes an inherently democratic activity in itself. As Starr puts it, everybody knows there is a conspiracy, and understands the self-interest of the conspiracists, but what galls is the level of deceit about such matters (2000: 8). Hence the shadowy activities of the Council on Foreign Relations, the Bilderburgers, US Business Roundtable, Trilateral Commission, World Economic Forum, Conférence de Montréal, Transatlantic Business Dialogue and so on are themselves treated as an inky threat. Rather excitingly, 'they' are organizing against 'us'.

Indeed, as if to demonstrate the power and range of books like the ones I have been writing about above (as well as the noisy protests, NGOs, shareholder activists, internet sites and so on), the empire continues to fight back. Hegemony, after all, is a battle of ideas. Neil Jacoby's *Corporate Power and Social Responsibility* (1973) was one of the first books to respond to the earlier range of critiques of corporate power that ended the post-war consensus. He goes through the charges levelled by 'reformists', 'leftists' and 'utopians' and concludes that all is basically well, and that only minor tinkering is needed. The same can be said for much of the business ethics literature which seeks to 'manage' corporate social responsibility in order to deal with the challenges of various protesters (see, for example, Cannon 1994). More recently, right-wing think tanks like the Brookings Institution in the US and the Institute of Economic Affairs in the UK have begun to publish a series of books intended to defend free trade against elitist insular protectionism. *Efficiency, Equity and Legitimacy*, for example, a book about the multilateral trading system, is edited by the IBM Professor of Business and Government at Harvard, the head of the Trade Policy Linkages Division of the OECD Trade Directorate in Paris, the deputy division chief of the African Department of the IMF, and the administrator of the Directorate-General for Trade of the European Commission (Porter et al. 2001). From Brookings too we have the clearly titled *Towards Free Trade in the Americas*, edited by trade advisors from the Organization of American States (Salazar-Xirinachs and Robert 2001). These are all *serious* people. People who have an investment, probably literally, in the globalization of world trade. On the other side of the Atlantic, the Institute for Economic Affairs has recently published a book arguing that Britain's trade interests would be advanced through participation in a global free-trade association. The book is written by a senior policy analyst at the Heritage Foundation, based in Washington, DC (Hulsman 2001). In another IAE publication, David Henderson (ex World Bank and OECD) argues that the liberal project is under threat from 'new millennium collectivism', an anti-liberal amalgam of 'pre-economic' ideas (2001). These oppositional groups (NGOs, academics, unions and so on) misunderstand the liberatory power of markets and sponsor a mistaken moralism of intervention to defend those perceived as 'victims of injustice'. In fact, Henderson argues, the poor are victims of regulation, of attempts to take away their freedoms. The IEA also publishes many other books intended to defend freedoms (smoking, taking drugs, wearing fur and so on) and question over-government and regulation.

The point of drawing attention to work like this is not to demonize it, or even to explain the counter-arguments in any detail,[13] but simply to show that the criticisms are beginning to bite. If senior figures feel the need to justify their stance with regard to the supposed benefits of corporate libertarianism, then perhaps we are seeing the beginnings of a serious debate. But this in itself brings problems. At the 2001 meeting in Davos, the World Wildlife Fund, Union Network International and the Third World Network were invited in to speak. High-profile philanthropy became fashionable and head-nodding about responsibility was all the rage. Head-nodding, that is, if the criticism was constructive. And so the constructive are separated from the destructive, the reformists from the revolutionaries, and the constructive reformists become easier to co-opt. This is a strategy that has worked nicely with other putatively critical groups. As the chapter on business ethics showed, being 'critical' of business can end up being remarkably supportive at times. Even 'critical management' academics, who paradoxically spend most of their working lives in Big Bureaucracies teaching managers how to manage, are easily distracted with some big grants, or manage to distract themselves with some big epistemological problems.[14] It is easy enough to claim that you are an ethical corporation because you are in dialogue with an NGO, or fund a chair in the social responsibility of business with money from big business.

But these are more personal issues as well. As I began by suggesting about Klein's *No Logo*, anti-corporatism is a form of branding itself. As Knobil says, with the caustic accuracy of the contemporary practitioner of marketing segmentation, 'If you choose Klein – Naomi, not Calvin – you want the world to know: "I am not someone who needs to depend on badges to convey who I am. I am an individual in my own right who despises brands and cares for society"' (2000). So, for Knobil, 'label-conscious liberals' ignore the huge corporate donations that help worthy causes, the generation of employment across the globe, and the importance of the reputational issues that come from having your brand exposed to the market-place. And these claims about branding can quickly turn personal preferences into Knobil's political programme. 'Research for Superbrands shows consumers feel Virgin and American Express are more trustworthy than the Conservative Party, Labour Party or royal family. Business leaders trust the likes of Visa, Cap Gemini, Sun Microsystems, Shell, Goldman Sachs, London School of Economics, Siemens and Microsoft to govern the country better than the European Parliament.' It seems like it might be time to embrace corporate citizenship as a working alternative to the discredited state variety.

And here we enter some territory where words no longer mean what they seem, where the ultimate form of democracy becomes the market, where freedom means the freedom of corporations, where regulation is an evil and the triumph of turbo-business our manifest historical destiny. Thomas Frank's *One Market Under God* (2000) is a splendid exposure of the ways in which corporate interests, business journalists, management gurus, left- and right-wing think tanks and 'cult stud' academics have effectively produced a new discourse – 'market populism'.

> Market populism decries 'elitism' while transforming CEOs as a class into one of the wealthiest elites of all time. It deplores hierarchy while making the corporation the most powerful institution on earth. It hails the empowerment of the individual and regards those who use that power to challenge markets as robotic stooges. It salutes choice and yet tells us the triumph of markets is inevitable. (2000: xv–xvi)

Market populism is a new way of solving the legitimacy problem for business which is, as I've argued in this book so far, not in itself a new issue. However, contemporary versions of cyber-libertarianism, organizational citizenship and community, the increasingly loud insanity of gurus like Tom Peters and Peter Senge, and politicians' and policy-makers' general faith in the market as the solution to all our problems adds up to an attempt to forge a new, stronger consensus. For Frank, this is a consensus based on the equation 'PRIVATIZATION + DEREGULATION + GLOBALIZATION = TURBO-CAPITALISM = PROSPERITY' (2000: 17). In linguistic terms Bourdieu and Wacquant (2001) call this the 'new planetary vulgate', a form of new liberalism that brings terms like 'new economy' and 'flexibility' together with 'identity' and 'fragmentation' to provide analyses of both 'employability' and 'exclusion'. Other words, such as 'capitalism', 'class' and 'exploitation' seem somehow vulgar, and the domestic political decisions and rhetorics that lead to globalization are presented as inevitabilities that only the conservative will oppose. Indeed, conservative has become a new word for reactionary, since conserving must mean defending the past.

Within this language, electoral democracy is traded for the diversity of the supermarket or the stock exchange where consumer choice is the ultimate form of democratic accountability. And anyone who rails against such choice is an elitist, an expert, a mass culturalist intellectual whose snobbish aim is to restrict and regulate what should be left alone.[15] So the Seattle and post protests were met by a wave of market populist outrage against those people (as the *Wall Street Journal* put it) who were 'standing atop the prone bodies of people who hunger for the fruits of free trade' (in Frank 2000: 69). So does the WTO become a kind of humanitarian relief agency, with its noble aims being sniped at by self-interested elitists or Stalinist interventionists who have learnt nothing from the collapse of the Berlin Wall. It does not matter that, as Chomsky (1996) has argued, the historical record tells us that the US has built its power on economic protectionism, massive state subsidy and covert or overt military intervention in states that threaten its interests. The new market populism doesn't need to be accurate in order to persuade.

What ties these issues together is the need for anti-corporate protesters to be able to name their enemy clearly and loudly. This is a manichean identity politics – 'them' (in their limos) and 'us' (on the streets).[16] But, as Klein's guilty fascination with branding shows only too painfully, there is really no 'pure' outside from which an outsider politics can be conducted. Seabrook (2001: 163) puts it nicely, 'the brand is neither quite marketing nor culture', both are complicit in each other. Market populism involves the marketing of popular taste and the popularization of the market, at one and the same time. Authentic culture can no longer be opposed to inauthentic marketing, since the tools of one are also the tools of the other (Smith 2001). The computers and mobile phones used to organize outside the conference centre. The publishing conglomerates and bookstores that sell the books I have summarized. The media stringers that sell pictures to multinationals all over the world. The branded *Adbusters* iconography on the mail-order T-shirt bought from the internet site, or the top ten sales chart for anti-capitalist books. Or even the Sony Play-station game 'State of Emergency', in which the oppressive American Trade Organisation (ATO) has taken over the world and your mission is to 'smash up everything and everyone in order to destabilize the ATO'. As with the arguments in chapters 3 and 4, where does *real* culture start and corporate culture stop? Is community here and now, and management over there? Making these distinctions becomes harder and harder as corporations adopt chameleon strategies for making themselves indistinguishable from the foliage. So, in WTO speak, 'participatory development' becomes a new code phrase for colonialism (Korten 1995), consumerism becomes a new form of citizenship and the highest expression of personal freedom (Frank 2000), environmental protection becomes a new area for corpora-tions and consultants to make money (Newell 2000: 110), and Anita Roddick shares many of the same enthusiasms as Klein et al., but heads a global retail franchise and writes books about meaningful change and responsibility (2000).

These are paradoxes that, sadly, cannot be resolved by a simple appeal to a 'them' and 'us' world, however much I might like that to be the case. Anti-corporate activism dramatizes the attractions and politics of being against management, but it also exposes the difficulties of what this might actually involve. As I have said, it is much easier to take the moral high-ground of opposition than to put forward practical and reasoned alternatives to the hegemonic ideas of the present age. But there is another way of thinking about all this, and that would be to reimagine what organization might be without corporate managerialism. After all, when anti-corporate groups demand that corporations themselves be torn down, no corporate response is sufficient. This at base, is the issue of scale I referred to above, and one that has echoed through this book (and the last two centuries) from de Gourney's diagnosis of 'bureau-mania' onwards. So, in the final chapter, I want to turn from my meandering about various forms of anti-managerialism to think about what I (and perhaps others) might be 'for', and not endlessly 'against'.

9

FOR ORGANIZATION

'Yet the noble despair of the poets
Is nothing of the sort; it is silly
To refuse the tasks of time
And, overlooking our lives,
Cry – 'Miserable wicked me,
How interesting I am.'
We would rather be ruined than changed,
We would rather die in our dread
Than climb the cross of the moment
And let our illusions die.'
                    W. H. *Auden,* The Age of Anxiety *(1948: 123)*

As Auden recognized, the hardest thing is to put forward alternatives. It is much easier to snipe from the sidelines than to risk having a Faustian supper with the devil. Most of this book has been concerned to pull a variety of forms of 'noble despair' together, and use them to construct a critique of managerialism. Hopefully, they add up to an interesting (if not coherent) story. Yet it is likely to have been a story which has conveniently confirmed the beliefs of anti-business readers, but has also confirmed a pro-business diagnosis that intellectuals like me are both jealous of power and incapable of realistic and useful thought about its exercise. So perhaps I will have changed no opinions and merely reinforced existing ones. You will have read this book through your existing prejudices, just as I said I would write it through mine.

This final chapter will do three things which are intended to open up a more productive debate on these matters. Firstly, I want to

182

clarify exactly who and what is my target in this book. I did a little bit of work on this in the introduction, but need to sharpen up my complaints a lot more in order that I can be clearer about what I am claiming to be against. Secondly, I will run through the various ways in which academics, filmmakers and activists have suggested that managerialism and corporate colonization might be resisted and think about their various strengths and limitations, differences and similarities. Finally, I will consider some of the grander themes which seem to tie this book together, most particularly the need to think about productive alternatives, to reinvigorate our organizational imaginations beyond the narrow confines that are currently accepted as immutable commonsense.

Against what?

Let me take the broadest sense of an answer to this question first, and dismiss it rapidly. It would, I think, be stupid to make a claim that I am 'against organization'. My understanding of human beings, one that is shared by most people who have thought about these things, is that we are organizing animals. That is to say, we make ourselves human through patterning our worlds, by categorizing people and things though language, by structuring our perceptions and our thoughts so that the world makes some kind of sense to us. Whether this is making the stars into constellations, or deciding what is food and what is not, or who is 'us' and who is 'them', we force an order onto the world and 'manage' its complexity in the general sense of 'coping' that I mentioned in chapter 1. If we did not, we would not be recognizable as human beings, in the social sense of that term. This reliance on organizing as a verb leads to us constructing organizations as things. These organizations become a kind of shorthand that embeds all sorts of acts of organizing into a relatively enduring pattern. So families, chess clubs, churches, universities, corporations and states are continually produced and reproduced through endless acts of ordering. Some last longer than others, or have meanings and consequences that echo across different spaces and time, but they all become 'things' that people invest in, to a lesser or greater extent.

In terms of the way that I have outlined it then, organizing makes organizations and vice versa. Since this is an inextricable part of our becoming human, it is not something that can be reasonably contested. However, the noun 'organization' is usually taken to refer to not all outcomes of organizing, which it could, but instead to some very specifically constituted formal organizations. But even this more limited group contains institutions that differ very considerably in their structural and cultural characteristics. If we consider churches, universities, corporations, states, small businesses, hospitals and so on, these have historically diverged considerably in their methods of organizing. There has not been, until fairly recently, an assumption that only one organizing principle is appropriate for all these different contexts. The use of hierarchy, methods of appointment, conceptions of mission, degree of member autonomy, professionalization, democratization of decision-making, degree of bureaucratization and so on have all differed, and these differences were not a matter for any particular concern or comment. I am not making any particular argument about some form of environmental determinism here, or indeed about the routinization of institutional histories or any particular reason why organizations have differed. All I wish to suggest is that there have been, and to a certain extent still are, many alternative ways of thinking about formal organizing and organizations, and this is true even if we discount less formal organizations like families or chess clubs.

So, there are a wide variety of potential models but, at the present time, it seems that the credibility of many aspects of these alternatives is being questioned through the generalized application of managerialism as the one best way. As I argued in the introduction, the dominant conception of organizing nowadays rests on the application of three forms of management as a generalized technology of control. The increasing celebration of the managerial class, the application of managerial language to more and more 'informal' areas of life, and the dissemination of particular forms of expertise by the B-School, are all combining to produce a hegemonic model of organization. This model has a certain air of inevitability to it, and other forms of organizing are hence increasingly articulated as archaic, as dinosaur survivals or quaint protected idiosyncrasies. Central to this diagnosis is some conception of management as being the only group, practice and intellectual discipline that is capable of responding to the stern demands of accelerating market societies. As many of the previous chapters illustrated, the story of globalizing turbo-capitalism, the breakdown of old slow certainties and the constancy of change leads to the conclusion that new experts are required. These experts will be a global managerial class, bred in the B-School and sent out to remodel the world. Like a new cohort of Jesuits, their missionary zeal will spread the message that the market is now king, and management its representative on earth. To be happy, efficient and progressive their mission must be embraced. And this applies to making widgets, organizing healthcare and education, encouraging 'development' in the third world or thinking about time, career or child-care (Grey 1999).

Rhetorically, then, the 'market' provides the legitimacy for the inevitability of managerialism. According to this logic, introducing the market into areas which were previously outside the market is both wise and inevitable since it can help to ensure both efficiency and customer satisfaction. But again, there is a very particular conception of the market at work here. After all, like organizing, markets can be done in many different ways. Despite what many economists have insisted, there is no one immutable market form. Markets are socially constructed sets of rules that provide legitimacy to certain transactions, so to homogenize them all as defined by the same sets of rules is rather like suggesting that all organizing can only be done in one way for it to be recognized as organizing (Callon 1998). Putting it another way, the market for an oatcake shop in Stoke-on-Trent, or a hamburger joint in Colorado, is not governed by the same rules, or even the same kind of rules, as the market for currency speculation in Frankfurt. To be sure, there are minimal similarities in terms of sellers and buyers, but there are also substantial differences – who can buy and who can sell, what can be bought and what can be sold, where these things can be bought and sold, how the parties establish some mechanism of exchange and expectations of information, acceptable levels of monopoly sellers or monopsonistic buyers, the degree of formalization or professionalization, the level of state intervention and/or moral constraints, the commonly expected time horizons, and (perhaps most importantly) definitions of success or failure. To treat all these differences as merely examples of the economists' *ceteris paribus*, everything else being equal, is to decontextualize a social practice and suggest that there is an ahistorical hidden hand that pushes and pulls in the same manner everywhere.

My point here is that words like market refer to common practices that regulate exchange, but that this actually tells us rather little about how specific markets are actually constructed and performed. Yet, for managerialists, the market is treated as if it were a global historical force that is sweeping everyone in the same direction. This abstract market, of perfect information and utility maximizing individuals, is then articulated as both a descriptive certainty and a prescriptive inevitability. Both of these add up to a kind of moral imperative, one that tells of progress away from war and famine and

185

towards the greatest good of the greatest number. For example, Thomas Friedman, in *The Lexus and the Olive Tree* (1999), argues that two countries with McDonald's have never been to war. Leaving aside the remarkably attenuated time horizon in this statement, as well as the fact it (knowingly) ignores civil wars and border conflicts,[1] the moral is presumably intended to be that the modernization represented by the corporate executive's Lexus will (and should) sweep away the community based around the olive tree. Swords will be turned into beefburgers as we realize the latter are more desirable than the former (though the market will probably encourage us to continue selling swords if there is a demand for them, and become a 'black' market if the state dares to intervene). According to this argument, the superiority of market logic applies everywhere and to everything. Universities, hospitals, armies are inefficient now, but they will be more efficient if marketized. As Schumacher put it,

> In the current vocabulary of condemnation there are few words as final and conclusive as the word 'uneconomic'. [. . .] Call a thing immoral or ugly, soul-destroying or a degradation of man, a peril to the peace of the world, or to the well-being of future generations; as long as you have not shown it to be 'uneconomic' you have not really questioned its right to exist, grow and prosper. (1993: 27)

But what is an efficient, or economic, university? One that gives all students a first-class degree, or that arranges a job on graduation, or that employs very few people and buys very few books, or that attempts to produce obedient citizens? Or, applying this logic to the globalization favoured by the WTO, will the University of Keele become more efficient by competing with the University of Colorado? Or workers in Thailand become more efficient because they are competing with workers in Stoke-on-Trent? These are nonsensical questions if they are answered in general terms because human beings do not universally agree on what they want, when they want it and how they are going to get it. Yet, as Frank (2000) graphically documents, the assumptions of market populism are that these questions can *all* be answered with recourse to markets – even if the practice does not correspond to the rhetoric. In practice, big sellers demand tax breaks, state subsidy and the protection of the WTO, at the same time that they insist on deregulation and flexibility for everyone else (Monbiot 2000: 351). Henderson (2001), for example, wants to defend liberal freedoms from the attrition of misguided regulationary zeal but needs to appeal to gigantically powerful 'free trade' associations in order to do so. In other words, even deregulation needs regulation. But this is not merely hypocrisy or confused thinking (though it is also both of these), but further illustration of my argument. What we call 'the market' is a mechanism of exchange constructed by particular interest groups at particular times, so the form of market being invoked by corporate managerialism reflects the interests of the 'ruling class' in this particular arena. The story they tell justifies the centrality of management, their high rewards and status, their 'right' to manage, and warns us of the disastrous consequences should we buck the 'law' of the market. There lies chaos, here is progress, and we can show you the way.

So, to summarize this section, in this book I am *not* trying to set this book up against organizing or organizations, or against the wide variety of ways in which human beings have transacted goods and services with each other. I *am* trying to argue that the very peculiar and particular notion of management that has been constructed over the past century is deeply implicated in a wide variety of political and ethical problems, and that it limits our capacity to imagine alternative forms of organizing. It seems to me that many of the arguments and ideas that I have covered in this book share, at base, a similar concern despite their surface diversity. The long-standing hostility to bureaucratic rationalization; more recent attempts to introduce notions of citizenship or community into the workplace; the idea that we need more social responsibility in business, or academic work which is critical of management; combined with the shift in both the climate of representation and the politics of protest, all add up to a widespread questioning of managerialism. This is not to say that I can add all these bits and pieces together and get a new social movement, one that homogenizes mannered seminar debates about whether stakeholder theory is a new variant of utilitarianism with angry class-war anarchists who want to burn the corporate Lexus outside the conference centre. However, I do think that these examples show that the hegemony of managerialism is being increasingly questioned on a wide variety of fronts. Hegemonic ideas require their legitimacy to be continually reinforced precisely because they are in permanent danger of being undone.

> The ultimate strength of capitalist global hegemony is that it continually works, and works very hard, to *persuade* people that the system is natural, fair and fundamentally better than any realistic alternative. [. . .] When the capitalist state has to use force, the army or the police, then this is clearly a failure of hegemony, though where people are

187

persuaded that the use of force is legitimate, this may actually increase hegemony. (Sklair 1995: 98–9, emphasis in original)

I do not believe that managerialism is a historically inevitable development, but that it has particular conditions of possibility and that these conditions can be changed. So, where might we look for challenges to this hegemony?

Sites of resistance

If the first half of the book considered the history of anti-bureaucratic thought then, in some sense, the second half of the book has translated this into contemporary anti-managerialism. Business ethics, CMS, cultural representations and anti-corporate protest all constitute ways of rethinking and challenging the assumptions of managerialism. However, at various different points, they also make claims about the problems and possibilities of certain key sites of reform or resistance. To put it very simplistically, business ethics seems to have a faith in the redemption of the manager, CMS in the role of academics, many contemporary books and films focus on the individual's capacity to resist the seductions of the group, whilst anti-corporate protest often focuses on NGOs or the state. This list is far too neat, because the four chapters do not map neatly on to my four sites, but it will do as a way to organize some thoughts. I'll move through each of the suggestions in that order.

Managers?

First, then, managers themselves, as a class who might be turned towards more socially responsible practices through some kind of ethical re-education, or even CMS evangelism. This, I think, is the most unlikely place to see much organized activity, apart from the further co-optation of common ideas about community, citizenship, social responsibility and the strategic use of business ethics. In 1921 Thorstein Veblen, a heterodox economist if ever there was one, suggested that 'the technicians, the engineers, and industrial experts are a harmless and docile sort, well fed on the whole, and somewhat placidly content with the full dinner-pail which the lieutenants of the Vested Interests habitually allow them' (in Rhodes 1999: 72). Nowadays, these people, whether docile functionaries, lieutenants, or the Vested Interests themselves, form the managerial class. For Veblen, managerial radicalism was unlikely, a view echoed by Whyte some forty years later in his analysis of the groupthink and conformity demonstrated by organization men (1961). Though these might be rather exaggerated condemnations, to all intents and purposes they can serve as a diagnosis for the present age too. Managers have too much invested in managerialism to make them likely to rebel en masse. They have identities, qualifications, salaries and status through being what they are, a full dinner-pail, so why should we assume that they will wish to disinvest and join movements for reform? This is not to say that particular individuals might not suffer from twinges of conscience, or generalized anxiety, or even find the whole job so painful that they decide to exit and do something else instead. But this is not the point. This book is not intended to be a criticism of the standards of morality of individual managers, and hence to portray these ordinary people as somehow demonic or lacking in sympathy.[2] The problem is a more general one, one that is created by the dominance of a particular form of acting and thinking. As Monbiot says, 'I find I cannot blame them: enterprising companies will always seek to maximize their opportunities'. (2000: 11). So this is not merely a matter of apportioning blame, but seeking explanations for why we have, to a large extent collectively, allowed the world to be organized in this way rather than another.

Yet, if mass radicalism is not on the cards, even more modest assumptions about change have not borne much fruit. As I noted in chapter 5, various writers in the 1930s seemed to be suggesting that the separation of ownership from control might mean that managers could do without Veblen's 'Vested Interests and their absentee owners' and act in more socially responsible ways. Yet the intervening period has not borne out this hope in any sustained fashion. Indeed, it could be argued that (despite the rise and rise of shareholder capitalism) we are now in a position which looks more and more like the robber baronial feudalism of the early twentieth century. Corporate power is on the increase, politicians and states seem to be embracing the accommodations of market populism, and the managerial orthodoxy is being disseminated in ever more sophisticated and institutionalized ways. Nonetheless, the structural contradictions and natural limits of global capitalism may still force managers to discipline each other. Newell and Paterson provide an interesting example of this when they suggest that some corporations might be forced to bring pressure to bear on others. The example that they use is insurance companies, worried about the huge climate disasters which may be the consequence of global warming, encouraging fossil fuel exploiters and the transport industry to investigate alternative sources of energy (1998). This seems a credible scenario, and it follows much of the literature on social responsibility and business ethics in turning corporate self-interest into action with wider benefits. However, managerialism as such is then assumed to continue unchecked. It might be forced to change its strategies in order to deal with the social unrest that follows from the huge inequalities it has created, or to sell itself to an increasingly cynical population, but the structural logic of corporate utilitarianism continues. So perhaps we need to look outside management itself for sources of resistance.

Academics?

The most obvious constituency to turn to next might be academics themselves, a group who, for CMS and (to a lesser extent) business ethics and anti-corporate protest, can act as muck-rakers and autonomous critics. As I noted in chapter 6, the idea of the free-floating intellectual who is capable of casting a detached eye over the present, and of universities as hotbeds of protest, has been a common enough myth, particularly since the 1960s. There is certainly some truth in this idea. Many, though not all, of the ideas I have been discussing in this book have been generated by academics. Even when they are not, as in some of the anti-corporate protest and most of the films and books, academics can and do play a role in shaping the conception and interpretation of contemporary ideas. For example, even if the makers of contemporary cyborg films and romantic work-based comedies are not self-consciously attempting to articulate a suspicion of managerialism, work like mine can hopefully shape the ways in which these films are seen, and hence perhaps the impact that they have. In some sense then, academics and universities are important agencies for the reproduction of ideas. Since managerial hegemony is a structure of ideas, then perhaps academics can play a role in changing them.

However, as I argued in chapter 6, suggesting that academics might be able to engage in critical politics is not the same as saying that they will. I explored much of my scepticism about tenured radicals in that chapter, but want to add a few things here. The most important point to make is that academics are just academics. That is to say, they are usually employees of large organizations who are paid a salary to engage in administration, the dissemination of canonical knowledge, and the production of highly specialist training for very specific audiences. There is nothing particularly heroic or romantic

190

about any of these activities and they can be found in many quasi-managerial jobs too. Further, in most of the first world, the institutions that they work in are becoming increasingly managerial and marketized, since they are subject to exactly the same demands for efficiency and relevance to the 'demands' of labour 'markets'. As with most other organizations, universities are becoming increasingly corporate – employing part-time and contract labour, tightening audit controls, reducing fixed costs wherever possible, and competing with each other for market share (whether students or grants). As Whyte put it forty years ago, 'many of the same academics who privately throw up their hands at the horror of materialistic culture act like so many self-abasing hucksters when it comes to pleasing grant givers' (1961: 102). To add to the difficulties for independent critique, most of the academics who are directly concerned with teaching and writing about management, corporations and markets are employed in B-Schools that earn their living by selling managerialism. For a B-School academic to thrive and have a career, they must sell their products, whether MBAs or research expertise, as really useful knowledge. To do otherwise would be like a professor of history to claim that history is bunk, or a physicist to deny the utility of the scientific method.

Taken together, this description adds up to a triple whammy, one which makes it much more likely that academics will conform rather than dissent when they are faced with claims about the superiority of managerialism, or the progressive nature of market populism. Of course, as I suggested about managers above, this is not an immutable law. Some academics will respond in other ways, but even then, they are just as likely to write an analysis of subjectivity or surplus value for a journal read mostly by their peers. Newell and Paterson's paper on climate change and politics which I referred to in the previous section, for example, claims to be a demonstration of the continued relevance of a Marxist international political economy (1998). It does this very well, but it is surely the case that framing the question in this way is unlikely to guarantee that their article is read much outside a very limited circle. P. J. O'Rourke, in his polemical defence of free markets, interviewed traders at the New York Stock Exchange, one of the hubs of global capitalism.

I asked David what kind of economic theories people who trade stocks believe in. Do they belong to the 'classical school', which says that the forces of supply and demand are uncontravenable and self-correcting? Are they Keynesians, who think that government programs can create

191

prosperity and full employment? Are they monetarists, who postulate
that economic cycles are tied to Federal Reserve policy?
  'I don't think they give two shits,' said David. (1998: 20)

In a good academic article, the language is too intimidating, the argument too dense, the scholarship too obtrusive to encourage most
people to give two shits. But that is exactly the kind of anal performance that gets published in what academics deem to be important
places. The remarkable hostility that gets thrown at academics who
write in more populist ways (Ritzer for example) or non-academics
who refuse the language of Theory (Klein for example) indicates
that having the correct manners is crucial to acceptability. Like an
Oxbridge high table, those who accidentally pass the port in the
wrong direction suffer being patronized or ostracized.[3]
  Almost all of the anti-corporate writers I covered in the previous
chapter do not have much faith in academics. Many of them document the corporate colonization of the university with considerable
anger but, more broadly, they seem to be very impatient with academics' cobwebbed quietism, or of the High Theory posturing that
masquerades as radicalism. Naomi Klein devotes some of her careful
bile to a condemnation of the US political correctness wars that led
to more concern about postmodern identity politics than 'issues
that were more about ownership than representation' (2000: 124).
In worrying so intently about the hall of mirrors that passes for truth,
and fragmenting the reflections into a thoroughly democratic kalei-
doscope that modestly claimed to do violence to no one, many academics became ostriches. Starr is similarly hostile to what she calls
'poststructural mudwrestling' (2000: 1), but amplifies the complaint
into a more damaging one too. In claiming that watching TV can be
rearticulated as resistance (2000: 37) she echoes Thomas Frank's condemnation of the way that the 'cult studs' have managed to celebrate
diversity and resistance without any serious analysis of the corporate
takeover (Frank 2000: 291). For Frank, the celebrations of mundane
agency found in cultural studies, such as demanding a burger without
pickles at McDonald's, are centrally complicit in building market
populism. As I showed in chapter 2, in suggesting that criticism of
consumer culture is elitist, the cult studs shift their focus from
production to consumption. Then consumption becomes celebrated
as the multi-faceted democracy of the market-place, whilst the systematic connections between marketing, managerialism and global
inequality are effectively unchallenged. The two most expansionist

disciplines of the academy over the last twenty years, cult studs and the B-School, then seem to be heading in very similar directions.

So much for academics, then. Some of them might do interesting and worthwhile things, but (because of the weight of the triple whammy) the prospects for revolt en masse are again not good. They have a full dinner-pail too, and are generally a docile bunch who did rather well at school, or at least wanted to. As Kierkegaard said of his age in the 1840s, so would I suggest about academics now. That their 'ability, virtuosity and good sense consists in trying to reach a judgement and a decision without ever going so far as action.' (1962 [1846–7]: 34). Yet managers and academics are not merely occupational groups, but individuals too. Perhaps radicalism will be better identified there, and not in the abstract constraints of particular jobs.

The individual?

In rather different ways, some notion of individual resistance and responsibility is deployed in all forms of anti-managerial critique. Weber apart, perhaps the classic example is Whyte's defence of individualism in the face of the organizational ethic, an ethic that subsumes individuality beneath an increasingly unthinking conformist consensus: 'We do need to know how to cooperate with The Organisation but, more than ever, so do we need to know how to resist it' (1961: 17). Whyte urges individuals to resist total involvement in any organization, to keep some part of themselves intact and separated from the seductions of Big Brother. It seems to me that this kind of account is exemplified and performed repeatedly in the films I covered in chapter 7. The narrative of a good person struggling against bad circumstances, or a bad person who becomes good after some kind of revelation, runs through many of these stories of people and organizations. Yet the notion of the good that they embody, or discover, is rarely some form of social change. More often, in a *Wizard of Oz* journey down the yellow brick road to enlightenment, they discover their own courage, love, intelligence, honesty and so on. Hence families, relationships, children, communities and so on are often used to represent a missing completeness – one that is revalued as the plot twists and turns to reward the virtuous and punish the guilty.

Versions of the individual in the other three areas are rather less romantic, and perhaps consequently, both less seductive and more practical. For business ethicists, education in social responsibility is often argued to comprise the cultivation of a moral character, or skills in understanding ethical argumentation. Individual managers with a conscience will hence find it more difficult to be persuaded to act against their new strongly held ethical codes, and consequently will contribute to reforming the unfortunate excesses of unrestrained managerialism. CMS scholars would tend to stress the agency and self-critique of academics themselves in resisting the seductions of the management orthodoxy. They, free-floating intellectuals rather than orthodox academics or unreconstructed managers, have the inde-pendence of mind to offer both powerful ideas and principled resistance – though the latter might also be seduced away from naive false consciousness or defensive subjectivities through CMS educa-tion. Finally, anti-corporate writers tend to use the individual as a rhetorical mode of address in order to locate the ultimate force for change. This individual does not occupy a specific occupational group, but responds to a general soliciting of everyday fairness and shared humanity. Once they understand the oppressive and unequal nature of global capitalism, then they will begin to act in many small ways that help to change things.

The latter position is the one that interests me most here, partly because it refuses to suggest that any particular group – managers, academics, politicians and so on – have a privilege in being the vanguard of social change. Like many of the film stories, this is an account of ordinary people doing extraordinary things, of connect-ing their private troubles to wider public problems: 'We must hold one thought clearly in mind: the global institutions of money have only the power we yield to them. It is our power. We can reclaim it' (Korten 1995: 324); 'There will be no messiah, no conquering hero to deliver us from the corporate leviathan. Most of our representa-tives have been either coopted or crushed. Only one thing can reverse the corporate takeover of Britain. It's you' (Monbiot 2000: 360). For anti-corporate activists and writers there seem to have been two common ways to express this appeal – the consumer and the activist. The first formulation sponsors informed consumption in shaping the economics of demand and hence supply. So, most explicitly, Klein (2000) suggests that shopping can put very powerful pressures on producers. Boycotting specific organizations – Nike, Starbucks, McDonald's – in protest at their policies on exporting jobs, destroy-ing local businesses, advertising to children or whatever, is then artic-ulated as a war of the flea that even corporates cannot resist. As I suggested in the previous chapter, this is an idea with a long pedi-gree. Though the consumer movement has often been no more than an attempt to ensure that products and services are fit for the purpose

194

for which they were sold, since the 1960s part of it has also become a much more politicized attempt to shape patterns of production and consumption. At minimum, then, the protesting consumer makes decisions within the market that reward the socially responsible through buying fair trade coffee, biodegradable washing powder, no sweat clothing, ethical investments and so on.

Yet it is very easy to argue that restricting protest to shopping does little to challenge the hegemony of consumption economics, and also reinforces the myth of the sovereign individual using the market as a form of proto-democracy. Thomas Frank's criticisms of the individualism that he finds in cyber-libertarianism, right-wing market ideologues and cult studs (2000) can easily be turned on to the notion of the heroic consumer who finds their conscience in the aisles of the supermarket. This would be an example of the commodification of politics and ethics, a moment when 'what it is to "be human" is subsumed under the rubric of efficient resource allocation and a means-oriented rationality' (Hancock 1999: 16) and utilitarian managerialism comes to constitute even our protests. In any case, and as Klein is well aware, marketing is now sufficiently sophisticated to sell us protest as a lifestyle choice. Not only can products be greenwashed, or kite-marked with care, but the information that consumers have in making consumption decisions is (to say the least) variable. When Shell claims X and Greenpeace claims Y, who are we to trust? Putting it simply, consumption is too important to be left to the whims of the individual consumer.

However, it is worth noting that none of the anti-corporate writers I surveyed in the previous chapter actually claim that some form of shopping is enough on its own. They all recognize that for consumers to be able to distinguish the fair trade brand from the exploitation brand, they need effective organizations that can disseminate information and exert countervailing pressures. And this is where my second character steps in, the activist. Of course the activist is likely to be a discriminating consumer too, but the difference is that the activist goes out looking for a fight. Further, the activist is usually a collective creature, not an individual consumer. In this sense, NGOs, single-issue pressure groups, alternative magazines and so on are all forms of collective activism. This is not to determine who or what they might name as their enemy, and what tools they will use against them. At a very broad level, Newell (2000) for example, suggests that NGOs might perform state-like regulation functions which use moral rather than legal or formal pressure. Activists might embarrass global corporations into doing things they would otherwise rather not do.

195

Or, they might fight at a very local level, protesting against specific developments such as the opening of a particular retail outlet, closure of a certain factory or building of a new road. They might engage in a campaign against a certain organization – the McLibel trial and www.mcspotlight.org being probably the best-known example – and use that as their Trojan horse. They might focus on a particular sector, clothing for example, and attempt to agitate for particular forms of compliance with new codes of conduct and labelling. Other strategies might be more cultural – adbusting or subvertising through websites, graffiti or alternative magazines. And, most spectacularly, they might use costumes, placards and bricks outside a fortified conference centre.

The point here is that activists are likely to do many things that managers and academics are unlikely to engage in. This is not to say that managers and academics might not also be activists, many of the latter clearly are, but rather that their occupational roles do not necessarily encourage these kinds of activities. The activist, whatever their other commitments, is a character who (by definition) engages in some form of overt politics, usually in concert with like-minded others. Anti-corporate writers are encouraging more people to occupy this role, partly by characterizing the activist as a romantic oppositional hero, as the conscience of the silent majority. So rather than beginning with managerial apologetics disguised as ethics, or the mud-wrestling of insular academics, anti-corporatism frames activism as a coherent and romantic individual and collective response. However, this leaves open the question as to what kind of activism has demonstrable and desirable effects. Whilst throwing bricks at police officers can guarantee media coverage, careful and informed pressure on pension funds might actually produce more important changes. On the other hand, entering into dialogue with the powerful might merely reinforce the legitimacy of power and allow for protest to be colonized. Voluntary codes of conduct produced after negotiations with pressure groups might be impossible to verify, but leave the impression that a particular issue had now been resolved to the satisfaction of all concerned. I don't propose to adjudicate on the relative merits of 'insider' or 'outsider' strategies in this book, save to say that there are some powerful arguments for breaking (what are believed to be) unjust laws in the name of (what is believed to be) a greater good. These are, in some sense, questions of tactics that cannot be measured against a moral or political absolute.

So faith in individual and collective activism does not finally answer the question of means or ends, but it does clarify the possible role of a particular form of collective individualism in resisting the advance of corporate managerialism. But there is a further twist to this tale. As the majority of anti-corporate writers acknowledge, the actor with potentially the most power of all is the state. If the state becomes an ally in these projects, however reluctantly, then the pressure that can be brought to bear on corporations will be magnified considerably. So Hertz, for example, expresses a faith in consumer and activist protest but goes on to argue that states must provide the structures of information, transparency and accountability that can make activism meaningful (2001: 126, 154). This is a crucial point, particularly with regard to my argument that the problem is not 'organization' as such, but a very particular form of pro-market managerialism. States, like the larger NGOs, are gigantic forms of organization which potentially constitute a force for collective resistance to globalizing managerialism. If the key decision-makers in states can, through the efforts of consumers, activists and NGOs, be persuaded that globalizing managerialism is harmful to their interests, then it will be much harder for market populism to win the arguments.

Politicians and states?

In this regard, there is a strange contradiction in much of the anti-corporate literature. On the one hand, the co-optation or corruption of politicians in the face of multi-national managerialism is condemned, and the increasing irrelevance of representational politics to citizens' everyday lives is bemoaned. As Monbiot puts it, 'Big business has become the leviathan of the third millennium, the monster before which our representatives feel obliged to prostrate themselves. The people we have appointed as the guardians of our liberties have delivered us into its maw' (2000: 352). Korten writes similarly of 'democracy for hire' and refers to the meaninglessness of elections within corrupted institutions (1995: 148, 294). Noreena Hertz's more recent 'end of politics' thesis is perhaps the most explicit presentation of these ideas. She writes about the widespread political apathy and disengagement which has resulted in the growth of activist and NGO politics, and characterizes governments as 'caught between a rock and a hard place; unwilling to risk losing the electorate's support by raising taxes, and unable to increase spending for fear of market censure'. (2001: 58) In a way that echoes the diagnosis of US politicians as being in the firm grip of the robber barons of the 1920s, where votes were bought and sold like any other commodity, here we have a characterization of the state as deeply permeated by corporate interests. The political rhetoric of turbo-capitalism, of the threats and opportunities of global competition, effectively means that state policies are aimed at wooing corporations and pacifying institutions like the WTO. This, for many countries or regions within countries, becomes a race to the bottom. Lower wages, lower taxes, lower environmental standards and minimal employment legislation all mean that your country is more likely to attract the interests of giant investors.

Yet there is an ambivalence here, simply because many of the solutions proposed as checks and balances on corporate power rely on the assumption of state intervention. So Klein writes of the importance of legislators 'raising the bar' on what counts as acceptable practice, or Hertz insists on the state's role as 'regulator of last resort' (2001: 190). In some sense, control of corporations requires legislation that can only be imposed through state, or multi-state activity. As I suggested in chapter 3, it is not enough to simply deploy the rhetoric of the rights and responsibilities of citizenship (whether individual or organizational) and assume that behaviour will therefore be changed. At some point the state, through its putative monopoly of legislation within a defined territory, must step in. Hence many, though not all, of the practical solutions proposed by anti-corporate writers are aimed at preventing corporations from doing things they would otherwise very much like to do. Korten, for example, spends some considerable time focusing on calming the damaging restlessness of the financial sector and argues that measures need to be put into place to reward 'patient capital' (1995: 324). He suggests capital gains taxes which are graduated to reflect the amount of time an investment has been held, the requirement that banks must have reserves equivalent to their lending, the rigorous enforcement of anti-trust laws as well as the preferential treatment of community banks and worker buyouts. Or, on a wider scale, a global 'Tobin tax' of 0.25 per cent per speculative transaction could raise $250 billion per year which could be used to pay off third world debt and also slow hot money down a little.[4]

The books I covered in the last chapter often end with these kind of suggestions. All are aimed at soliciting forms of regulation and producing more locally responsible forms of market. However, it is important not to fall into the trap of seeing this as a policy debate between well-meaning constraint and libertarian freedoms. As I have already argued, there is no one pure market form within which the hidden hand does its impartial work. To accept this is to limit im-

198

aginable alternatives to an unacceptable degree, and drift into believing that there are no alternatives to a market populist end of history. All markets are social constructions constituted by different assumptions about people, things and rules of exchange. Even Adam Smith was clear that the state had a vital role to play in ensuring that social benefit was widely spread and monopolies did not dominate the market for their own ends. The WTO wishes to regulate markets too. The question is really what form of regulation, at what level, and in whose interests? Or, to put it another way, how do we wish to socially construct forms of exchange?

The problem is that these questions are not seen clearly, largely because the dominant interests in most states – like most organizations – is currently wedded to the managerialist model of representing market interests. This becomes clearer if we consider one of the most radical suggestions put forward by anti-corporate writers, that corporations should face the threat of dissolution if they violate standards deemed appropriate within a given state. Monbiot notes that the first English corporations were charitable institutions – hospitals, schools, churches – which used incorporation to avoid death duties and so on (2000: 11). Having a licence from the Crown meant that, in certain defined circumstances – which did not include profit-making – they would be treated as legally constituted bodies. When, by the end of the sixteenth century, similar charters were awarded to trade associations, this gradually led to the construction of large profit-making companies of shareholders like the East India Company. As he argues, the invention of this corporate being was a contested one, with a clear recognition that immunities could be granted, but could also be taken away. Korten tells a very similar story for the US context, though happening about a century later (2000: 53). Now, it seems that these debates are in the past, and we have a situation where commercial organizations are treated as having immutable rights, but comparatively few responsibilities. They are an organizational form that has become taken for granted as part of the landscape of capitalism. Indeed, it might be argued that the rhetoric of market managerialism is in practice the voice of these supra-individual entities. Like the Frankenstein's monster stories I covered in chapter 7, it is as if our creations are now becoming our masters. The legal system has been adjusted to meet their needs, the media acts as their voice, universities as their training and research centres, tax-avoidance is legitimized and state subsidies act as a tithe paid to keep the baron happy.

Yet the ultimate sanction that the state still holds, though largely too co-opted to use at present, would be the destruction of a corporation that has failed to meet agreed standards of public benefit. This is not such a remarkable suggestion. If corporations are treated as a historically contingent social construction, then it becomes perfectly legitimate to make their continued existence a matter for debate. If a particular corporation repeatedly pollutes, underpays, harms its employees, breaks the law or whatever, then there is no particularly good reason why it should not be wound up. I am treating this as an organizational matter, a question of how human beings wish to organize themselves. To avoid using this sanction is to effectively say that these arrangements are beyond the popular will, or to argue (probably more honestly) that the interests of shareholders and executives come before the interests of local residents, employees or ordinary citizens. Of course, given that many corporations are licensed outside the countries that they operate in, it may not be possible to take such dramatic action. Instead, it must be possible to refuse to allow a particular organization to operate within a certain state. Unless this sanction is possible, and the WTO are doing their best to ensure that it is not, then this very particular organizational form is guaranteed a form of immunity that ordinary mortals do not share.

But then perhaps this should not surprise us. Both states and corporations are big organizations, and both are increasingly imagined through the hegemonic lens of market managerialism. Unless this hegemony is challenged, and alternative organization forms are re-legitimized, then we are unlikely to see the state biting the hand that feeds it. So, what kind of alternatives?

Alternative organization

So here I finally get to the topic of what will have to become another book. My exploration of the limits of market managerialism has been an attempt to unsettle some very deeply embedded assumptions. To put it simply, I do not believe that there is only one best way for human beings to do organization. In the first part of this book I explored some of the ways in which terms like administration, bureaucracy, culture, citizenship, community, management and so on have been articulated. Often we are told that these words can be arranged as a century-long evolution of efficiency and humanization. This is the B-School story of progress that fuels the frantic search for the latest and most marketable new technology of organizing.

However, a more nuanced and historically informed reading of these ideas demonstrates that there are actually some very strong continuities in terms of the themes that characterize twentieth-century theories of organization. Ideas about individual versus collectivity, control versus consent, formal versus informal and so on seem to oscillate – each periodically providing the rhetorical other to justify its novelty. So what really seems to have been solidified in this mythical story is the centrality of management (as occupational group, process and form of knowledge) combined with the celebration of a very particular form of market. This story is not a neutral one, in other words. It is an account that elevates top-down versions of power, that legitimizes the separation of conception from execution and the growth of huge disparities in status and reward. Further, in the case of the corporation (perhaps the most highly developed form of market managerialism), it is a story that is spreading across the globe and having disastrous ramifications for the human and non-human environment and for the autonomy of states and local communities.

However, as I argued in the second half of the book, there are many sites on which this story is being contested. I chose to focus on four.[5] The first was the rise of business ethics and corporate responsibility as a largely 'internal' conversation concerned to reinforce the moral legitimacy of the business organization. This was then contrasted with critical management studies as an 'external' critique, though one that is currently shaped in some rather constraining ways by its location in university departments of business and management. The third moves us to a wider change in the climate of representation of business that can be found in films, novels, cartoons and so on from the 1970s onwards. If anything, I am taking this to indicate that there has been something of a sea-change in popular representations of management and the corporation. Finally, I spent a chapter on the current explosion of activity and interest in anti-corporate protest which seems to exemplify a more explicit impatience with the supposed inevitability of market-led globalization, and forms of managerial utilitarianism that justify inequality and environmental damage.

I am not particularly interested in determining chains of cause and effect here, more to establish that the hegemony of market managerialism is being challenged in a variety of ways. As I said in chapter 1, I wished to collect these diverse texts and practices together because it seemed to me that they were (however broadly) suggesting that there is no inevitability to the way that the world is organized at the moment. That sense of fate, of there being no reasonable alternative, is probably the most disabling assumption of all in terms of progressive social change. When organizing, as an open-ended and polymorphous collective project, gets reduced to managerialism then it might seem that there is nowhere else to turn. But I do not believe that this is the case. Recognizing the historical and social specificity of managerialism is very important in this respect. For most of human history, and in most cultures, organizing has been done without managers and markets as we now understand those terms. Why then should we assume that all these other organizational forms are now redundant, doomed to irrelevance in the face of B-School expertise?

I need to expand on this a little though. It is all very well to claim that more imagination is needed, but what kinds of organizing am I suggesting as alternatives? The first point to make here is something about scale. From Weber to Klein, one of the common complaints has been that organizations are getting too big to be human. As Fritz Schumacher put it in his *Small is Beautiful*, attacking 'gigantic groups motivated by greed, envy and the lust for power',

> Small scale operations, no matter how numerous, are always less likely to be harmful to the natural environment than large scale ones, simply because their individual force is small in relation to the recuperative forces of nature. [. . .] It is moreover obvious that men organized in small units will take better care of *their* bit of land or natural resources than anonymous companies or megalomaniac governments which pretend to themselves that the whole universe is their legitimate quarry.' (1993: 22–3, emphasis in original)

Schumacher was originally voicing these complaints almost thirty years ago, but today the even greater size of some corporations has exacerbated certain consequences. Firstly, they have a great deal of power and influence which allows them to effectively side-step many formal and informal constraints on their activities. Secondly, their spatial dispersion and levels of hierarchy means that people who make decisions will rarely be confronted by their effects. Further, assumptions about economies of scale, and the accelerating speed of mergers and acquisitions, result in the destruction of smaller businesses and an increasingly homogenized set of choices for consumers. 'Were we to tell the corporations dominating some sectors that, dissatisfied with their services, we shall take our custom elsewhere, they would ask us which planet we had in mind' (Monbiot 2000: 16).

For these reasons, opposing giganticism seems an obvious first step. Creating and protecting a range of small, local organizations

that provide goods and services might then provide meaningful alternatives for both employment and consumption. There is no particular reason why corporations should not be forced to split into smaller
units if they pass a certain size. In theory, this requirement does exist
but (as the recent Microsoft trial showed) it has become very difficult to enforce. Yet if organizations were smaller, local forms of
formal and informal regulation and pressure would be more likely to
have an effect on changing their behaviour. As Hertz (2001: 50) puts
it, bypassing the local causes a 'breakdown in solidarity' and runs the
danger of 'perpetuating selfishness', by which she seems to mean the
unrestrained growth of shareholder value. This is not to claim that
'communities' are always kind and tranquil places – I have said
enough about this in chapter 4 – merely that they can encourage more
face-to-face senses of responsibility. In economic terms, it is more
difficult to externalize your costs if this involves damage to local
resources, labour markets or reputation. For Korten, this intimate
sense of the local is the logical starting point for an 'ecological
revolution' (1995: 261). Monbiot additionally suggests that this
localism is also likely to revitalize a craft tradition of pride in work,
not necessarily for its own sake, though this might be a welcome side-
effect, but rather because this is precisely what is likely to guarantee
the success of a particular enterprise. Rather than relying on globally
slick marketing, or putting all your competitors out of business
through offensive pricing or acquisition, the small local organization
has to do what it claims that it will do. If it doesn't, it will probably
go out of business. According to Eric Schlosser, citing the example of
Conway's Red Top Restaurant in Colorado Springs, even fast food
can be high quality, but only if stays small and local (2001: 257).

Interestingly, Korten makes the argument that there would also
be a corresponding impact on big government (1995: 317). If the
regulatory power of gigantic states is no longer needed to counter the
predatory instincts of big corporations, then government can itself
shrink and become more local. 'Rolling back the state' does not need
to imply rolling out the red carpet for trans-national corporations.
Genuine forms of regional autonomy, of subsidiarity, might then be
a practical alternative. This would, of course, entail some form of
protectionism – a word that is now usually deployed to mean selfish
insularity rather than defending people and practices that a particular community happens to care about. Protection of jobs, local organizations and markets, the built and natural environment and so on,
would have to be relegitimized as credible. The mythic naturalism of
a market-led managerialism that sweeps away inefficiencies in the

name of consumers needs to be exposed as a practice that effectively hollows out localities and benefits the powerful in the corporate centres. 'If corporate globalization is causing the insecurity, then it – not community – is the enemy of diversity.' (Starr 2000: 222) Once again, this is a question of interests. Hegemonic definitions of the efficiencies of scale beg the question of 'efficient for whom'? If efficiency involves transporting a product away from where it was grown or made, packing and labelling it somewhere else, sending it to distribution centres somewhere else again, and then sending it to be sold at a gigantic warehouse that has destroyed many small businesses, we might begin to question the conflation of efficiency with shareholder value.

But scale is not the only issue here, simply because there are also many other dimensions upon which organizing might be reimagined. For example, the Scott Bader Commonwealth, a chemical company, has a constitution that in 1973 (amongst other matters) limited its size, guaranteed 1:7 maximum income differentials, and refused to engage in any war-related production (Schumacher 1993: 234). The company is still going strong eighty years after it was founded (www.scottbader.com). There are plenty of other examples of successful non-standard organizations, the most common of which is probably the co-operative, which can potentially be fairly large. Indeed, since Owen, Fourier and the Rochdale pioneers in the nineteenth century, worker co-operatives have been a small but significant feature of contemporary industrial capitalism.[6] In an ideal co-op, all members would share in the profits and the risks, but no one outside the co-op would be allowed to have shares. In its literal meaning, this means that the organization is a venture that must rely on the co-operation of all members for its success. Starr describes the co-op as socialism in practice (2000: 95), but this seems to me to understate the very practical benefits that might follow from this form of organization in favour of her ideologically driven definition. Co-operatives might have extended managerial hierarchies, elaborated divisions of labour, and engage in forms of production that other constituencies might find objectionable. Or they might be feminist, egalitarian and driven by a concern to avoid forms of exploitation. But this is not the point. What co-operatives can achieve is a collective organization that is ultimately responsible to its members, and not to a faceless group of investors spread across the globe. This might make them locally responsible, but it will certainly make them more democratic than present forms of managerialism.

This brings me on to potentially the most underdeveloped set of ideas. When organizational structure is discussed in B-Schools, it is usually framed as a set of immutable imperatives or contingencies which depend on environmental constraints. So stable markets support machinic structures, whilst newly turbulent and hyper-competitive markets require organic structures, or some version of that argument. But this is to reduce the engineering of organizations to a remarkably narrow set of choices – managed bureaucracy or managerially induced flexibility. It seems to me that these are 'choices' which still largely reflect certain narrow assumptions about control, skill and rationality, and that are by no means inevitable or neces-sary. For a start, in empirical terms it is easy enough to assert that actual processes of organizing can never be captured in a simple dualism, but that they differ from organization to organization depending on local histories and understandings. In these terms authors such as Gouldner (1954) and Pugh and Hickson (1973), for example, have suggested that organizations may, in practice, be more or less bureaucratized. In Gouldner's case he distinguished between 'mock', 'punishment centred' and 'representative' bureaucracies, for Pugh and Hickson the terms 'full', 'workflow' and 'personnel' were favoured. This seems to indicate that there may be other ways of organizing even *within* supposedly bureaucratic structures that have rather different consequences for the members of the organization, and that this may have rather little to do with the prescriptions found on the organization chart. The same argument holds in reverse for organizations that are labelled as 'flexible', 'commitment oriented' or having a 'strong culture' (see Kunda 1992, or Watson 1994a, for example). Just because the mission statement claims that the organi-zation is a community, it doesn't mean that everybody understands this term in the same way.

Now these descriptions of the ways that organizing is actually done (whatever the label attached to it implies) seem to open up the pos-sibility that there might be many different solutions to the same problem. As has been pointed out many times (see chapter 2), to see Weber's writings as some kind of one best way solution is a crudely prescriptive interpretation of his 'ideal type' concept. However, I would like to propose instead that we might read Weber's descrip-tion of bureaucracy as a formulation of general problems that all complex organizations need to negotiate. Thus there need to be some rules, some internal differentiation, some way of making decisions and so on. However, the way that these problems are practically negotiated is contingent on local circumstances and choices. These are problems that any organizer needs to address and not ready-made solutions that the organization must adopt. They are alternatives, but they are alternatives within limits of possibility. This kind of approach can show quite clearly that new-wave managerialism of the citizenship or community varieties does not simply reverse all the tenets of bureaucracy – despite what its proponents like to claim. In practice it is still largely assumed that managers will occupy the top of some form of hierarchy with significant inequalities of status and reward; that this kind of organizing requires special (but generalizable) skills; and that there will be top-down instruction or inspirational leadership from the strategic apex.[7]

One way of illustrating this is to argue that Weber has pointed to the importance of any organization having some kind of co-ordination mechanism. For any complex organization to function it requires that there is some method of ensuring that the constituent parts are functioning in a way that is mutually supportive and meets the explicit goals of the organization. However, the usual resolution of this problem is the formulation of a hierarchy with the co-ordination mechanism at the apex. Yet, as Marglin argued, 'The social function of hierarchical work organization is not technical efficiency, but accumulation.' (in Thompson and McHugh 1990: 49)

There is no necessary structural reason why the co-ordinators should be considered as a separate group, or that they should be given a higher status and reward position within the organization. Indeed, they could simply be seen as another part of the organization, no more or less functional or central than other parts. As Ricardo Blaug (1999) has argued in his lovely paper on the defeat of the well-organized XXth Roman legion by a swift and invisible Germanic tribe in AD 9, 'hierarchism' inspires a kind of blindness to other organizational forms. It is very common to assume that what exists, that what we can see easily, must be the one best way. As a result, other forms of non-hierarchical organization are often ignored, by both organizers and theorists, even when their successes are painfully obvious.[8] The same argument can be used for other parts of the bureaucratic model too. Specialization is undoubtedly a functional result of complexity: if an organization did not have more or less specialized roles it would not be able to perform complex tasks. Yet the permanent association of particular persons to particular roles is not a logical consequence of this and neither is the assumption that some specialisms are more important than others. In addition, the assumptions that particular roles have to be carried out by one person, rather than a group, and that such roles are fixed, and not negotiable, may also be unjustified. With regard to rules it is again taken as read that organizations need rules in order that they be constituted as 'organized'. Yet it does not follow from this that the rules are not periodically renegotiable and contingent on the members' perceptions of the organization's central task. A metaphor might help to illustrate the point. A durable building of any kind must have foundations, walls, roof and so on. Were it not to possess these features it would not be fit for the purpose it was intended. Yet these limitations do not prevent architects elaborating the structure according to their conceptions of aesthetic rationality or indeed the building being used by many different people for many different things. The shell is necessary, just as the formal organization is necessary, but the use to which it is put and the arrangement of the internal partitions can be largely up to the inhabitants.

Consider an organization that did not attend to Weber's description at all. This would simply not be an organization as most people understand the term since it would continually refuse any structure or internal differentiation. It would have no task specialization, no hierarchy (therefore no promotion) and no rules. Members would drift in and out according to their own interests and make no distinction between their identities in the organization and their identities outside it. Though this may be an appealing chaos for some, perhaps not unlike the 'orgunity' I proposed in chapter 4, this kind of thought experiment reveals the importance of Weber's ideal type as a set of structural problems for any organization. The anti-organization seems to me not to be able to handle many of the complex tasks that we require organizations to perform – trains would not run on time if there were no way of ensuring that the driver knew that she should perform a particular set of duties at a particular time. If we desire a world that benefits from organizing and organizations, that has railways and buildings, then the anti-organization is unlikely to be an adequate response.

But this still leaves a great many choices for imagining organizations that are not based on a market managerial model. These would be organizations that would recognize the functional imperatives of complex organizing whilst refusing the definitions of the solution that have now become hegemonic. Thus there might be a form of limited task specialization that acknowledged areas of expertise but would not imply that only experts, professionals or managers have power over particular areas of the organization's activity. Specified roles could be replaced by negotiated allocations of personnel to cope with particular problems or opportunities. There would probably (but not necessarily) still need to be a centre which was responsible for strategic decision making and co-ordination but its power may be continually renegotiated by the members of the organization. Promotion might be replaced by an agreement that a particular individual or group had certain skills that required them to take a certain position within the organization for a determined period. Further, any organization must depend on certain rules, such as the circulation of decision-makers, but its members may choose to treat these as guides and not determinations – there might be no final appeal to the 'rulebook'. Debate about the organization's means could be just as important as debate over the organization's ends, with individual members having a genuine chance to influence the overall direction in ways that they felt were desirable. A continual encouragement of public debate about the nature of the organization would therefore be necessary to ensure that members felt committed to all or part of its activities. In sum, it might be possible to treat organization as a verb rather than a noun, an on-going institution within which assumptions about both means and ends are continually being renegotiated. Following the line of experimentation already found in anarchism, feminism, situationism and utopian communities,[9] this might help prevent the organization becoming too stratified, and hence work against the possibility that any one group might become dominant within the organization. Playing with these structural descriptions seems both theoretically possible and, to my mind, politically attractive. The structural arrangements that pertain within a given organization could then be treated as ways of doing politics, and not merely attempts to re-engineer managerialism as a new brand.

One of the interesting consequences of these experiments in organizational size, ownership and structure is that the clarity of the boundaries between work and leisure, the public and the private, production and consumption and so on, begins to look increasingly vague. If work is conceptualized as wage labour, and often labour that is fairly meaningless for those people who engage in it, then alternative organizational forms such as those I have described here can be seen as attempts to make work more meaningful. But, in case this sounds like another version of managerial humanism, we might need to expand what the word 'work' could mean. As Beder (2000) argues, the virtues of a narrow version of the work ethic have been sold through the kinds of technologies discussed in much of this book. Work, however badly paid, alienating or destructive has been

208

articulated as a virtue in itself and has been counterposed to the dangers of idleness and sloth. But this is to strangle the meaning of the word to an unacceptable degree. If work is instead seen as one of the ways in which human beings can be creative, and perhaps is an element of being part of co-operative organization, then it might be rescued from market managerialism. For Beder, this might involve remembering and revitalizing older conjunctions of work and leisure. After all, there have been other times and places where work was part of a productive, creative, informal and perhaps even familial setting. Work, in other words, could be one of the ways in which we become human, and not just a job performed in particular times and places for money. This suggests a humanist Marxist way of thinking about how the potential relationship between human beings and their world might be understood in terms of creative labour, and how capitalist conceptions of 'work' serve to alienate people from this possibility and make labour into something external and wearisome.

Finally, then, what of management? Is this a word and associated set of concepts that can also be reimagined and expanded in more imaginative and emancipatory directions? This, it seems to me, is more difficult. As it is presently constituted, management is premised on separation of intellectual and practical labour. It is intimately tied up with a particular professionalisation project, with certain ideas about expertise and personhood, as well as the huge legitimation industry associated with the B-Schools, training centres, consultancy firms, magazine and book publishers and so on. Yet it is presented as if it were a neutral and progressive technology of organizing, often by borrowing its legitimacy from a version of science aimed at the systematic improvement of the human condition. As Watson (1994b) puts it, the question is whether management can be non-managerial. In other words, can management become simply another term for co-ordination? This would mean that those who engaged in co-ordination, this necessary function in complex organizations, did not recognize themselves (and were not recognized by others) as being in some way more special than those that do other things. At the present moment, and following Grey (1999), I doubt it. This is a word that simply has too much invested in it, too many other ideas and interests encrusting its meaning for it to be stripped down to a more modest role. As I said in chapter 1, common sense currently tells us that only management can do organization, and that organizing always involves permanent hierarchies of status and reward, B-School credentialism, the separation of conception from execution, the dominance of the market and so on. If these are all objectionable features of the present age, and I believe that they are, then management must be actively resisted.

To be clear though, this is not a question of doing away with co-ordination, merely ridding ourselves of the assumption that manage-rialism is constitutive of organizing. It is not a question of who manages, of substituting bad management for good management, but a question of the construction of manageability (Grey 1996: 602). That is why this book begins and ends 'against' management. Against a historically specific construction of the manager and the managed, against the vastly unequal distribution of rights and responsibilities that now seems to follow in lockstep from this originary distinction between those who rule and those who are ruled. Managerialism is an excuse for a particular form of domination, one that is taken and one that is given. Management can borrow the terminology of bureaucracy, community, citizenship, culture and so on, or can end-lessly claim to be 'beyond' management, but in every case it uses these as further justifications for forms of social engineering that are essen-tially managerial. Co-ordination, in the sense of bringing people and things together in productive ways, is not necessarily managerial. Organization, in the most general sense of patterning and arranging, is not necessarily managerialist. But management must manage something or somebody. At its heart it contains a self-serving claim to centrality, one that is now welded to the reproduction of a global capitalist market-place. At the present time, management cannot be reimagined, but it can be refused.

Nostalgia and utopia

It is easy enough to refuse the present, to wallow in noble despair and refuse the tasks of time. Critique, particularly for academics like me, has become a fine and principled position. When I write about alternatives, as I have done all too briefly above, they seem silly, unrealistic and smell of the perfumed air of 1960s' radicalism. Being green, pro-feminist, co-operative, anti-capitalist and so on seems dull and dutiful in comparison with wrestling with post-structuralism and negative dialectics, or complaining about the dreadful food in McDonald's. In part, this is because it is just so easy to dismiss all these 'alternatives' as failed, and hence to position them as nostalgic and, as I suggested in chapter 2, part of an essentially conservative lament for a world which we have lost. All very nice, and well intentioned no doubt, but so deeply unrealistic, essentialist and romantic. As George Boas wrote in 1932,

> In my boyhood in Providence I used to see men, women and children trudging to the mills at six-thirty in the morning, tin dinner pails in hand [. . .] to return at six-thirty at night. They were pale and rickety, God knows, and nothing for the mill owners to look in the eyes. But that does not mean that their contemporaries on the farms were red-cheeked and stocky, effervescing with vitamins, sleeping late in the morning and going to bed early, delighting in robust rural pleasures. (in Rhodes 1999: 114)

Well, perhaps, but let's pause a bit before we give nostalgia a bad name. This is a book about organizing, and specifically about the narrowing alternatives for organization that characterize the hegemony of market managerialism. I am not, and have been explicit about this in several places in the book, attempting to claim that communities were happy and jolly places, that co-operatives always co-operate, or that the division of labour has brought nothing but unhappiness and misery. The past was not necessarily any better than the present. Neither am I against technology, or progress, or organization. But the contemporary atrophy of ideas about alternatives means that they must be solicited from somewhere, and the past is one of the obvious places to look. Yet, and this is where I diverge from authors like George Ritzer, the point of this strategy is that it is not a disabling sickness but a resource which can be used to reimagine the future. What frightens me deeply, and saddens me greatly, is that the remarkable range of alternative ways in which human beings might come together to do things is being narrowed down to a choice of one.

The enemy that needs to be named, then, is not managers as such, or business gurus, or the WTO, or compliant politicians, but lack of radical imagination. Being against management and managerialism, in the way that I want to end this book, is not meant to stop with an unquestioned sense of my own righteousness but to (again) lay the foundations for an endless utopian project that experiments with different ways of organizing ourselves. Utopianism. Another word with a bad name. But this is a word that always sets itself against the sclerosis of the present, and attempts to think other forms of future into being. For Thomas More, the father of utopian thought, a vision of meritocratic managerialism would have been a vast improvement on the inherited cruelties of Henry VIII's England. As I suggested of

Saint-Simon in chapter 1, managerialism could be seen as a bourgeois revolution which is now all too complete, and the radicals of a previous era have become the new world order. However, More also provides us with some fine language to contest what this revolution has become:

> In fact, when I consider any social system that prevails in the modern world, I can't, so help me God, see it as anything but a conspiracy of the rich to advance their own interests under the pretext of organizing society. They think up all sorts of tricks and dodges, first for keeping safe their ill-gotten gains, and then for exploiting the poor by buying their labour as cheaply as possible. Once the rich have decided that these tricks and dodges shall be officially recognized by society – which includes the poor as well as the rich – they acquire the force of law. Thus an unscrupulous minority is led by its insatiable greed to monopolize what would have been enough to supply the needs of the whole population. (More 1965 [1516]: 130)

Utopianism then might not be so different from utopianism now, but it should be aimed at management and not the cruel king. It is also, perhaps, a word that suggests that organizational arrangements, particularly those naturalized as market managerialism, are a form of politics made durable (Parker 2002b). If we can begin to see the political assumptions built into the present ways in which we organize ourselves more clearly, then we can also begin to think about alternative politics built into alternative structures. It seems to me that theorists of organization, particularly those who are uneasily positioned within the B-School, are peculiarly well placed to take up this challenge. But, in case this seems like yet another version of the heroic academic changing the world from their office, these writings will surely not be sufficient on their own. They will need to be echoed in a wide variety of other places, and escape the confines of books like this, before the world even starts to change even a little bit.

My hope is that this is an argument whose time has come. Business ethics, critical management studies, the climate of cultural representation and the anti-corporate movement by no means represent a coherent response or political manifesto. But they do tell us something about the spirit of the age. A spirit, perhaps, which is coming to a realization that market managerialism is not the end of history, but just another oppressive form of commonsense that needs to be addressed more directly. Monbiot, writing on the same theme, suggests that 'there are issues that divide us', which is to understate the matter considerably, but that 'we have discovered an oppositional accord which overrides our differences' (2001: 22). I hope that he is right. Whether this can be built into 'some countervailing power, some force that resists the imperatives of profit in the name of economic democracy' is another matter (Frank 2000: xvii). As this chapter has shown, there *are* organizational alternatives to market managerialism and corporate domination. History does not have to end with global capitalism, even though there are powerful forces who are trying to persuade us that there are no alternatives. Dissent is difficult under such circumstances, when commonsense seems colonized and 'noble despair' a preferable option. But commonsense is not the end of thought or action, and despair feeds only on itself. Alternatives can be built, and should be built, but this is only to suggest how the story might begin.

NOTES

1 For example, the vagaries of employees who might become HIV positive can now be costed through the 'AIDS Impact Calculator' created
   by Lifeworks. Increases in pay and insurance costs can be predicted on
   a country by country basis, allowing for the management of hiring decisions. (*Newsweek* new year special issue 2000: 41).
2 This was not what Whyte believed, but how he characterized the professionalization of management.
3 Which I have, for the sake of clarity, probably over-stated.
4 See Grey (1999) for a further discussion of the expansion of management in these directions.
5 Perhaps it degrades into something like this book.
6 Though not all. See chapters 5 and 6.
7 Indeed, it might be suggested that organization is a general description
   for what human beings do. Organizing involves making patterns that
   endure in some way. When we organize something we give it a shape,
   a direction, a meaning. This is not to say that this pattern necessarily
   lasts, that the 'pool of order' coheres for very long (see Law 1994) but
   is to point to the importance of looking at organizing as a process, not
   as a finished outcome (Cooper and Law 1995). This is how humans
   make sense with their worlds, and the organization which is thereby
   produced becomes what sociologists sometimes call social structure
   (M. Parker 2000a).

CHAPTER 2   McBUREAUCRACY: LIBERALISM AND THE IRON CAGE

1 Gaetano Mosca, *Elementi di Scienza Politica*, 1895, translated as *The
   Ruling Class* in 1939; Robert Michels *Zur Soziologie des Parteiwesens*

in der modernen Demokratie, 1911, translated as *Political Parties* in 1915.

2 See M. Parker (2000a) for a fuller description of this literature.

3 This part of the chapter is based on my 'Nostalgia and Mass Culture: McDonaldization and Cultural Elitism' (1998) which appeared in M. Alfino, J. Caputo and R. Wynyard (eds), *McDonaldization Revisited: Critical Essays on Consumer Culture*, Westport, CT: Praeger.

4 It is important that the reader should not forget that this book is written by a European and reflects this in a variety of ways. I am, for example, well aware that 'Americanization' may mean something rather different in the home of McDonald's.

5 A suggestion made even more tragic after the events of 11 September 2001.

6 See Ritzer 1994: 131–8 for an account of a how 'a New Yorker with a sophisticated palate' learned to dislike McDonald's.

7 For more on these and other forms of resistance to McDonald's see www.mcspotlight.org or Klein 2000: 387.

8 The McTextbook style of *McDonaldization* – now in its third 'new century edition' – is a curious illustration of this point. Whilst it has enabled the book to reach a very wide audience, it also glosses over the contested political and theoretical issues that I have been discussing. Ritzer's own self-publicity for McDonaldization as 'a key idea in sociology' (1994) further abbreviates the possibilities of 'public discourse' by radically simplifying the issues at stake. Of course, as Ritzer himself acknowledges, getting cited does not guarantee quality in academic publications – just as personal marketing does not guarantee good publicity.

CHAPTER 3   CITIZENSHIP: THE CORPORATE STATE

1 This chapter is a rewritten version of my 'Organizations and Citizenship' (1997), *Organization*, 4/1: 75–92.

2 For example, Silver 1987; Miller and Rose 1990; du Gay 1991; Kunda 1992; Willmott 1993; Hancock 1997; and Thompson and Findlay 1998.

3 For example, Marshall 1950; Giddens 1982; Barbalet 1988; Plant and Barry 1990; Turner 1990, 1991; and Ahrne 1996.

4 The exception, alarmingly, is Handy (1998).

5 Du Gay 2000 is particularly useful as a critical review of the anti-bureaucracy versions of this argument.

6 For example, Miller and Rose 1990; Miller and O'Leary 1993; du Gay et al. 1996; Pritchard 1996; and du Gay 2000.

7 In chapter 7, I will argue that these efforts at corporate propaganda are remarkably similar to those that took place after the earlier legitima-

tion crisis of the 1920s and 1930s. See also Beder (2000) for a similar historical context.

8 For example, Knights and Willmott 1989; Kunda 1992; Willmott 1993; and Grey 1994.

9 Though, given the rise of corporate universities (Beder 2000: 212), these may be over-optimistic assumptions.

10 Hancock, for example, has suggested that this argument is really a form of neo-feudalism which completely underplays the coercive power of capitalist ideology (1997). I fear he may be right, but I hope he is not.

CHAPTER 4   COMMUNITY: THE FREEDOM TO WORK

1 This chapter is a rewritten and expanded version of 'Organization, Community and Utopia' (1998), *Studies in Cultures, Organizations and Societies*, 4/1: 71–91.

2 This is not, by any means, a new story. It has been told endlessly over the last century at least. See Whyte (1961: 43), for example, in which he argues that this story has been used to legitimize a moralization of belonging against the tragedy of industrial societies.

3 See, for example, Willmott 1993, but many of the references in the footnotes to the previous chapter are relevant too.

4 A message they re-emphasized, despite 'downsizing, mergers and reengineering' in their 2000 reprise of the book.

5 In the armed forces, for example. These organizations are a particularly interesting example of intense forms of community feeling existing within elaborated bureaucratic structures.

6 A diagnosis that, from Northern Ireland to Afghanistan, has some tragic implications.

7 A theme I will return to in more detail in the final chapter.

8 Indeed, du Gay suggests that strong senses of community are more fascist than democratic and diverse (2000: 50), a point echoed by Starr (2000: 205) in terms of an uncritical faith in community as a counter to capitalist globalization.

9 Though I hope I am wrong about this.

10 Particularly with regard to the mass culturalist dismissal of the passions and identities of ordinary people. See chapter 2.

CHAPTER 5   THE BUSINESS OF BUSINESS ETHICS

1 This section of the chapter is developed from a part of 'Business, Ethics and Business Ethics: Critical Theory and Negative Dialectics' (2002) which appeared in M. Alvesson and H. Willmott (eds), *Critical Management Studies* (2nd edn), London: Sage.

2   See also Kjonstad and Willmott 1995; ten Bos 1997; Willmott 1998.
3   It also legitimizes much of the anti-corporate protest movement that I will be covering in chapter 8, but this is rarely mentioned by ethicists.
4   Though see Castro 1996, the brief opening chapters in Cannon 1994, and some chapters in Frederick 1999 for exceptions.
5   A US version of the beginnings of such an engagement can be found in Freeman and Phillips 1999.
6   In this context, mine would be very high.
7   This section of the chapter is based around part of 'Against Ethics' (1998) in my edited book *Ethics and Organization*, London: Sage.
8   See, for example, Sorell and Hendry 1994; Pearson 1995; and Pearson and Parker 2001.
9   See Watson 1994a; Howell 1997; Callon 1998, for example, and the comments in chapter 1.
10 This is also a helpful move in terms of my suggestion that I am not 'against' managers, but 'managerialism'. I do not, for example, wish to suggest that all managers are unethical, but do wish to argue that management is a political problem.
11 Though the 'blindness' of utilitarianism is more rhetorical than real, simply because who and what counts as stakeholders is a political issue that reflects prior decisions.
12 Postmodernism is a difficult and confusing word, but has had a remarkable influence within social theory generally and organization theory specifically. See, for the former, Lyotard 1984 [1979], and for the latter, Cooper and Burrell 1988; M. Parker 1992; and Chia 1996.
13 This section is influenced by Derrida 1978 [1967]; Caputo 1993; and Chia 1994.
14 Though see Kjonstad and Willmott 1995; ten Bos 1997, 2002; and many of the chapters in M. Parker 1998.
15 See, for example, Nodoushani 1996; Feldman 1997; Reed 1997; and Thompson et al. 2000.

CHAPTER 6   CRITICIZING CRITICAL MANAGEMENT STUDIES

1   The previous chapter should have demonstrated that well enough anyway.
2   Given that this book will, hopefully, be read outside CMS too, this chapter is perhaps the most risky. It needs to avoid getting stuck within very specific debates (and perhaps satisfying one audience) without reducing them to a simplistic parody (and perhaps satisfying another audience). Such is the problem of writing about things that you know about for people that you know, something that hasn't troubled me in the rest of the book. So, apologies to all my friends whose work I have pasticheed so cruelly and inaccurately in this chapter.

3   For example, Thompson and McHugh 1995; Alvesson and Willmott 1996; Wilson 1999; Barry et al. 2000; Jackson and Carter 2000; and there are others.

4   At the present time, and at the risk of hubris, Keele is probably the most pre-eminent amongst these, but Cambridge, Essex, Exeter, King's, Lancaster, Strathclyde, UMIST and Warwick might also be identified as places with smaller colonies.

5   aom.pace.edu/cms/aboutcmsw/manifesto.html (accessed 19/6/01).

6   A point which has been extensively discussed in CMS already, of course. See Alvesson and Willmott 1996, particularly chapter 7.

7   Grey's (1996) earlier critical discussion of managerialism is explicitly based on Kantian ethics.

8   Schlosser's documentation of accidents in meat-processing plants in the US might stand as an example here (2001).

9   See M. Parker 2000a for a full discussion of this literature.

10   See du Gay 2000 for an illustration of this, and M. Parker 2000b for more examples.

11   An outline of the argument can be found in M. Parker 1999 and almost entirely challenged in Thompson et al. 2000. Various positions are also articulated in a special issue of *International Studies of Management and Organization* edited by Grugulis, Willmott and Knights (2001).

12   Peter Armstrong, at the 2001 Labour Process Conference, Royal Holloway College.

13   Which, of course, includes me. See M. Parker 2002a.

14   A quality that this book exhibits all too painfully. When I told fellow academics that I was writing a book about anti-corporate protest, they often responded with something like 'that should sell well'. No doubt it was meant as an optimistic comment that was meant to cheer me up, but I often understood it as a veiled criticism of my motives. Academics are not meant to be too fashionable.

15   For example, in July 2001, Paul Adler (the chair of CMSW) circulated a list of well over 100 activist websites to the CMS mailing list, and David Boje (a management professor at New Mexico State University) has been tireless in his activist and academic work on Nike's sweatshop activities.

16   For example, when Alvesson and Willmott write about the possibilities for changing consciousness through 'micro-emancipation' (1996), I wonder why they are so modest in their aims.

CHAPTER 7   THE CULTURE INDUSTRIES AND THE
DEMONOLOGY OF BIG ORGANIZATIONS

1   A point that Klein makes about the TV airing of Michael Moore's *TV Nation* and her publishing of a book with anti-corporate themes by a

publishing conglomerate (2000: 187). See Barnet and Cavanagh 1994 and Sklair 1995 for an account of globalization, capitalism and the culture industries.

2 Though the word itself was coined by his brother Josef (Scholes and Rabkin 1977: 29).

3 See Seltzer 1992, who compares this discipline to Baden-Powell's control of the bodies of boy scouts.

4 Frank 2000: 38; Morris 2000: 153; Hertz 2001: 205.

5 A book which was reprinted in 2000 to sit alongside Klein, Frank, Monbiot and so on.

6 A contemporary book which has been compared to Sinclair is Schlosser's (2001) *Fast Food Nation*. See, especially, chapter 8.

7 The following section contains fragments from 'Cyborganization: Cinema as Nervous System' (1998, with Bob Cooper), in J. Hassard and R. Holliday (eds), *Organization – Representation: Work and Organization in Popular Culture*, London: Sage; and 'Manufacturing Bodies: Flesh, Organization, Cyborgs' (2000) in J. Hassard, R. Holliday and H. Willmott (eds), *Body and Organization*, London: Sage.

8 See also Ballard's 1973 novel *Crash*, made into a film by David Cronenberg in 1996.

9 Baran and Sweezy made a similar point about representations of business organizations in fiction in the mid-1960s. They claimed that the focus had moved from the hero who built an empire at the expense of his soul to the soul-destroying features of corporations more generally (1966: 33).

10 Though see Byers 1990 and some comments in Shaviro 1993 and Corbett 1995.

11 A sequel which, of course, also reflects the imperatives of Hollywood entertainment corporations.

12 This plot was borrowed, complete with the evil CEO of 'Scorex Industries', for *Inspector Gadget* (1999).

13 A sub-theme about heartless Japanese organizations runs through other films too – *Gung Ho* (1986) and *Rising Sun* (1993) for example.

14 See De Cock 2001 for a combined review.

15 Michael Lewis's *Liar's Poker* (1989), an insider book about the 'big swinging dicks' on Wall Street, covers very similar territory, and the corporate executive discovering his humanity plot is reprised in the context of an efficiency expert in the Australian film *Spotswood* (1991).

16 Indeed, I had to prevent this section from becoming just such a list, by not mentioning films with a variety of anti-work themes such as *Save the Tiger* (1973), *Blue Collar* (1978), *Matewan* (1987), *Falling Down* (1992), *Clerks* (1994), *Jerry Maguire* (1996), *Brassed Off* (1996), *Office Space* (1999), and the list goes on.

17 See Joanna Brewis and Ruth Holliday's chapters in Hassard and Holliday 1998 for further discussions of some of these films.

18 Which probably also includes the 'intellectuals' who practise business
    ethics and critical management studies too.

CHAPTER 8   ANTI-CORPORATE PROTEST

1   A different version of this review of No Logo appeared in Organiza-
    tion 9/1: 181–4 (2002).
2   Almost exactly the same book-size, black and white photo of the author,
    and colour scheme was used to package Noreena Hertz's (2001) The
    Silent Takeover.
3   Though the analysis is more like Packard's The Waste Makers (1960)
    in its scope.
4   The remarkable hostility of academics to 'popularizers' was also illus-
    trated in the reception of Alain de Botton's harmlessly therapeutic Con-
    solations of Philosophy (2000). As I noted and exemplified in chapter
    two, Ritzer has received similar treatment.
5   In Genoa, on 20 July 2001, Carlo Giuliani was shot and then run over
    by a police van.
6   See Jacoby 1973; Plant 1992; Klein 2000: 282; and Böhm 2001.
7   The fact that four are by women – Klein, Beder, Starr and Hertz – is
    interesting in itself, though I don't want to draw any speculative con-
    clusions from that fact.
8   See also Barnet and Cavanagh 1994 for an earlier account.
9   The role of 'corporate universities' in the colonization of higher educa-
    tion is described in Beder 2000: 212, and some of its prehistory, with
    particular reference to Warwick University, can be found in Barnet and
    Müller 1974: 115.
10 Its worth mentioning that he takes this metaphor from a Star Trek
    episode in which the inhabitants of Stratos, a beautiful city in the sky,
    live off the misery of those who live on the surface of the planet below
    (Korten 1995: 103).
11 Mindful of the last chapter, these are the themes covered in the films
    Wall Street and Other People's Money. See Michael Lewis's Liar's Poker
    (1989) for an insider story of this 'greed is good' lifestyle.
12 A tension also exemplified in terms of the Taliban, obviously a deeply
    patriarchal regime, but one that shared a similar diagnosis of 'Ameri-
    canization' to many anti-globalization protesters.
13 As I said in the introduction, this is not a balanced book. There are
    plenty of places where the reader can imbibe the public relations of
    the corporate libertarians and have management's right to manage
    explained in detail.
14 Something I have been busily engaged with for quite some time.
15 On the more specifically cultural aspects of this change, see John
    Seabrook's Nobrow (2001).

16 It was pointed out on the CMSW email discussion list (see chapter 6) that both protesters and WTO probably walked away from Seattle feeling righteous. As a CMS academic, the author took this to mean that more reflexivity and theory was needed.

CHAPTER 9 FOR ORGANIZATION

1 McDonald's, at the time of writing, operates in 120 countries. These include China, Colombia, Croatia, El Salvador, India, Israel, Kuwait, Northern Ireland, Russia, Turkey and Yugoslavia.
2 This is an important point. The managers I have taught on MBAs and interviewed in organizations are not uniformly 'bad' people. They often do things that I disapprove of, but they are things that I would almost certainly do if I were in their shoes.
3 Whether this book falls into that category is a moot point. I think I would be rather disappointed if it doesn't, and I fear that (despite my efforts) it is still far too mannered to be read much outside universities.
4 *Guardian*, Thursday 8 Feb 2001: 15. For some similar suggestions concerning scale and public shareholdings in joint stock corporations, see Schumacher 1993: 241.
5 I can imagine that there will be many readers who will say that my four topics were unrepresentative, and that I have missed out huge literatures in radical economics, development studies, feminist and anti-imperialist politics and so on. I have to agree with them, but also ask them if it makes my arguments less compelling?
6 See Gould 1979; Leidner 1991; Korten 1995: 296; and Cheney 1999.
7 Some of the ideas below are developed from the model of a 'neo-bureaucracy' in K. Ramsey and M. Parker (1992) 'Gender, Bureaucracy and Organizational Culture', in M. Savage and A. Witz (eds) *Gender and Bureaucracy*, Oxford: Blackwell, 253–76.
8 An argument that could just as easily apply to anti-corporate protesters, the IRA, the Zapatista and al-Qaida.
9 For example, Reedy 2002 on anarchism, Sargisson 1996 on feminism, Plant 1992 on situationism, and Berneri 1971 on the utopian communities of Owen, Fourier and Saint-Simon.

BIBLIOGRAPHY

Adler, P. (2000) Critical in the Name of Whom or What? CMSW editorial essay. http://aom.pace.edu/cms, accessed 26/6/00.

Adorno, T. and Horkheimer, M. (1972) *Dialectic of Enlightenment*. New York: Seabury Press.

Ahrne, G. (1996) Civil Society and Civil Organizations. *Organization*, 3/1: 109–20.

Alvesson, M. and Willmott, H. (eds) (1992) *Critical Management Studies*. London: Sage.

Alvesson, M. and Willmott, H. (1996) *Making Sense of Management: A Critical Introduction*. London: Sage.

Amis, K. (1969) *New Maps of Hell*. London: New English Library.

Auden, W. H. (1948) *The Age of Anxiety*. London: Faber and Faber.

Ballard, J. G. (1973) *Crash*. London: Jonathan Cape.

Bamyeh, M. (1993) Transnationalism. *Current Sociology*, 41/3: 1–95.

Baran, P. and Sweezy, P. (1966) *Monopoly Capital*. New York: Monthly Review Press.

Barbalet, J. (1988) *Citizenship*. Milton Keynes: Open University Press.

Barnet, R. and Cavanagh, J. (1994) *Global Dreams: Imperial Corporations and the New World Order*. New York: Touchstone.

Barnet, R. and Müller, R. (1974) *Global Reach: The Power of the Multinational Corporations*. New York: Simon and Schuster.

Barry, J. et al. (2000) *Organization and Management: A Critical Text*. London: Thompson Learning.

Baudrillard, J. (1985) The Ecstasy of Communication. In H. Foster (ed.), *Postmodern Culture*, London: Pluto Press, 126–34.

Bauman, Z. (1989) *Modernity and the Holocaust*. Cambridge: Polity.

Bauman, Z. (1993) *Postmodern Ethics*. Cambridge: Polity.

Bauman, Z. (1996) On Communitarians and Human Freedom. *Theory, Culture And Society*, 13/2: 79–90.

Beder, S. (2000) *Selling the Work Ethic: From Puritan Pulpit to Corporate PR*. London: Zed Books.

Bennett, T. (1981) *Popular Culture: Themes and Issues 2*. U203 Popular Culture course, Block 1, Unit 3. Milton Keynes: Open University Press.

Bennis, W. and Slater, P. (1998 [1968]) *The Temporary Society*. San Francisco: Jossey-Bass.

Berle, A. (1955) *The Twentieth Century Capitalist Revolution*. London: Macmillan.

Berle, A. and Means, G. (1932) *The Modern Corporation and Private Property*. New York: Macmillan.

Berneri, M. (1971) *Journey Through Utopia*. New York: Shocken.

Bierce, A. (1996 [1911]) *The Devil's Dictionary*. Ware: Wordsworth Editions.

Bishop, L. (2000) Stranger from a Strange Land. CMSW editorial essay. http://aom.pace.edu/cms, accessed 20/9/00.

Blaug, R. (1999) The Tyranny of the Visible. *Organization*, 6/1: 33–56.

Böhm, S. (2001) '010501'. *Ephemera* 1/2: 163–81. [www.ephemeraweb.org].

Bottomore, T. and Rubel, M. (eds) (1963) *Karl Marx: Selected Writings*. Harmondsworth: Penguin.

Bourdieu, P. (1984) *Distinction: a Social Critique of the Judgement of Taste*. London: RKP.

Bourdieu, P. and Wacquant, L. (2001) NewLiberalSpeak: Notes on the New Planetary Vulgate. *Radical Philosophy*, 105: 2–5.

Braverman, H. (1974) *Labor and Monopoly Capital*. New York: Monthly Review Press.

Burns, T. (1955) The Reference of Conduct in Small Groups. *Human Relations*, 8: 467–86.

Burns, T. and Stalker, G. (1961) *The Management of Innovation*. London: Tavistock.

Burrell, G. (1997) *Pandemonium*. London: Sage.

Byers, T. (1990) Commodity Futures. In A. Kuhn (ed.), *Alien Zone: Cultural Theory and Contemporary Science Fiction Cinema*, London: Verso, 39–49.

Calhoun, C. (1993) Nationalism and Civil Society. *International Sociology*, 8: 387–411.

Callon, M. (ed.) (1998) *The Laws of the Markets*. Oxford: Blackwell.

Cannon, T. (1994) *Corporate Responsibility*. London: Pitman.

Caputo, J. (1993) *Against Ethics*. Bloomington: Indiana University Press.

Carr, A. (1968) Is Business Bluffing Ethical? *Harvard Business Review*, 48/1. Reprinted in R. Larmer (ed.), *Ethics in the Workplace* (1996), Minneapolis: West Publishing, 4–10.

Castro, B. (ed.) (1996) *Business and Society*. Oxford: Oxford University Press.

Chambers, I. (1986) *Popular Culture: The Metropolitan Experience*. London: Methuen.

Cheney, G. (1999) *Values at Work: Employee Participation Meets Market Pressure at Mondragon*. Ithaca: Cornell University Press.

Chia, R. (1994) The Concept of Decision: A Deconstructive Analysis. *Journal of Management Studies*, 31/6: 781–806.

Chia, R. (1996) *Organizational Analysis and Deconstruction*. Berlin: de Gruyter.

Chomsky, N. (1996) *Powers and Prospects*. London: Pluto.

Clegg, S. (1990) *Modern Organizations: Organization Studies in the Postmodern World*. London: Sage.

Clutterbuck, D., Dearlove, D. and Snow, D. (1992) *Actions Speak Louder. A Management Guide to Social Responsibility*. London: Kogan Page.

Cohen, A. (1985) *The Symbolic Construction of Community*. London: Ellis Horwood.

Cohen, A. (1994) *Self Consciousness: An Alternative Anthropology of Identity*. London: Routledge.

Cooper, R. (1990) Organization/Disorganization. In J. Hassard and D. Pym (eds), *The Theory of Philosophy of Organizations*, London: Routledge, 167–97.

Cooper, R. and Burrell, G. (1988) Modernism, Postmodernism and Organizational Analysis. *Organization Studies*, 9/1: 91–112.

Cooper, R. and Law, J. (1995) Organization: Distal and Proximal Views. *Research in the Sociology of Organizations*, 13: 237–74.

Corbett, J. M. (1995) Celluloid Projections: Images of Technology and Organizational Futures in Contemporary Science Fiction Film. *Organization*, 2: 467–88.

Dawe, A. (1987) The Two Sociologies. In K. Thompson and J. Tunstall (eds), *Sociological Perspectives*, Harmondsworth: Penguin, 542–54.

Deal, T. and Kennedy, A. (1988 [1982]) *Corporate Cultures*. London: Penguin.

Deal, T. and Kennedy, A. (2000) *The New Corporate Cultures*. London: Texere.

De Botton, A. (2000) *The Consolations of Philosophy*. London: Penguin.

De Cock, C. (2001) Through a Glass Darkly: Tales of Super-Capitalism. *Ephemera*, 1/1: 80–91. [www.ephemeraweb.org].

Derrida, J. (1978) [1967]) *Writing and Difference*. London: Routledge and Kegan Paul.

Drummond, J. and Bain, B. (eds) (1994) *Managing Business Ethics*. Oxford: Butterworth-Heinemann.

du Gay, P. (1991) Enterprise Culture and the Ideology of Excellence. *New Formations*, 13: 45–61.

du Gay, P. (2000) *In Praise of Bureaucracy*. London: Sage.

du Gay, P., Salaman, G. and Rees, B. (1996) The Conduct of Management and the Management of Conduct. *Journal of Management Studies*, 33/3: 263–82.

Durkheim, E. (1991 [1893]) *The Division of Labour in Society*. Basingstoke: Macmillan.

Eliot, T. S. (1948) *Notes Towards the Definition of Culture*. London: Faber and Faber.

Etzioni, A. (1961) *A Comparative Analysis of Complex Organizations*. New York: Free Press.

Etzioni, A. (1993) *The Spirit of Community: The Reinvention of American Society*. New York: Simon and Schuster.

Featherstone, M. (1987) Lifestyle and Consumer Culture. *Theory, Culture and Society*, 4/1: 55–70.

Featherstone, M. and Burrows, R. (eds) (1995) *Cyberspace, Cyberbodies, Cyberpunk*. London: Sage.

Feldman, S. (1997) The Revolt against Cultural Authority: Power/Knowledge as an Assumption in Organization Theory. *Human Relations*, 50/8: 937–55.

Felstead, A. (1993) *The Corporate Paradox*. London: Routledge.

Fineman, S. (ed.) (1993) *Emotion in Organizations*. London: Sage.

Fournier, V. and Grey, C. (2000) At the Critical Moment: Conditions and Prospects for Critical Management Studies. *Human Relations*, 53/1: 7–32.

Frank, T. (2000) *One Market under God*. London: Secker and Warburg.

Franklin, H. B. (1990) Visions of the Future in Science Fiction Films from 1970 to 1982. In A. Kuhn (ed.), *Alien Zone: Cultural Theory and Contemporary Science Fiction Cinema*, London: Verso, 19–31.

Frederick, R. (ed.) (1999) *A Companion to Business Ethics*. Malden, MA: Blackwell.

Freeman, R. and Phillips, R. (1999) Business Ethics: Pragmatism and Postmodernism. In R. Frederick (ed.), *A Companion to Business Ethics*, Malden, MA: Blackwell, 128–38.

Friedman, A. (1977) *Industry and Labour*. London: Macmillan.

Friedman, M. (1995 [1970]) The Social Responsibility of Business is to Increase its Profits. Reprinted in W. Hoffman and R. Frederick (eds), *Business Ethics*, New York: McGraw-Hill, 137–41.

Friedman, T. (1999) *The Lexus and the Olive Tree*. New York: Farrar Straus & Giroux.

Galbraith, J. (1967) *The New Industrial State*. Boston, MA: Houghton Mifflin.

Gerth, H. and Mills, C. (eds) (1948) *For Max Weber*. London: Routledge and Kegan Paul.

Gibson, W. (1986) *Neuromancer*. London: Grafton.

Giddens, A. (1982) Class Division, Class Conflict and Citizenship Rights. In A. Giddens, *Profiles and Critiques in Social Theory*, London: Macmillan.

Gould, M. (1979) When Women Create an Organization: The Ideological Imperatives of Feminism. In D. Dunkerley and G. Salaman, *The International Yearbook of Organization Studies*, London: RKP.

Gouldner, A. (1952) The Problem of Succession in Bureaucracy. In R. Merton et al. (eds), *Reader in Bureaucracy*, New York: Free Press.

Gouldner, A. (1954) *Patterns of Industrial Bureaucracy*. Glencoe: Free Press.

Gray, J, (1992) *The Moral Foundations of Market Institutions*. London: Institute of Economic Affairs.

Greer, G. (1971) *The Female Eunuch*. St Albans: Paladin.

Grey, C. (1994) Career as a Project of the Self and Labour Process Discipline. *Sociology*, 28: 479–97.

Grey, C. (1996) Towards a Critique of Managerialism: The Contribution of Simone Weil. *Journal of Management Studies*, 33/5: 591–611.

Grey, C. (1999) 'We are All Managers Now'; 'We Always Were': On the Development and Demise of Management. *Journal of Management Studies*, 36/5: 561–85.

Griseri, P. (1998) *Managing Values*. Basingstoke: Macmillan.

Grugulis, I., Willmott, H. and Knights, D. (2001) The Labor Process Debate. Special issue of *International Studies of Management and Organization*, 30/4.

Hall, S. (1982) The Rediscovery of Ideology. In M. Gurevitch et al. (eds), *Culture, Society and the Media*, London, Methuen.

Hall, S. and Jefferson, T. (1976) *Resistance through Rituals*. London: Hutchinson.

Hancock, P. (1997) Citizenship or Vassalage? Organizational Membership in the Age of Unreason. *Organization*, 4/1: 93–111.

Hancock, P. (1999) The Management of Everyday Life: The Idea. Paper presented at 1st International Critical Management Studies Conference, Manchester.

Handy, C. (1998) *The Hungry Spirit*. London: Arrow.

Hare, R. (1993) Universal Prescriptivism. In P. Singer (ed.), *A Companion to Ethics*. Oxford: Blackwell, 451–63.

Hassard, J. and Holliday, R. (eds) (1998) *Organization-Representation*. London: Sage.

Hatch, M. (1997) *Organization Theory*. Oxford: Oxford University Press.

Haug, W. (1986) *Critique of Commodity Aesthetics*. Cambridge: Polity.

Hawley, N. (2000) Creating Corporate Mini-Mes. *Business 2.0*, July, 80.

Hebdige, D. (1979) *Subculture: The Meaning of Style*. London: Methuen.

Hebdige, D. (1985) 'The Bottom Line on Planet One'. *Ten.8*, 19: 40–9.

Henderson, D. (2001) *Anti-Liberalism 2000*. London: IEA.

Hertz, N. (2001) *The Silent Takeover: Global Capitalism and the Death of Democracy*. London: Heinemann.

Hetherington, K. (1994) The Contemporary Significance of Schmalenbach's Concept of the Bund. *Sociological Review*, 42/1: 1–25.

Hetherington, K. and Munro, R. (eds) (1997) *Ideas of Difference: Social Ordering and the Labour of Division*. Oxford: Blackwell.

Hickman, C. and Silva, M. (1985) *Creating Excellence*. London: Unwin.

Hirschman, A. (1996) Rival Interpretations of Market Society. In B. Castro (ed.), *Business and Society*, Oxford: Oxford University Press, 250–9.

Hobsbawn, E. and Ranger, T. (eds) (1983) *The Invention of Tradition*. Cambridge: Cambridge University Press.

Hoffman, W. and Frederick, R. (1995) *Business Ethics: Readings and Cases in Corporate Morality.* New York: McGraw-Hill.

Hoggart, R. (1958) *The Uses of Literacy.* Harmondsworth: Pelican.

Howell, S. (ed.) (1997) *The Ethnography of Moralities.* London: Routledge.

Hulsman, J. (2001) *The World Turned Rightside Up.* London: IEA.

Huxley, A. (1994 [1932]) *Brave New World.* London: HarperCollins.

Jackson, J. (1996) *An Introduction to Business Ethics.* Oxford: Blackwell.

Jackson, N. and Carter, P. (2000) *Rethinking Organizational Behaviour.* London: Pearson.

Jacoby, N. (1973) *Corporate Power and Social Responsibility.* New York: Macmillan.

Jacques, R. (1996) *Manufacturing the Employee: Management Knowledge from the 19th to the 21st Centuries.* London: Sage.

Jameson, F. (1985) Postmodernism and Consumer Society. In H. Foster (ed.), *Postmodern Culture,* London: Pluto Press, 111–25.

Jancovich, M. (1996) *Rational Fears: American Horror in the 1950s.* Manchester: Manchester University Press.

Janssens, M. and Brett, J. (1994) Coordinating Global Companies. In C. Cooper and D. Rousseau (eds), *Trends in Organizational Behaviour,* Chichester: Wiley, 31–46.

Jaros, S. (2001) Labor Process Theory. *International Studies of Management and Organization,* 30/4: 25–39.

Jary, D. and Jary, J. (eds) (1991) *Dictionary of Sociology.* London: Collins.

Kaghan, B. (2001) Where Corporate Executives Live and Work. Message on c-m-workshop@jiscmail.ac.uk, 22 March.

Kierkegaard, S. (1962 [1846–7]) *The Present Age.* London: Fontana.

Kjonstad, B. and Willmott, H. (1995) Business Ethics: Restrictive or Empowering? *Journal of Business Ethics,* 14: 445–64.

Klein, N. (2000) *No Logo: Taking Aim at the Brand Bullies.* London: Flamingo.

Knight, P. (2000) *Conspiracy Culture.* London: Routledge.

Knights, D. and Willmott, H. (1989) Power and Subjectivity at Work. *Sociology,* 23: 535–58.

Knobil, M. (2000) 'No Logo – No Comeback'. *Observer,* 3 December.

Korten, D. (1995) *When Corporations Rule the World.* West Hartford, CT: Kumarian Press.

Kuhn, A. (ed.) (1990) *Alien Zone: Cultural Theory and Contemporary Science Fiction Cinema.* London: Verso.

Kunda, G. (1992) *Engineering Culture.* Philadelphia: Temple University Press.

Law, J. (1984) How Much of Society can the Sociologist Digest at One Sitting? *Studies in Symbolic Interaction,* 5: 171–96.

Law, J. (1994) *Organizing Modernity.* Oxford: Blackwell.

Leavis, F. R. (1930) *Mass Civilization and Minority Culture.* Reprinted in F. R. Leavis, *Education and the University* (1979), Cambridge: Cambridge University Press.

Leidner, R. (1991) Stretching the Boundaries of Liberalism: Democratic Organization in a Feminist Organization. *Signs*, 16/2: 263–89.

Lessard, B. and Baldwin, S. (1999) *Netslaves*. New York: McGraw-Hill.

Lewis, M. (1989) *Liar's Poker: Rising Through the Wreckage of Wall Street*. New York: W. W. Norton.

Likert, R. (1961) *New Patterns of Management*. New York: McGraw-Hill.

Linstead, S. (2000) Dangerous Fluids and the Organization-without-Organs. In J. Hassard, R. Holliday and H. Willmott (eds), *Body and Organization*, London: Sage, 31–51.

Lyotard, J.-F. (1984 [1979]) *The Postmodern Condition: A Report on Knowledge*. Manchester: Manchester University Press.

Lyotard, J.-F. (1988 [1983]) *The Differend: Phrases in Dispute*. Minneapolis: University of Minnesota Press.

MacIntyre, A. (1981) *After Virtue*. London: Duckworth.

Maffesoli, M. (1995) *The Time of the Tribes*. London: Sage.

Mangham, I. (1995) MacIntyre and the Manager. *Organization*, 2/2: 181–204.

Marcuse, H. (1964) *One Dimensional Man*. London: Routledge and Kegan Paul.

Marshall, T. H. (1950) *Citizenship and Social Class and Other Essays*. Cambridge: Cambridge University Press.

Marx, K. (1976) *Capital: Volume 1*. Harmondsworth: Penguin.

Marx, K. and Engels, F. (1967) *The Communist Manifesto*. Harmondsworth: Penguin.

McGregor, D. (1960) *The Human Side of Enterprise*. New York: McGraw-Hill.

Meyer, S. (1996) Assembly Line Americanization. In B. Casto (ed.), *Business and Society*. New York: Oxford University Press, 43–50.

Miller, P. and O'Leary, T. (1993) Accounting Expertise and the Politics of the Product. *Accounting, Organizations and Society*, 18, 2/3, 187–206.

Miller, P. and Rose, N. (1990) Governing Economic Life. *Economy and Society*, 19/1: 1–31.

Minson, J. (1993) *Questions of Conduct*. Basingstoke: Macmillan.

Mintz, M. and Cohen, J. (1971) *America Inc: Who Owns and Operates the United States*. New York: Dial Press.

Mitchell, G. (1968) *A Dictionary of Sociology*. London: Routledge and Kegan Paul.

Monbiot, G. (2000) *Captive State: The Corporate Takeover of Britain*. London: Macmillan.

Monbiot, G. (2001) Dissent is in the Air: Take to the Streets. *Guardian*, 8 February.

More, T. (1965 [1516]) *Utopia*. London: Penguin.

Morris, J. (2000) Mid-Late Twentieth Century: 'An Unprecedented Moral Quagmire'. In A. Pollard (ed.), *The Representation of Business in English Literature*, London: IEA, 137–82.

Mulhall, S. and Swift, A. (1992) *Liberals and Communitarians*. Oxford: Blackwell.

Munro, R. (1998) Masculinity and Madness. In J. Hassard and R. Holliday (eds), *Organization-Representation*, London: Sage, 185–99.

Nelson, M. (1985) Bureaucracy. In A. Kuper and J. Kuper (eds), *The Social Science Encylopedia*, London: Routledge and Kegan Paul, 79–81.

Newell, P. (2000) Environmental NGOs and Globalization: The Governance of TNCs. In R. Cohen and S. Rai (eds), *Global Social Movements*, London: Athlone Press, 117–34.

Newell, P. and Paterson, M. (1998) A Climate for Business. *Review of International Political Economy*, 5/4: 679–703.

Nietzsche, F. (1990 [1889]) *Twilight of the Idols*. London: Penguin.

Nodoushani, O. (1996) The Problems and Prospects of Postmodern Management Discourse. *Management Learning*, 27/3: 359–81.

O'Rourke, P. (1998) *Eat the Rich*. London: Picador.

Organ, D. (1990) The Motivational Bases of Organizational Citizenship Behavior. In B. Staw and L. Cummings (eds), *Research in Organizational Behavior*, vol. 12, Greenwich, CT: JAI Press.

Ottensmeyer, E. and McCarthy, G. (1996) *Ethics in the Workplace*. New York: McGraw-Hill.

Ouchi, W. (1981) *Theory Z*. Reading, MA: Addison-Wesley.

Packard, V. (1957) *The Hidden Persuaders*. London: Longmans, Green and Co.

Packard, V. (1960) *The Waste Makers*. Harmondsworth: Penguin.

Packard, V. (1962) *The Pyramid Climbers*. Harmondsworth: Penguin.

Parish, J. and Parker, M. (eds) (2001) *The Age of Anxiety: Conspiracy Theory and the Human Sciences*. Oxford: Blackwell.

Parker, M. (1992) Post-modern Organizations or Postmodern Organization Theory? *Organization Studies*, 13/1: 1–17.

Parker, M. (ed.) (1998) *Ethics and Organization*. London: Sage.

Parker, M. (1999) Capitalism, Subjectivity and Ethics: Debating Labour Process Analysis. *Organization Studies*, 20/1: 25–45.

Parker, M. (2000a) *Organizational Culture and Identity*. London: Sage.

Parker, M. (2000b) The Sociology of Organizations and the Organization of Sociology: Some Reflections on the Making of a Division of Labour. *Sociological Review*, 48/1: 124–46.

Parker, M. (2002a) 'The Romance of Lonely Dissent': Intellectuals, Professionals and the McUniversity. In M. Dent and S. Whitehead (eds), *Managing Professional Identities*, London: Routledge, 138–56.

Parker, M. (ed.) (2002b) *Utopia, Ideology and Organization*. Oxford: Blackwell.

Parker, M. and Jary, D. (1995) The McUniversity: Organization, Management and Academic Subjectivity. *Organization*, 2/2: 319–38.

Parker, S. (1976) *The Sociology of Leisure*. London: Allen and Unwin.

Pascale, R. and Athos, A. (1982) *The Art of Japanese Management*. Harmondsworth: Penguin.

Pearson, G. (1995) *Integrity in Organizations: An Alternative Business Ethic*. Maidenhead: McGraw-Hill.

Pearson, G. and Parker, M. (2001) The Relevance of Ancient Greeks to Modern Business? A Dialogue on Business and Ethics. *Journal of Business Ethics*, 3/4: 341–53.

Perrow, C. (1973) The Short and Glorious History of Organizational Theory. *Organizational Dynamics*, 1/1: 8–20.

Peters, T. and Waterman, R. (1982) *In Search of Excellence*. New York: Harper and Row.

Piercy, M. (1992) *Body of Glass*. London: Penguin.

Plant, R. and Barry, N. (1990) *Citizenship and Rights in Thatcher's Britain*. London: IEA Health and Welfare Unit.

Plant, S. (1992) *The Most Radical Gesture. The Situationist International in a Postmodern Age*. London: Routledge.

Pollard, A. (ed.) (2000) *The Representation of Business in English Literature*. London: IEA.

Poole, R. (1991) *Morality and Modernity*. London: Routledge.

Porter, R., Sauvé, P., Subramanian, A. and Beviglia-Zampetti, A. (eds) (2001) *Efficiency, Equity and Legitimacy*. Washington, DC: Brookings Institution.

Postman, N. (1987) *Amusing Ourselves to Death*. London: Methuen.

Potter, D. (1994) *Seeing the Blossom*. London: Faber and Faber.

Prendergrast, M. (1994) *For God, Country and Coca-Cola*. London: Phoenix.

Pritchard, C. (1996) Making Managers Accountable or Making Managers? *Educational Management and Administration*, 24/1: 79–91.

Pugh, D. and Hickson, D. (1973) The Comparative Study of Organizations. In G. Salaman and K. Thompson (eds), *People and Organizations*, Harlow: Longman.

Punch, M. (1996) *Dirty Business*. London: Sage.

Ransom, D. (2001) Shrink It or Sink It. *New Internationalist*, 334, May, 9–11.

Reed, M. (1997) In Praise of Duality and Dualism: Rethinking Agency and Structure in Organizational Analysis. *Organization Studies*, 18/1: 21–42.

Reedy, P. (2002) Keep the Black Flag Flying. In M. Parker (ed.), *Utopia, Ideology and Organization*, Oxford: Blackwell.

Reich, C. (1970) *The Greening of America*. New York: Random House.

Rhodes, R. (ed.) (1999) *Visions of Technology*. New York: Simon and Schuster.

Riesman, D. (1961) *The Lonely Crowd*. New Haven: Yale University Press.

Rippin, A. (1993) From Factory-Floor to Corporate Confessional: the New Meaning of Total Quality Management. *SCOS Notework*, 12/1: 22–30.

Ritzer, G. (1994) *Sociological Beginnings: On the Origins of Key Ideas in Sociology*. New York: McGraw-Hill.

Ritzer, G. (1996) *The McDonaldization of Society* (revised edition). Thousand Oaks, CA: Pine Forge.

Roddick, A. (2000) *Business as Unusual*. London: HarperCollins.

Roy, D. (n.d.) *Global Corporate Citizenship*. Washington, DC: Hitachi Foundation.

Roy, D., Banzhaf, J. and Regelbrugge, L. (1993) *Global Citizenship*. Washington, DC: Hitachi Foundation.

Ryan, M. (1988) Postmodern Politics. *Theory, Culture and Society*, 5/2–3: 559–76.

Salazar-Xirinachs, J. and Robert, M. (eds) (2001) *Towards Free Trade in the Americas*. Washington, DC: Brookings Institution.

Sanders, S. (1979) The Disappearance of Character. In P. Parrinder (ed.), *Science Fiction: A Critical Guide*, London: Longman, 131–47.

Sargisson, L. (1996) *Contemporary Feminist Utopianism*. London: Routledge.

Schlosser, E. (2001) *Fast Food Nation*. London: Penguin.

Scholes, R. and Rabkin, E. (1977) *Science Fiction: History, Science, Vision*. New York: Oxford University Press.

Schumacher, E. (1993) *Small is Beautiful*. London: Vintage.

Seabrook, J. (2001) *Nobrow. The Culture of Marketing and the Marketing of Culture*. London: Methuen.

Seltzer, M. (1992) *Bodies and Machines*. New York: Routledge.

Selznick, P. (1957) *Leadership in Administration: A Sociological Interpretation*. New York: Harper and Row.

Semler, R. (1994) *Maverick*. London: Arrow.

Shaviro, S. (1993) *The Cinematic Body*. Minneapolis: University of Minnesota Press.

Shepherd, J. et al. (eds) (1977) *Whose Music?* London: Latimer.

Silver, J. (1987) The Ideology of Excellence: Management and Neo-Conservatism. *Studies in Political Economy*, 24: 105–29.

Sklair, L. (1995) *Sociology of the Global System*. Hemel Hempstead: Prentice-Hall.

Smircich, L. (1983a) Organizations as Shared Meanings. In L. Pondy, P. Frost, G. Morgan and T. Dandridge (eds), *Organizational Symbolism*, Greenwich, CT: JAI Press, 55–65.

Smircich, L. (1983b) Concepts of Culture and Organizational Analysis. *Administrative Science Quarterly*, 28: 339–59.

Smith, W. (2001) Conspiracy, Corporate Culture and Criticism. In J. Parish and M. Parker (eds), *The Age of Anxiety: Conspiracy Theory and the Human Sciences*, Oxford: Blackwell, 153–65.

Smith, C., Child, J. and Rowlinson, M. (1990) *Reshaping Work: The Cadbury Experience*. Cambridge: Cambridge University Press.

Solomon, R. (1992) *Ethics and Excellence*. Oxford: Oxford University Press.

Sorell, T. (1998) Beyond the Fringe? The Strange State of Business Ethics. In M. Parker (ed.), *Ethics and Organizations*, London: Sage, 15–29.

Sorell, T. and Hendry, J. (1994) *Business Ethics*. Oxford: Butterworth-Heinemann.

231

Sotirin, P. and Tyrell, M. (1998) Wondering about Critical Management Studies. *Management Communication Quarterly*, 12/2: 303–36.

Spark, A. (2001) Conjuring Order: The New World Order and Conspiracy Theories of Globalisation. In J. Parish and M. Parker (eds), *The Age of Anxiety: Conspiracy Theory and the Human Sciences*, Oxford: Blackwell, 46–62.

Sparkes, A. (1991) *Talking Philosophy*. London: Routledge.

Starr, A. (2000) *Naming the Enemy: Anti-Corporate Movements Confront Globalization*. London: Zed Books.

Stauth, G. and Turner, B. (1988) Nostalgia, Postmodernism and the Critique of Mass Culture. *Theory, Culture and Society*, 5/2–3: 509–26.

Stephenson, N. (1992) *Snow Crash*. London: Roc/Penguin.

Stewart, D. (1996) *Business Ethics*. New York: McGraw-Hill.

Street, J. (1986) *Rebel Rock*. Oxford: Blackwell.

Swales, J. and Rogers, P. (1995) Discourse and the Projection of Corporate Culture. *Discourse and Society*, 6/2: 223–42.

ten Bos, R. (1997) Business Ethics and Bauman Ethics. *Organization Studies*, 18/6: 997–1014.

ten Bos, R. (2002) Machiavelli's Kitchen. *Organization*, 9/1: 51–70.

Tester, K. (1997) *Moral Culture*. London: Sage.

Thompson, D. (1973) *Discrimination and Popular Culture*. Harmondsworth: Penguin.

Thompson, P. (2001) Progress, Practice and Profits: How Critical is Critical Management Studies. Paper presented to the 19th Labour Process Conference, Royal Holloway College, March.

Thompson, P. and Findlay, P. (1998) Changing the People: Social Engineering in the Contemporary Workplace. In A. Sayer and L. Ray (eds), *Culture and Economy after the Cultural Turn*, London: Sage.

Thompson, P. and McHugh, D. (1995) *Work Organizations*. London: Macmillan.

Thompson, P., Smith, C. and Ackroyd, S. (2000) If Ethics is the Answer, You Are Asking the Wrong Questions: A Reply to Martin Parker. *Organization Studies*, 21/6: 1149–58.

Tomlinson, A. (1991) *Cultural Imperialism*. London: Pinter.

Trevino, L. and Nelson, K. (1999) *Managing Business Ethics*. New York: John Wiley and Sons.

Tudor, A. (1989) *Monsters and Mad Scientists: A Cultural History of the Horror Movie*. Oxford: Blackwell.

Turner, B. (1987) A Note on Nostalgia. *Theory, Culture and Society*, 4: 147–56.

Turner, B. (1990) Outline of a Theory of Citizenship. *Sociology*, 24: 189–217.

Turner, B. (1991) Further Specification of the Citizenship Concept. *Sociology*, 25: 215–18.

Vaneigem, R. (1992 [1967]) *The Revolution of Everyday Life*. London: Left Bank Books and Rebel Press.

Van Maanan, J. (1991) The Smile Factory. In P. Frost, L. Moore, M. Louis, C. Lundberg and J. Martin (eds), *Reframing Organizational Culture*. Newbury Park: Sage.

Vinten, G. (ed.) (1994) *Whistleblowing: Subversion or Corporate Citizenship*. London: Paul Chapman.

Walton, J. (1992) *Fish and Chips and the British Working Class*. Leicester: Leicester University Press.

Warnock, M. (ed.) (1962) *Utilitarianism*. London: Collins.

Watson, T. (1994a) *In Search of Management*. London: Routledge.

Watson, T. (1994b) Towards a Managerially Relevant but Non-Managerial Organization Theory. In J. Hassard and M. Parker (eds), *Towards a New Theory of Organizations*, London: Routledge, 209–24.

Weekley, E. (1967) *An Etymological Dictionary of Modern English*. New York: Dover Publications.

Whyte, W. H. (1961) *The Organization Man*. Harmondsworth: Penguin.

Williams, R. (1961) *Culture and Society 1780–1950*. Harmondsworth: Penguin.

Williams, R. (1976) *Keywords*. London: Fontana.

Willmott, H. (1993) Strength is Ignorance; Slavery is Freedom; Managing Culture in Modern Organizations. *Journal of Management Studies*, 30/4: 515–52.

Willmott, H. (1998) Towards a New Ethics. In M. Parker (ed.), *Ethics and Organizations*, London: Sage, 76–121.

Wilson, F. (1999) *Organizational Behaviour: A Critical Introduction*. Oxford: Oxford University Press.

Wray-Bliss, E. and Parker, M. (1998) Marxism, Capitalism and Ethics. In M. Parker (ed.), *Ethics and Organizations*, London: Sage, 30–52.

Zamyatin, Y. (1993 [1924]) *We*. New York: Penguin.

INDEX

Index compiled by Zeb Korycinska